# THE FEMINIZATION
# OF RACISM

# THE FEMINIZATION OF RACISM

## Promoting World Peace in America

Irene I. Blea

Westport, Connecticut
London

**Library of Congress Cataloging-in-Publication Data**

Blea, Irene I. (Irene Isabel)
    The feminization of racism : promoting world peace in America / Irene I. Blea.
      p.   cm.
    Includes bibliographical references and index.
    ISBN 0–275–96375–6 (alk. paper)
    1. Minority women—United States.  2. United States—Race relations.  3.
Feminism—United States.  I. Title.
    HQ1421.B57   2003
    305.48′8′00973—dc21        2002072822

British Library Cataloguing in Publication Data is available.

Library of Congress Catalog Card Number: 2002072822
ISBN: 0–275–96375–6

First published in 2003

Praeger Publishers, 88 Post Road West, Westport, CT 06881
An imprint of Greenwood Publishing Group, Inc.
www.praeger.com

Printed in the United States of America

The paper used in this book complies with the
Permanent Paper Standard issued by the National
Information Standards Organization (Z39.48–1984).

10  9  8  7  6  5  4  3  2  1

*To Raven, who has the courage to sing,*
*a bird like you has never taken wing.*

# Contents

# *Tables*

# *Acknowledgments*

Several women listened to me discuss my research for this book. They tossed around a sea of ideas with me. I especially want to thank two sisters, Chelo and Espie, for being my friends, my nurses, and my packing and moving assistants when I was riddled with pain and sometimes unable to plan my next step. Thank you to Patricia and Nancy for making U.S. Bureau of the Census data and projections for the next decade available to me. Thank you Kathy, Paulina, and Margaret for sharing your network and welcoming me home. Gracias Martha from the Asian and Pacific Island Women's Leadership Institute, who reminds us about the starfish that gets thrown into the sea and keeps returning to the shore. Thank you Georgiana and other Native sisters for inviting me to walk this earth walk with you.

# Introduction

The September 11, 2001, attacks on the World Trade Center and the Pentagon prompted Americans to ask, "Why do they hate us?" As the months have passed, I have reflected on this question and come to the realization that part of the answer is within our own national boundaries. As the media coverage of the war and the people of Afghanistan entered our homes via the Internet, television, print, and radio, I, like many others, began to see patriotism foster racism. I also saw the plight of Afghan women being used to promote hatred of the enemy. In witnessing the human rights atrocities of the war, I decided to write about how to heal from war, hatred, and intolerance, and promote global tolerance in our own country.

After September 11, people kept saying the world would never be the same. They said it as if the United States and the world were the same thing. Contrary to what U.S. ethnocentrism assumes, the world and the United States are not the same thing to all those who live outside the United States, and often to those who live within it but are disenfranchised from the mainstream. Perhaps what changed the most after the infamous blasts that crumbled symbols of America was that many more Americans were saying what I had maintained over a period of more than thirty years. In my last five books I have called for the people of the United States to unite, to respect and celebrate our differences, to learn to live together, and teach the world to exist in peace. It is true now more than ever, and I say it more loudly.

This book is also firmly linked to media images of dark-complected women covered in shrouds, being shot, beaten, and beheaded in the stadiums and streets of Afghanistan. At the time of the attacks I flashed back on another image that took place in another stadium and also received heavy media attention. I was in China in 1995, attending the U.N. Fourth World Women's Conference, and as I entered the stadium something powerful connected; the majority of women in the world are women of color. By the end of my business at the U.N. conference in China, I knew I would henceforth write books that placed U.S. women in a global context. I have always written about women of color, but when I wrote *U.S. Chicanas and Latinas in a Global Context* (Praeger, 1997), I had to exclude several global issues. One I did not exclude was how women of color in the United States and the world experience not only sexism, but also racism. *Chicanas and Latinas in a Global Context* ends with a suggestion that even though women of color in the United States are in the minority, they should reconceptualize themselves as part of the global majority of women. They should cease referring to themselves and not accept others referring them as a minority. In fact, U.S. women of color share many similarities with the majority, women from "underdeveloped" countries, sometimes more than they share with their white sisters in their own country.

In this book, *The Feminization of Racism: Promoting World Peace in America*, I have decided to compare and contrast the experiences of Chicanas and Latinas, Native American, Asian American, and African American women and link them to global issues of war, racism, and sexism. I present the similarities and differences among these women, and offer suggestions for healing U.S. society from within. In understanding why "they" hate us, we come to understand our internal weaknesses and can emerge stronger. After we have defined our weak points, we can address them and share with the world how to live in peace.

This book, as well as my others, suggests that periods of significance for men, as recorded by men for men, are not as significant in the same manner, and with the same results, as they are for women. How American men conceptualize the world is only one way of looking at the world. Very often women see it differently. In the United States women and people of color observe the world and act in it differently from white men and women. I want to render insight into how U.S. women of color conceptualize their reality based upon their history and their social surroundings to make the following points: The Americas consist of much more than the United States of America, and to some extent the United States is misnamed. There are "united states" in countries throughout the Americas, where advanced civilizations existed prior to the appearance of European (white) males.

In addition, there is a misconception that the United States is a nation of immigrants. It is not. African Americans and Vietnamese were imported into the country. Native Americans (Indians) are indigenous to South, Central, and North America. Chicanas and Latinas are a mixture of indigenous and Spanish European blood. Contrary to how Chicanas and Latinas engage in self-identity, their European ancestry does not cancel out the fact that they are also indigenous. Yet some women have more shallow roots in the United States, while others have histories that go back hundreds or thousands of years. These historical experiences feed their social and political consciousness, and only some are shared with immigrant Latinas. In spite of their immigrant status, many immigrant women have not totally abandoned the indigenous and ethnic or cultural traditions from their countries of origin. This does not mean they are stuck in the past. In fact, they are highly contemporary women with contemporary issues and successes.

Contemporary women of color are complex. Those lighter in skin color have better social experiences because they do not inherit the legacy of discrimination against people of darker skin tones; that is, until they speak their native language or speak English with an accent. The groups discussed in this book have contributed much to the structure and function of language, and they are presented in the historical order in which they have been incorporated in the United States. This book demonstrates how they have balanced being "Americans," people of color, and female. Attention is paid to their income, education, health, political power, experience in the criminal justice system, and spirituality, and how they create in spite of misunderstandings, mistreatment, and stereotypes.

Perhaps my most important focus is on the aging of American women of color. I stress the need to pay attention to the 75 million aging baby boomers who will, by 2006, be the largest senior population in the world. Of major concern to feminists should be the need for services and service providers, home care, insurance, and prescription-drug cost regulation. Because more than half the baby boom population is female, women now face living alone longer than ever before. They also have certain health risks, plus the propensity for accidents as they get older, and often fall victim to the predatory practices of marketing strategists. Many older women will live alone for the first time in their lives.

I wrote this book because women and a feminist perspective on racism are instrumental in healing the world and maintaining global peace. I write to inform, to motivate action in preparation for the next U.S. Women's Conference. Mostly I write because I love. Because I know that everyone and everything is my relation. I am related to all, to the flower, the fauna, the Earth, the sky, and all things that walk, swim, or crawl.

CHAPTER 1

# *Radical Feminists*

Most American media contended that on September 11, 2001, terrorism was felt in the United States for the first time; most of the country was shocked, some of it became irate that anyone would dare attack the land of the brave with freedom and justice for all. When two American planes that were said to be controlled by something evil charged into the World Trade Center towers, the media almost immediately began to stress how America had changed, how it was no longer the safe place it once was. The next day the plight of brown women in the Middle East became an American media focus on the violence of the Taliban. During that time I frequently flashed back to the summer of 1995, when I entered the stadium for the beginning ceremonies of the U.N. Fourth World Women's Conference in Beijing, China. I was struck by the presence of 30,000 women from all over the world. They had come there to address the impact of patriarchy and sexism upon their human rights. I was also struck by the fact that perhaps 80 percent of those 30,000 women were women of color. At that moment I knew in my heart what I had known in my mind for a long time: The majority of the world's women are women of color. On September 11, 2001, I also remembered that this was not the first time the United States had experienced terrorism. An earlier attack on the World Trade Center came to mind. So did the fact that American people of color knew terrorism at the hands of white people within the land of the brave, where the Constitution promised freedom and justice for all.

## TERRORISM AND WOMEN OF COLOR
## IN THE LAND OF THE FREE

The women being shown on television as being oppressed by the Taliban looked like women of color I knew. I remembered how women at the U.N. conference were encouraged by what was interpreted as a giant step for womankind. We had received much media coverage, and felt that at last the word was going global about women's oppression. U.S. women, regardless of color, returned encouraged. A few years after we returned home, things for women of color in the United States reverted to what they had been. In the beginning there was much excitement about building coalitions, but it had died down, and on September 11 I wondered what function the media focus on women in Afghanistan was serving. What did the world gain by exploiting all that was wrong with the Taliban and women who lived under it? The answer was simple. Americans had to learn to loath the Taliban and women were a vehicle in that promotion, that conveyance, of hate. Thus, sympathy for the enemy would be curtailed by showing the United States how "bad" women were treated in Afghanistan and other Middle Eastern countries.

The startling images and the news that women were restricted to wearing the shroudlike *burqa* was astonishing. The Islamic *hejab* (veil) that completely covered the women and allowed them no peripheral vision aroused in women in "the land of the free" feelings of claustrophobia, fear of being locked in, smothered. For the first time in America, the land of justice for all, the public saw women being executed and heard reports about them being stoned to death for walking alone and for infidelity. Other information was equally as startling: the lack of education, the inability to work, and not being able to walk or talk with men who were not relatives.

Over the Internet there appeared more astonishing images, reports, and stories about how shrouded women were forced to kneel and then were flogged while Taliban men had the stadium pulsating with the chants of onlookers. There were other descriptions of how crowds fell silent only when two female thieves were driven into the arena and pushed to the ground. Physicians using surgical scalpels promptly carried out the hand amputations. Holding the severed hands high by the index fingers, a Taliban soldier warned the huge crowd, "These are the chopped-off hands of thieves, the punishment for any of you caught stealing." Then the women were driven in a jeep once around the stadium and the crowd rose to their feet, cheering.

My flashbacks to the fourth U.N. conference on women reminded me that I attended the conference in an effort to lobby the U.N. delegates to make racism a feminist issue. I was also there to attend the NGO (nongovernmental organization) conference to talk about the effects of racism upon American women of color, specifically Chicanas and Latinas in my own country, the United States of America. As I listened to the testimony of women from all over the world, I came to know more fully how racism affects women on a global level. Most of them had experienced war, and like most of the conference women began their presentations with personal experiences. Many of the women's experiences living under Taliban rule were also personal, but they were indicative of trends, tendencies, and policies in that country. The experiences of women of color in the Untied States reflect tendencies and policies of the United States. Frequently those social trends and official policies have terrorized them.

U.S. feminism began with personal experiences shared and analyzed with documented social trends and policies that had developed over time. The contemporary experiences of prejudice against women came to full consciousness during the 1960s, when discrimination was openly discussed throughout the country. Unfortunately, gender and class struggles kept women of color highly peripheral to the white-dominated women's movement. During this early part of feminine politicization, knowledge was key. Women of color, sometimes for the first time, discovered the death and destruction of their own people by their own government within the civil rights movement. This created radical feminists, a term that many nonfeminists related to with hatred and mistrust.

Soon after the explosions of September 11, 2001, and the bombardment of the Pentagon and eradication of the World Trade Center, there spawned an epidemic of patriotism never before seen in my lifetime of fifty-six years. Along with some of my colleagues, and Ifeared that Americans were learning basic hatred, which is essential to ingraining into the human psyche that there is an enemy and that we, the good guys, are right in hating them, the foreigner. The we–they dichotomy made it acceptable to react against anything that was not "democratic." The American flag flew everywhere. It became representative of all that was good, right, and just.

For feminist women's advocates (there are women's advocates who are not feminist), especially women of color, September became a confusing time. After considerable thought, it is my opinion that in the name of patriotism the September 11 incidents took work done by civil right activists in the United States and diminished it to the status of relative unimportance. This was especially true for women of color, who had spent four decades addressing the combined effects of racism and sexism in the United States. At the same time patriotism appeared to unite the nation, it took the practice of international racism and sexism to a global level of war in the name of fighting terrorism. Perhaps this was done purposefully in an effort to globalize democracy and expand it around the world, and not everyone wants it. I am not saying that Americans know they are playing a role in the worldwide phenomena of racism and sexism; what I am saying is whether we know it or not, this is what American patriotism is supporting. Because women are not seen as a viable threat, propaganda efforts, for the first time, present Middle Eastern women as humans enduring sexism so we can hate the real enemy, men of color.

The question then emerges: Does not patriotism serve to do away with racial discrimination and sexism by instilling pride in uniting the United States as one country and exposing the humanity of Afghan women? Yes, on the surface it does. On a deeper level, it not only relinquishes racism within America to a level of relative unimportance, it also makes feminists in the United States look ridiculous. The general public has noted that at least American women have more freedom than women under the Taliban did. More freedom? Yes, but that freedom, especially for women of color, is relative to that of U.S. males, especially white males.

Feminists believe that women in the United States have been terrorized, and terrorism is especially stored in the historical memory of women of color as real and very recent. One only needs to look back at film footage of Vietnamese women being shot at and scrambling to escape their country to see terror. American Indians still feel the terror of mass carnage, imprisonment, and the disarming effects of alcoholism and diabetes. African Americans carry the social–psychological scars of slavery and resistance to prejudice. They and Latinos are highly familiar with racial profiling, and Chicanas, sisters to Indian women, have experienced the rape of war on their very own land.

Some can accept historical evidence of murder and attempted genocide, as they note that at least Americans have freedom of religion. Women of color know forced conversion and that Americans are free to practice Christianity in several forms. Indian, African, Mexican, and Asian women have evidence of the suppression of religious expression. It was not long ago that women were burned at the stake after being falsely charged with practicing witchcraft. American Jews and Muslims have long been singled out, called names, and had their places of worship burned or defaced. In the majority of churches the ministers are still men. And in many religions women cannot lead prayer or speak or be priests or ministers. This is forbidden not only by religious doctrine, but also by cultural patriarchy ingrained in marriage and political relations.

Poor women of color have tried hard, with little success, to shape radical feminism. In the 1970s feminism recognized poverty as socially and psychologically dysfunctional. It rendered a unique perspective that has grown as the understanding of the experiences of poor women has grown. White feminists are now aware of this experience and a few have tried to do something about it.

The next step in American feminism is to act upon making racism a feminist issues. The fact that most of world's women are women of color also holds true in the United States, where many Americans feel feminism and racism are leftover radical ideas from the 1960s. They do not comprehend the two in the light of human rights at the national, much less the global, level. Instead, Americans concentrate on what racism and sexism means to them as individuals with little or no attention to what it means to the human race. If they are white people who mostly relate to whites, then there is no racism, but if they are people of color there is racism and it permeates their lives.

However, when people of color, especially women, act outside of traditional cultural roles, the media pays attention and it is pointed out to whites.

When they act to gain control over their own lives, they endure the consequences. When women do this at minimum they are called names, labeled "bra burners," "bitches," whores," and "lesbians." At an extreme there is always violence, some type of physical punishment that results in being sequestered, beaten, raped, and relegated to a lifetime of poverty. For many women the consequences include all of these. Such was the case for women who resisted the Taliban.

## U.S. FEMALE DEMOGRAPHICS AND FEMINISM

Women of color first openly resisted such consequences in the 1960s, when baby boomers became critical of various forms of injustice in the United States. As that large number, 75 million, matured, consciousness about racism and sexism matured, especially when they found out they outnumbered men. Thus far the higher number of women has not translated into more power. In 1990 there were about 127.5 million women in the United States. This number represented over 51 percent of the population. It is projected that there will be 195 million women in the United States by 2050 (U.S. Bureau of the Census, 2000a), and that women will again represents about 51 percent of the total population.

The women's statistics news releases by the U.S. Bureau of the Census (2000a, 2000b, 2000c, 2000d, 2000e) indicate that the American male population grew faster than the female population during the last decade (see Tables 1.1 and 1.2). There are about 6 million more women than there are men. A closer review of the U.S. Commerce Department's Census Bureau reports reveals the percentage that the male population has grown. The number of men grew by 13.9 percent and the number of females grew by 12.5 percent over the 1990s. This not only resulted in a lessening of the gap between the number of men and women; many feminists find this troubling because they feel that numbers are powerful. What is more powerful is how much power those numbers represent.

The male-to-female ratio declined with age. For persons age eighty-five and over, it was 49 males for every 100 females. In addition, the nation's baby boom population (fifty-plus years of age with about a 51-percent female population) is expected to grow by 50 percent during the current decade (U.S. Bureau of the Census 1996a). This fact continues to be good news for feminists.

According to government statistics based on U.S. Census 2000, the nuclear family has revived a bit (see U.S. Bureau of the Census 2001). But three in ten households were maintained by women (see U.S. Bureau of the Census 1995b), and family composition is changing (see U.S. Bureau of the Census 2001b). The U.S. family is continuing to look female dominant. Not only are there are more single-parent households, but the age at which women are first marrying is rising. This is also good news for feminists because unmarried women spend more time "in the world" and gain more of a feminist consciousness.

The March 2000 population survey indicated that about one-half (51 percent) of women fifteen years of age and over were living with a spouse (U.S.

**Table 1.1**
**Total U.S. Resident Population**
**Estimate by Percentage and**
**Gender**

| | |
|---|---|
| Population | 276,059 |
| Percentage of total | 100.0 |
| Median age (years) | 35.9 |
| Mean age (years) | 36.6 |
| Male population | 134,979 |
| Female population | 141,080 |

*Source*: Population Estimates Program, Population Division, U.S. Census Bureau, Washington, D.C. (Internet release date January 2, 2001).

*Note*: Projection to November 1, 2000. Numbers in thousands.

Bureau of the Census 1997). Twenty-five percent had never married, 13 percent were divorced or separated, and 10 percent were widowed. One in five women who have never married have children. Records also indicate that the numbers of divorced and never married adults is increasing, and that most of those women have a high school diploma. At 84 percent, the high school completion rate for women age twenty-five and over equals the rate for men. Twenty-four percent of the women counted had bachelor's degrees or higher, and among adults ages twenty-five to twenty-nine, women typically were better educated than men. This is also good news for feminists, because better-educated women tend to have a higher level of feminist consciousness. In addition, many feminists are women who have been married, experienced the limitations of that role, gained a social political consciousness about relations between men and women, and adopted feminists perspectives. This, of course, leads to the stereotype that feminists are women who have "lost at love" or are "women scorned" and are simply angry with men.

The majority of our nation's residents (people who actually live within the U.S. borders) are female. Female residents outnumbered males (U.S. Bureau of the Census 2000a) by 6 million, 140 million to 134 million. The latest information documents just how much American women have changed over the past thirty years. They marry and have children later in life, they stay in school longer, and they work more. The median earnings for women who work full time and were fifteen years of age and over was $26,300. This is was 72 percent of the median earning rates for their male counterparts, who earned $36,500. Thus, in spite of a grand civil rights movement in the 1960s, forty years later discrimination in the workplace continues. Women still make less money than men, but make more money than ever before.

**Table 1.2**
**Total U.S. White Resident**
**Population Estimate by**
**Percentage and Gender**

| | |
|---|---|
| Population | 226,861 |
| Percentage of total | 82.2 |
| Median age (years) | 37.0 |
| Mean age (years) | 37.5 |
| Male population | 111,502 |
| Female population | 115,359 |

*Source*: Population Estimates Program, Population Division, U.S.
Census Bureau, Washington, D.C.
(Internet release date January 2,
2001).

*Note*: Projection to November 1,
2000. Numbers in thousands.

Some of these tendencies are expected to continue. For example, 61 percent of women sixteen years of age and over work. These women are concentrated in three different occupational groups: 58 percent are in administrative support (including clerical), 24 percent have professional specialty appointments, and 18 percent work in the service (U.S. Bureau of the Census 2000a). This number does not include domestic laborers, the 16 percent of private household workers, an area in which women of color are concentrated.

In the 1990s, men outnumbered women until the age of twenty-five. From twenty-five to thirty-four, there were about the same number of women as men. Beginning at age forty, women outnumbered men, and by age sixty-five women outnumbered men three to two. The 2000 census reveals that the male and female populations were 138.1 million and 143.4 million, respectively. Females made up 50.9 percent of the population. In 1990, females comprised 51.3 percent of the population.

The greatest increase in the male–female ratio between 1990 and 2000 was in the age group from seventy-five to eighty-four. There the percentage increased from 59.9 to 65.2. Alaska led all states with the highest male–female ratio (107.0), followed by Nevada (103.9), Colorado (101.4), Wyoming (101.2), Hawaii (101.0), Idaho (101.0), and Utah (100.4). The lowest male–female ratios were recorded in the District of Columbia (89.0), Rhode Island (92.5), and Massachusetts (93.0). The female population grew at a faster rate than the male population in only three states: Alaska, California, and Hawaii.

The Census Bureau cautions that the 2000 estimates should not be confused with Census 2000 results, which are not scheduled for periodic release until 2003. However, estimates indicate that the average life expectancy for women born between 1940 and 1950 is between sixty-five and seventy-one years of age. For women born between 1950 and 1970 it is seventy-one to seventy-five years of age, and for women born since 1975 the life expectancy is seventy-seven to nearly seventy-nine years of age. Further, one in four females was a college graduate and one in seven employed women worked in executive, administrative, or managerial occupations (U.S. Bureau of the Census 2000d). In the last decade, 75 percent of women finished high school; 18 percent completed a bachelor's degree. This is compared to 76-percent high school and 23-percent college graduation for men. At the beginning of the new millenium, most women have a high school diploma. In fact, at 84 percent, the high school completion rate for women age twenty-five and over equals the rate for men. In addition, 24 percent of women have a bachelor's degree or higher, somewhat lower than the 28 percent of men with the same degree. Among young adults ages twenty-five to twenty-nine, women typically are better educated than men. Thirty percent have at least a bachelor's degree, compared with 28 percent of men.

## FAMILY VALUES

Many link family values to women marrying and raising children. The most common age for women to have gotten married in 2001 was between twenty-five and twenty-nine years old. The second most common age was twenty to twenty-four. However, the greatest increase in birth rates occurred among women thirty to thirty-four years old. Although many feel that women who delay marriage and work outside the family threaten the family, they do not. This changes the face of who dominates in the family. When a women earns money and that money is used to maintain the family, women have more decision-making power. Tied to making money is higher education. Most women in college major in traditional fields, such as education or nursing, and most, according to student service and career advisors at the University of New Mexico and California State University, want to get married. Yet a growing number of women are choosing nontraditional education in forensic medicine, law, engineering, and business. Graduate degrees can take as long as ten years to obtain, postponing marriage and having children to a later age (U.S. Bureau of the Census 2000a). Past thirty, women have fewer babies and cannot delay childbirth for too much longer (U.S. Bureau of the Census 2000a). At this time this is not threatening family values. What it means to feminists is that women are thinking more of their self-interest and often find it not in their interests to begin families as early as their mothers and grandmothers did.

In 1997 there were about 3.9 million births in the United States and a total fertility rate (TFR) of 2.0 births per woman. Minorities represented over 40 percent of all births, although they made up only 28 percent of the population. By 2000 the minority percentages continued to grow. Some reasons minorities accounted for a disproportionate share of births are a high immigration rate, a larger proportion of minority women are in their childbearing ages (they are younger), and minority women also have more children than non-Hispanic white women, on average.

In 1997 whites had an average of 1.8 births per woman, compared with 1.9 births among Asian Americans, 2.0 births among Native Americans, 2.2 births among blacks, and 3.0 births among Hispanics. With an average of three births per woman, the 1997 total fertility rate among Hispanics rivaled that of the total U.S. population in the early 1960s (U.S. Bureau of the Census 1997), during the tail end of the baby boom. Blacks are the only group who experienced a substantial decline in fertility rates over the 1990s. Since 1993 the number of Hispanic births has outnumbered births to black women. On a final note, half of all mothers with infants return to the labor force after giving birth (U.S. Bureau of the Census 2001). This is a trend that is likely to continue as the Hispanic population grows (U.S. Bureau of the Census 2000b), and the trend toward working mothers will continue to question the structure of family and its values in the United States.

To add fuel to this discussion, Census 2000 reported that revenues for women-owned businesses show continued growth (U.S. Bureau of the Census 2001). The number of women-owned businesses represents a third of all domestic firms and nearly 50 percent of all retail and service firms. Within retail, women were dominant in apparel and accessory stores. They owned one-half of all firms and miscellaneous retail stores, but on March 21, 2001, the Current Population Survey indicated that 13.2 percent of females and 10.3 percent of males were in poverty. In fact, families supported by women are six times more likely today to be in poverty as married-couple families (U.S. Bureau of the Census 2001). By 2005, employed women should almost reach the 48th percentile. The Department of Labor Women's Bureau estimates that most women work year round and full time (U.S. Bureau of the Census 2000b).

March 2000 census data also show that women have almost achieved educational parity with men. As of June 1998, younger women surpassed young men in educational attainment (U.S. Bureau of the Census 1998). This threatens some men, and a few women, who also feel that the increased median earnings of women age twenty-five years and over who worked full time, year round disrupts the family and the "natural (Biblical) order" of male–female relationships. Another threatening factor to them is that during the last thirty years the number of women living alone has doubled from 7.3 million to 15.3 million (U.S. Bureau of the Census 1998). The percentage of women who lived alone rose for every age group in 2000, except those ages sixty-five to seventy-four.

A scrutiny of the data reveals that women "dominated" seven occupations: secretaries, kindergarten through twelfth-grade school teachers, cashiers, registered nurses, managers and administrators, bookkeepers and accounting clerks, and nursing aides, orderlies, and attendants. Most of them are in administrative support (emphasis on support) and service (emphasis on service) occupations. These are historical occupations for women. At the beginning of this century, over 79 percent of the people working in administrative support (including clerical) were female, as were 95 percent of those employed as service workers in private households (U.S. Bureau of the Census, October 2000). As stated, when condensed, at the turn of this century nearly three out of four women age fifteen and over worked in four occupational groups: administrative support, including clerical (24 percent); professional specialty (18 percent); service workers, except private households (17 percent); and executive, administrative, and managerial (14 percent). We will see later that the lower the job rating and pay, the higher the number of women of color.

Because of women's prescribed social roles, they spend nearly 15 percent of their potential work years away from paid work, compared with 2 percent for men. These rates vary by race and ethnicity, but in January 2001, fewer white women were unemployed than were Hispanic or black women (U.S. Bureau of the Census). Of the nearly 57 million women in the civilian labor force, about 7 million have work disabilities, and women with work disabilities are nearly three times as likely as nondisabled women to be unemployed. Two-thirds of all part-time and nearly three-fifths of all temporary workers are women. Women disproportionately representing workers earning wages has had a severe impact on feminist consciousness among women of color, because when women enter the workforce they encounter both sexism and racism more frequently, but when they bring home incomes, their power within the household increases. Women's power increases regardless of culture when they earn money. Thus, family values are also a concern among people of color.

This leads to a discussion on how, although women make up a little over 51 percent of the 253.7 million U.S. citizens, there are many differences. These differences are most apparent when one concentrates on women of color, but some tendencies among minority women are maintained. The 2000 Census of Population and the Current Population Survey indicated that the median age for black females was almost thirty years of age; for black men it was lower, at about twenty-seven years. About 31 percent of black women were married, 38 percent had never married, 8 percent were separated, 12 percent were widowed, and 11 percent were divorced. Among elderly African Americans, women dominate: 62 percent of the elderly were women, and a woman maintained 44 percent of black households with no husband present.

An interesting slide presentation by the Ethnic and Hispanic Branch of the Population Division of the U.S. Bureau of the Census (2000) reveals that unlike African American women, over half of the 7.2 million Asian and Pacific Islanders were females in the West. Further, Asian females had a median age of thirty-one, compared with twenty-nine for Asian males. Asian men are, on average, older than African American men. Asian women had lower high school graduation rates than Asian men (74 versus 82 percent). Pacific Islander women and men had very similar rates of high school graduation rates (75 and 77 percent), but the female rate was lower. Sixty percent of Asian women and 63 percent of Pacific Islander women were in the labor force, compared with 57 percent of all women in the United States. Women maintained 12 percent of Asian households with no husband present. This was lower than the 19 percent of Pacific Islander households, and the lowest for all women.

One-half of the approximate 34 million Hispanics and Latinos in the United States during the 1990s were women. Fifty-two percent of Hispanic females were in the labor force, compared with 57 percent of all women in the United States. Families maintained by females with no husband present made up about 20 percent of Hispanic families, and about 9 percent of Hispanic females lived alone or maintained a household that did not contain family members. In this decade the issue of family values is especially important for Latinos and Hispanics because the extended family is so important to cultural definition.

In review of the more than 215 million whites in the United States, 51 percent are female. Over three-fourths of white women have a high school degree and 18 percent have a bachelor's degree or higher. Fifty-six percent of white women participate in the labor force, and about 14 percent of white households are headed by women. When compared to women of color, some conditions are glaring. For example, the Asian and Pacific Island female median age is higher. Asian women have higher labor-market participation rates and African American women maintain more households with no male present while Asian women maintain the least number of households with no male present. Some questions arise: What are the social factors that account for the differences? How do social factors impart the data, and how legitimate are the findings? One gained insight to these questions during the 1960s, when women in the civil rights movement placed women's concerns at the forefront. In the process, women of color increased both their race and gender consciousness to render insight into the quality of their lives.

Quality of life issues are important to racial and ethnic people, especially among the elderly. In the future there will be greater racial and ethnic diversity among the nation's elderly because the population that is aging is more diverse. Based on trends from the last three decades, 80 percent of whites and Hispanics, 71 percent of American Indians, and 66 percent of blacks live to age sixty-five (U.S. Bureau of the Census 2000c). Of these, one-fourth will live until they are ninety. Among those who live to the age of eighty-five, black women are likely to live longer; an additional 6.6 years compared with 6.3 years for white women.

## AGE AND AGING AS A FEMINIST ISSUE

Most white middle-class senior citizens assume that democracy is in place. As they age past eighty years they begin to experience limitations contingent upon the deterioration of their physical and sometimes mental faculties. This often prevents them from continued participation in the social and political affairs of the nation. The American Association of Retired Persons (AARP) notes that several states now have more than 1 million elderly citizens. California and Florida have the largest number of people sixty-five and older (AARP 2002). It is estimated that the number of older women will more than double worldwide in the next quarter century. This is of concern to feminists because all people age. Information from the 2000 Census and the Current Population Survey indicates that the elderly population will more than double during the next forty years in the United States, and, as has been mentioned, the leading edge of the baby boom generation will turn sixty-five by 2011. Women will outnumber men three to two, and if history is our teacher, it is in the feminist self-interest to organize now.

AARP also reports that three-fourths of the elderly die from heart disease, cancer, or stroke. After age eighty-five, influenza and pneumonia are the major causes of death. Women are more likely to die of strokes than men are. Those over seventy-five are especially more likely to die from heart disease than men (71 versus 44 percent). Elderly women also tend to have more long-term, chronic, disabling health problems, such as arthritis and hip fractures, while men tend to develop relatively short-term fatal diseases.

Very often senior citizens are disappointed that their children and grandchildren do not come to visit anywhere near as often as they would like them to visit. Elderly women are much more likely to live alone than elderly men. In 2000, the Public Information Office of the U.S. Bureau of the Census reports that women maintained over half (54 percent) of the households run by persons seventy-five and older (2000a). Thus, women are living longer and live alone much longer, and many feel the sting of loneliness. This is often disappointing, because women are the primary caregivers for children and they sometimes feel abandoned by their offspring in their old age. However, women are a large proportion of elderly care providers.

Seniors are healthier than ever before. Less than 10 percent of people sixty-five to sixty-nine years old need assistance with everyday activities. Between ages eighty and eighty-four, 31 percent need assistance, but at eighty-five and older the need for assistance increases to 50 percent. Public funds, primarily Medicare, pay for about 60 percent of health care needs for the elderly. Thus, what happens to Medicare is an issue for senior women. What most young Americans believe, however, is that they will never get old. This value for youth has not only distanced youth from seniors; it has also caused a lack of respect and a multitude of stereotype about seniors. This phenomena is manifest in discrimination, or ageism, against senior citizens. This, coupled with gender, places senior women at risk for bad health, poverty, and various crimes, including home robbery, marketing fraud, physical attack, and rape.

Because women are increasingly likely to have been in the labor force and/or looking for work, by 2010 many will have retirement incomes of their own. But women who are currently seniors often receive benefits through their husbands. The death of a husband often marks a point of economic reversal for the surviving wife. She has to learn to live on less money, but she also has to learn how to manage her own resources. For women of color those resources are highly limited, because if they worked it was in areas where employers did not contribute to retirement and/or social security benefits.

Aging can be a taxing process for women who have not consciously prepared for it, and most women have not. For middle-income seniors, mental and physical ailments do not significantly reduce economic resources until after age eighty. In 2000 women made up nearly 60 percent of the total elderly population, but 75 percent of the elderly population were poor. These statistics appear enough for aging to become a feminist issue, especially in light of the 75 million baby boomers approaching senior citizenship as this book is read. This book stresses the importance of elderly women in cultural maintenance, the exchange of life experiences, and promoting peace. But because the aging baby boomers will soon be a very large population of seniors, and because well over 50 percent will be female, aging must become a feminist issue in the United States. The major concerns of feminists should have to do with the cost and access to health facilities and for housing in a society that has had little appreciation for those who are not young enough to provide for themselves.

In my role as an AARP New Mexico State Legislative Committee member and as vice president of my local AARP chapter, I have found that added to the stresses of aging is the loneliness that comes from the fact that in most households making a living for a younger family of four now takes two full-time wage earners. This leaves little time for working persons to spend quality time with elderly persons living outside their homes. This often leaves the elderly person depressed, with anxiety disorders and the willingness not to live longer. This mental health deterioration increases accidents and the predatory practice of younger service providers like those in home improvement and telemarketing.

There is good news, however. There are some tendencies for people of color and a few whites to keep the elderly home and to offer them more respect. The Americanization process, however, is making this less true for people of color. Families of color are subjected to the same stresses of earning a living and raising children, but women of color also feel the stresses of racism and sexism and ageism combined. They often feel a lack of cultural continuity, which is fostered by a connection between generations (Blea 1988). Because of the limitations of age, seniors attend fewer community gatherings; also few community gatherings that consider the needs of seniors are taking place, and seniors are increasingly looking toward the family for support.

They often are disappointed and feel disillusioned with their families. Many are relinquished to the role of unpaid babysitter, leaving them feeling exploited but with the family's best interests in mind. Exploitation can be emotional, but it can also be material. Five million children lived with a grandparent in 2000; 81 percent of the children who lived with a single parent and a grandparent lived in the grandparent's home (U.S. Bureau of the Census 1995c). However, if the child lived with two parents and a grandparent, they were most likely to live in their parents' home. Sometimes the elderly are able to contribute, but generally the presence of another adult stresses the family living space and emotional stability. On the bright side is that children gain senior role models and historical and social continuity from having a senior at home.

The concerns of the elderly (age and gender) are not disconnected from public policy that impacts women and people of color. Foremost among them is prescription drug cost. In addition, recent attacks on affirmative action, such as Proposition 209 in California, seriously affected women and people of color. Affirmative action has kept college, university, and employment practices open to fair treatment of women and people of color, thereby allowing them to earn a decent living and to prepare for old age. To resist the attacks on affirmative action policy, white women and some men, plus women and men of color, formed coalitions. They were unsuccessful in defeating the attacks, and their coalitions did not succeed past the issue because they forgot they would get old.

There have been a few people of color and white coalitions. Some of the early ones were on bilingual education. Unfortunately, not many feminists saw defending bilingual education as part of their working longevity. Proposition 227 did away with bilingual education in California beginning in August 1998. Bilingual parents of girls took little note of the fact that sexism exists in the schools, and that bilingual girls, like other girls, need a feminist orientation to their studies if we are to promote not only the feminization of racism but the feminization of ageism.

Although putting a senior female face on some issues seems ludicrous, there are some connections. The summer of 1997 witnessed numerous efforts to get the citizens of the Golden State to vote no on Proposition 5, which sought to prevent gambling on Indian land. The pro-gambling side claimed that Las Vegas money had been invested in the campaign against gambling in order to limit competition from the Indian reservations. I lived in California when I witnessed that the other side claimed that Indians could buy land anywhere, and that building over 100 casinos would ruin the quality of life for whites, especially white seniors who would become addicted to gambling in their spare time. Those who wanted gambling claimed that the resisters were misrepresenting the truth. Other sides warned that treaties guaranteeing American Indians the right to become self-sufficient were being violated. It was a confusing mess, coalitions were difficult to form, and persons of good conscience did not know what to think. The issue divided Indian tribes and distanced some tribes from one another. Some attempt was made to note that money from these establishments often goes to build hospitals, clinics, and schools that benefit both men and women, but the racism involved insured that fragmentation of women and men of color from other citizens continued. Some noted that racism was an offense against self-sufficiency and humanity. Additional revenues would help alleviate Indian poverty; if this was not done, everyone suffered.

## POVERTY AS A MODEL FOR THE
## FEMINIZATION OF RACISM

In the 1960s poverty became a feminist issue only after a long debate dominated by white middle-class women insensitive to poverty. The feminization of racism has taken a much longer time to be realized as a feminist issue because white women think it does not affect them. It does. They have lived lives based upon white privilege. In 1964 Lyndon B. Johnson implemented the Civil Rights Act of 1964. The legislation prohibited discrimination based on race, color, religion, sex (including pregnancy), and national origin. This legislation did little to change social relations in the United States. The efforts to produce it defined racism as a major contributor to the existence of poverty. During this period racism appeared to be a black and white phenomenon.

The media consistently featured African Americans as the minority, with little national attention paid to Asians, Latinos, and American Indians. Johnson, however, was sensitive to the Mexican American experience and attacked poverty with Kennedy's idea by declaring a war on poverty. Some believe part of Johnson's incentive was to declare war on a domestic issue to divert attention from the war in Vietnam, which the United States was losing.

The war on poverty was utilized by people of color, especially women, to better the quality of their lives. It was during this time that Medicare and Medicaid, Head Start, financial aid, and legal aid were first made available to poor people. Medicare and Medicaid provided health care to the elderly and the poor. Head Start was an early childhood development program attempting to break the cycle of poverty by assisting children to prepare for school. Financial aid assisted poor students in attending universities across the countries. Legal aid provided legal assistance to the poor.

During my lifetime I have witnessed that together, the Civil Rights Act and the pressure it applied to begin the war on poverty changed the political climate in many states, especially in areas with large populations of people of color. It was in recreation centers, mental health centers, and other war on poverty programs that women of color gained electoral and nonelectoral political experiences in large numbers. In these programs, "minorities" first began to work with white people, but many whites did not want change. They saw no need for restitution to poor people of color for past wrongs committed against them. In 2002 some still believe poverty is caused by laziness. Conversations with Chicanos and Pueblo Indians in New Mexico have revealed to me that they believe whites want to enjoy white privilege and the comforts it brings them, and have no interest in watching people of color acquire equality. Some take direct action to prevent it. In the past these actions were most dangerous in the South and Southwest, where they threatened, injured, and killed civil rights workers. These memories do not die easily.

Historically, the first allies of poor people appear to have been women. In the Southwest, several white nuns supported the Chicano civil rights movement. Women protested the fact that they could not gain admittance to certain schools, vote, or hold political office. They had to obey laws conceptualized and passed by men. For some women, this was unbearable. As early as the 1840s, two of the best-documented women, Elizabeth Cady Stanton (1815–1902) and Susan B. Anthony (1820–1906), fought for equal rights, the right to vote, plus other social, political, and economic rights enjoyed by men.

In the 1960s this history was revitalized and another phase of the women's movement emerged with force. The women's movement had been led by middle-class white women. This resulted in a tremendously fragmented effort because of the hesitancy to address issues of sexual preference and orientation, racism, and class discrimination. There have been a few women of color highly involved in the mainstream movement, but this information has not reached the majority of U.S. women. It has taken the movement years to even recognize that women of color endure racism and class prejudice at the same time they endure sexism. This results in a multivariable existence that was first explored by women of color in the 1960s.

To assist in healing the nation from the ravages of racism, the feminist movement must quickly act to voice that racial discrimination is a feminist issue, just as poverty is a feminist issue. Women of color have to insist upon this. They have to challenge the privilege and often weak power base of white women to correct the perceptions of women of color and the wrongs this perception has done to them and their people. This will bring them more in step with what is happening globally. Women around the world are not going to respect, much less trust, white American feminists until they do this. U.S. women represent powerful potential and can make major world-changing contributions, but they lack legitimacy and credibility in the areas of justice and morality.

The advancement of global peace hinges upon redefining some social conditions as crimes. The feminization of global racism will move humans toward a more humane existence. A more humane existence pivots upon bettering the quality of life for women across the globe, and this is now a stated priority of the United Nations. Further, putting a feminine face on racism is consistent with the platform of action of the U.N. Fourth World Women's Conference.

## PREVENTING CRIMES AGAINST HUMANITY

If I write that discrimination fosters crimes against humanity, many would think me ludicrous. But I feel this way, and especially cruel is the multifaceted interaction of racism and sexism. Sexism allows the commitment of political, economic, and educational offenses against women. It subjects them to the assaults of poverty; trespasses on their human right to have adequate shelter, eat nutritiously, and dress adequately; and in the process batters their children. A lack of commitment against sexist infractions also leaves women open to physical and emotional abuse, including the crimes of murder and rape.

The U.S. Crime Index rates per 100,000 inhabitants went from 1,887.2 in 1960 to 5,897.8 in 1996 (FBI 2001b). According to the statistics totaled by state by the FBI (2001, 2002) by 1996 the crime rate was 313 percent the 1960 crime rate. In 2000 the risk of being a victim of a crime is categorized to include stolen or damaged property, murder, forcible rape, robbery, aggravated assault, burglary, larceny theft, and vehicle theft. Crime in the United States accounts for more death, injuries, and loss of property than all natural disasters combined. The murder rate in the United States last year was the lowest in thirty-five years. According to the FBI (2002), Americans were victims of slightly fewer serious crimes reported to police. The FBI's final figures for crimes reported in 2000 showed very slight decreases in the number of murders, robberies, assaults, and burglaries (2001a). The same report showed small increases in rapes, larcenies, and auto thefts. The rate—meaning the number of incidents per 100,000 residents—dropped for all of those crimes. The report marked the nation's ninth consecutive year of fewer reported crimes and a 22-percent decrease since the last decade.

The reduction in crime is attributed to tougher sentencing rules, which prompted a prison-building boom to accommodate more inmates and longer sentences. Some argued that the strong national economy under Bill Clinton, and the historically low unemployment rate that accompanied it, played a large role in pushing down the number of crimes reported. But analysts note that demographics are a key factor, as the last of the huge baby boomer generation moved beyond their crime-prone years. Whatever the reason, the number of people in young age groups (middle teens to middle twenties) is expected to swell again in the early 2000s (U.S. Bureau of the Census 2000b). Keep in mind that 51 percent of the baby boomers are women and that women will disproportionately outnumber men as they get older. This leaves older women more vulnerable to crime, not only because of their gender, but because of their age.

By the end of the last century the crime rate fell 3 percent. In 1999 it fell to 506 per 100,000 residents, the lowest level since 1978. The number of people murdered was down to less than 0.1 percent. Cities had a 0.7-percent increase in murders, with the most pronounced increase, 11.7 percent, originating in towns with fewer than 10,000 residents. The number of forcible rapes of women increased for the first time in eight years, by 0.9 percent to 90,186 offenses (FBI 2001). However, the rape rate went down 1.6 percent. Rape is a social as well as an individual mental disease that causes physical and psychological trauma to predominately female victims. Worldwide, feminists find it essential to stop the rape of women, the lifegivers of humanity. At an international level, prosecuting rapists during wartime is rare. Only through the efforts of women has the legal right not to be raped been enforced. There are still problems with how rape is handled by authorities, but now women have more female political representatives in the judicial and medical communities and some gains have been made on the home front.

In summary, overall crime rates were highest in the South and lowest in the Northeast. The crime rate dropped the most in the Northeast, and the least crime was in the West. The FBI crime report is based on data reported voluntarily by 17,000 local and state law enforcement agencies, which represent 94 percent of the U.S. population. It reported a total of 9,524 hate crimes in 2000. Most hate crimes are crimes of intolerance, reported by 11,700 law enforcement agencies (FBI 2001b).

To understand the development of feminist consciousness among women of color in the United States, one must know the gender, racial, and class histories of these women. There is also the importance of the 1960s civil rights movement, which fostered feminist consciousness, gaining insight into the power relations between men and women. For social activists this includes doing something about it, taking action to change the power relationships, and enduring the consequence of their decisions within the social and political context in which the action was taken.

The first generation of contemporary feminists of color received nonelectoral and electoral political experience during the 1960s. Prior to this, women meandered alone, with a friend or family member, through their attitudes about the nature of their powerlessness in their lives. If they questioned their lives they were generally told that things were simply that way, not to "make waves" or "upset the apple cart," and to forget about it. Because racism was so intense, many women of color tried to forget about it.

White women were more fortunate than women of color because they had a history of a feminist movement in their background. The majority of women of color did not know their feminist history. The combined factors of racism and sexism had denied them the knowledge of their people's history. The white feminist movement of the nineteenth century impacted a few African American women, but there is no record that it touched the lives of American Indians, Asians, or Chicanos.

Prior to the civil rights movement, most women did not have a language like feminism and racism, and a voice to express their concerns. The civil rights movement remedied most of this. It provided a vehicle for them to gather in groups to render opinions, ask questions, and talk about their feelings and experiences and how to put their ideas into action. During this period they were able to evaluate the civil rights movement, criticize it, and implement changes for women. Thus, with regard to oppressing a feminist consciousness, the Taliban was correct in limiting interaction among women. This does not make it right, or good, or moral, but it did keep women in a subservient position to the males in control. Women around the world have known this as a male strategy and still strive against it.

The experience of women under Taliban rule demonstrated that periods of historical significance are not significant to all people in the same manner. Women have a different experience, dictated by gender and the social significance of their sex. As U.S. women of color worked in small groups themselves, they experienced both male and female resistance, retaliation, and even violence because of their feminist views. Not only did their communities turn against them, racist whites ridiculed them and their people for claiming civil liberties. Thus, the first civil rights organizing among women of color was clandestine, just as Afghan women met privately to resist their oppression. From this we learn more about the nature of resistence. It begins small, sometimes quietly, for women.

White feminists of the 1960s were also not highly supportive. They asked women of color to choose between organizing against racism and struggling against gender discrimination. Women of color could not socially, psychologically, biologically, or spiritually separate the fact that they were female from the fact that they were persons of color. In addition, selecting to fight a feminist battle did not do away with the white privilege white women wanted to cling to. Women of color of that period could not join forces with white feminists, the hippies, or the anti–Vietnam War protests for very long. Racism and the privileges it granted to some was so firmly engrained in the psyche of white activists that they thought only they could lead. People of color were tired of following strategies that did not work for the betterment of all, and women generally retreated from the white feminist movement into their own cultural movements to resist sexual discrimination.

## PROMOTING TOLERANCE AND
## GLOBAL DEMOCRACY

The U.S. civil rights movement gained world attention and consisted of various interests with various factions. One of its aims, however, was to build a true democracy that could be respected worldwide. Most Americans believe the movement is the African American movement, but it was much more. It was not, and still is not, solely a black–white struggle. It was and is a struggle of people of all colors attempting to create a just and more peaceful world. The elimination of racism was a goal among Mexican Americans in the form of the Chicano civil rights movement. American Indians emerged with a civil rights movement characterized by the highly verbal American Indian movement (AIM). Indians and Chicanos presented issues relevant to land, the use of their native languages, and religion. Asian Americans participated, with increased attention to the need for bilingual education and a humane immigration policy. Japanese citizens finally talked about their incarceration during World War II, and the Chinese voiced their experiences with discrimination through a public policy that excluded them. Of major concern to all groups were political representation, employment, and integration of ethnic and racial history into educational curricula, increased health care, and lower incarceration rates.

This took place with minimal white support. White youth was receiving much media attention for their rejection of dominant forms of authority via the "flower child" or "hippie" movement. They wanted freedom of linguistic and sexual expression, to be free of social pressure to conform, creative freedom, and an end to the Vietnam War. The civil rights movement advocated these concerns, but it was on the Vietnam issue that the youth of the 1960s, regardless of color, came together the most.

The 1960s activism worried the U.S. government, which was frightened about what would happen to its military, economic, and political presence in Southeast Asia under communism. U.S. soldiers were fighting in Vietnam to insure that U.S. interests would remain firm, but young Americans wanted love, not war. However, the coalitions with white youth on this issue also did not last long. More generally, what happened was that each group held mass demonstrations linking the war to their own issues and featuring their own male leadership. It was racism, the inability of youth of all colors to unite, that prevented revolution in the United States, not the National Guard, nor the election of presidents, nor federal government infiltration of the movements, nor the killing or incarceration or imprisonment of the leadership, nor the cooling off of tempers.

The 1960s were important to the baby boom generation, who are now fifty-five to sixty-five years old. In their youth this generation took over state and federal buildings, burned records, and even bombed buildings. Those who sought to stop them were not called terrorists. The youth were called "radical," the worst thing one could be in the United States in the 1960s. It was mostly adults, using the media to launch propaganda against social change, who undermined the civil rights movement. Those of privileged status called the youth overprivileged kids with unrealistic dreams and nothing better to do in the media. Young men were stereotyped as draft dodgers, the women as "loose."

A public television program, "1968: The Year That Stopped a Generation" (Oregon Public Broadcasting 1998), clearly spells out how this was class and age warfare. It placed adult Americans against its young and brought open rebellion into homes, on the television, and in the streets. White adults were shocked to see civil disobedience, and cloaked it in a language that attempted to diminish and disarm. Conservative Americans could not believe that males were burning their draft cards and that females were appearing in public without bras. Many angry Americans were disgusted with the marches against the Vietnam War, and many youth were infuriated by the fact that they were being told the war was not a war. Most shocking to them was that policemen were beating them up and spraying with them mace for publicly demonstrating and resisting accepting conditions as they were.

The violence boiled to a fever pitch at the 1968 Democratic Convention, where the city of Chicago armed itself against 10,000 demonstrators, who were mauled when the U.S. flag was lowered and defiled. Some adults now hated the youth and what they stood for, especially youth of color, who were addressing issues of racism. White adults had gone from ridiculing and demeaning them to taking prohibitive action by coming down hard with billy clubs on all youth; the stereotypes had escalated from name calling, frustration, pushing, and kicking to full-scale violence. On May 4, 1970, a riot during a Vietnam War protest at Kent State College in Ohio left four students dead, one permanently paralyzed, and eight others wounded. These assassinations entered the front rooms of Americans via television on the evening news.

People of color were not shocked by the violence exerted by the National Guard against the students. They knew people would die advocating change. Violence against people of color for criticizing and taking action against injustice was common at the time in the form of police brutality. They also knew violence in other ways: psychologically, spiritually, and by government policies that limited their civil and human rights.

The television program about the 1960s noted here has a title that implies that the only losers of that generation were the youth themselves. I lived through the 1960s and was active in the Chicano movement. The television program blamed the victim, as if mainstream society did nothing to aggravate the situation. The documentary renders some insight into the concerns of people of color, and it informs us that the civil rights movement was international. It was a human rights movement that also took place in Germany, Japan, Mexico, and France. It was violently controlled one piece at a time, but not without rejuvenating the Socialist Party. In Mexico City students held a demonstration on October 2, 1968, seeking freedom from one-party political rule. They were massacred in Taloloco, in Plaza de las Tres Culturas, where the Spanish had massacred the Aztec Indians in 1521. This was a turning point in Mexican politics, and a turning point in the United States. Some government officials, and many citizens, charged that communists infiltrated the civil rights movements. I remember how critics maintained that outside insurgents, seeking to overthrow democracy, were at the root of youth unrest. They simply could not believe that youth had the ability to be critical and act upon their conclusions. Even today this attitude of outsiders coming into the United States "riling up" American youth has been fueled by the attacks on youth in Tiananmen Square in Beijing, China, in 1989 where the government was communist. In other words, the civil rights movement was a communist plot.

The civil rights movement launched phenomena that not only changed the nation, they also changed the world. It brought foreign policy into the living rooms of most Americans. Communist infiltration was suspected on November 24, 1963, when President John F. Kennedy was killed by an assassin's bullet in Dallas, Texas. This agitated the conservatives, who hated not only communists but suspected them as involved in the civil rights movement. On June 4, 1968, the president's brother, Robert Kennedy, was killed. The Kennedys had supported civil rights for people of color in the United States and their deaths signaled to the world that not all was well in America. To make matters worse, on April 4, 1968, civil rights leader Martin Luther King, Jr. was also shot and killed in Memphis. In the national and international media emerged stories of America's dead national heroes. Accompanying these stories were film, video, and photographs of the heroes' wives dressed in mourning. The now famous renderings of Jackie and Ethel Kennedy and Coretta Scott King dressed in black, burying their slain husbands, proved to the world that fighting for civil and human rights in America was dangerous. Many Americans lost their innocence and their idealism. Youthful women of color became more skeptical and more critical of their own country and the people who ran it. The skepticism persists, and was evident in the loudness of their silence when two jets tumbled the World Trade Center and another crashed into the Pentagon.

## STRATEGIES FOR HEALING

It has been my experience that analyzing and balancing contradictions and the values attached to adjusting U.S. history to make it inclusive is highly difficult but necessary if we are to gain global respect. To have a more inclusive society we need to know the history of indigenous populations and how they differ from immigrant populations. We need to discuss this in a context of war and conquest, one that focuses on war and conquest, and includes people of color living under colonialism or other characteristics of war. This means that when attention is paid to Asian women, the focus should not tend to be upon the Chinese and Japanese cultures with little attention to their diversity. Attention must be paid to them and to Korean, Vietnamese, and Cambodian women and the consequences of war upon their lives. This attention must be extended to Pacific Island women, who also get caught up in the mental and political boundaries of being indigenous and conquered on their own land and Asian at the same time.

We must redefine the fact that U.S. citizens need to have categories and niches in which to place people. These categories and niches, if they must continue, must be rooted in reality and not the denial that has Americans wanting to simplify and romanticize how they think about their own people. Is it possible? Yes, with a massive education program that includes not just retribution but atonement and forgiveness as well. Do not all groups, even animals, have a hierarchical order? It does not matter. Humans have placed themselves at the top of the evolutionary scale and now must act as if they are above being animalistic. Diversity, violence, and population control are the rule in the United States, as they are in most countries. We can only heal if we know social control works to separate citizen and nations.

To escape our denial we must acknowledge and engage in discussions on African American women and how we must include attention to atrocities committed against them during slavery and how this experience informs and shapes Americans. We also have to focus on the contributions of African American and other women as entrepreneurs, authors, and entertainers at the same time we acknowledge the large middle income and other contributions of Hispanics and African Americans. These populations have many of the same problems as other people, but they have special concerns because they have had the experience of people of color.

Women must also write, publish, and make their presence felt in other media, but there are some problems attached to documenting women of color. It is impossible to generalize and remain politically correct. In some ways "political correctness" has limited expression. It is difficult to gather reliable data and use politically correct labels and language. In addition, there is also the burden of filtering through the artificial boundaries, categories placed not only on data and historical documentation, but also in our minds. These artificial boundaries consist of settlement patterns of the United States from east to west and redefining it as initially a south to north movement.

U.S. women and those of the world cannot afford the dual impact of man-made boundaries and categories, plus the definitions and limitations they have imposed upon themselves. The social circumstance of women is too grave. It is so serious that men and generations of children plus other women do not know nor appreciate women, their gifts and contributions, and the fact that they have answers that can heal the divisions imposed upon them and upon the world. The U.N. World Women's Conference addresses all this. The aim is to create world agreement among member nations on the nature of women's rights and how to protect them. This protection is especially important in time of war, when women are seized as part of the prize and experience rape at alarming rates. I am not alone, there are millions of women of color and other feminists who share this worldview.

## REFERENCES

AARP. 2002. Material distributed at New Mexico State Legislative Committee. Santa Fe, New Mexico. June 13.

Blea, Irene. 1988. *Toward a Chicano Social Science*. New York: Praeger.

Oregon Public Broadcasting System. 1998. "1968: The Year That Stopped a Generation." Produced by Steve Talbot.

U.S. Bureau of the Census. 2001a. Ethnic & Hispanic Statistics Branch. Population Division. Washington, D.C.: U.S. Government Printing Office. (See also slide presentation: slide 3 of 22; last revised: January 4, 2001).

———. 2001b. "The Nuclear Family Rebounds." Public Information Office. Report by Jason Fields, April 13. Washington, D.C.: U.S. Government Printing Office.

———. 2001c. "Revenues for Women-Owned Businesses Show Continued Growth." Washington, D.C.: U.S. Government Printing Office.

———. 2000a. "Census Facts for Womens History Month," and "Women-Owned Firms Compared to All U.S. Firms by State." (CB97-FS.02.) (See also memo from Laverne Vines Collins, Chief of the Census Bureau's Public Information Office, February 2, 2000. Washington, D.C.: U.S. Government Printing Office. Also available at <http://www.census.gov/Press-Release/cb96-07.html>).

———. 2000b. "Half of All Mothers with Infants Return to Labor Force after Giving Birth." Washington, D.C.: U.S. Government Printing Office.

————. 2000c. "Profile of the Nation's Women." Public Information Office. Washington, D.C.: U.S. Government Printing Office.

————. 2000d. "Women in the United States: March, 2000." PPL-121. Washington, D.C.: U.S. Government Printing Office.

————. 2000e. "Women-Owned Firms Compared to All U.S. Firms by State: 1992–2000." Washington, D.C.: U.S. Government Printing Office.

————. 1998. "Younger Women Surpass Young Men in Educational Attainment." Washington, D.C.: U.S. Government Printing Office.

————. 1997. "We Measure: Women and Their Racial and Ethnic Backgrounds." Washington, D.C.: U.S. Government Printing Office.

————. 1996a. "Age at First Marriage at Record High." Public Information Office. Washington, D.C.: U.S. Government Printing Office.

————. 1996b. "One-Third of Nation's Businesses Owned by Women." Washington, D.C.: U.S. Government Printing Office.

————. 1995a. "About 40% of Food Stamp Mothers Never Married." Washington, D.C.: U.S. Government Printing Office.

————. 1995b. "Never-Married Women Have Children," Washington, D.C.: U.S. Government Printing Office.

U.S. Department of Labor, Womens Bureau. 1993. "We Measure America: Women and Work." Washington, D.C.: U.S. Government Printing Office.

U.S. Federal Bureau of Investigation (FBI). 2002. "United States Crime Statistics: United States Crime Index: Rates per 100,000 Inhabitants." Crime Index Public Information Office. Washington, D.C.: U.S. Government Printing Office.

————. 2001a. "United States Crime Index: Rates per 100,000 Inhabitants." Washington, D.C.: U.S. Government Printing Office.

————. 2001b. "U.S. Crime Statistics Total and by State: United States Crime Index: Rates per 100,000 Inhabitants." Public Information Office. Washington, D.C.: U.S. Government Printing Office.

————. 1996. "Women's Statistics News Release." (Last update 3/14/96). "United States Crime Index: Rates per 100,000 Inhabitants." Public Information Office. Washington, D.C.: U.S. Government Printing Office.

# CHAPTER 2

# Indigenous Women and the American Holocaust

Contrary to popular belief, women of color are highly diverse and they are not all immigrants. In addition, not all of them are delighted with their lives in the United States. A great number of them are offended because they and their men are targeted as potential terrorists. They believe this to be a blatant racist act. One of the most racist terrorist acts was committed against American Indians. Indigenous women and their people suffered what they refer to as "America's holocaust." They were hunted, enslaved, not allowed to speak their language, and taken by force as young as the age of four to be schooled, to have the Indian "removed" from them. They not only lost their independence; they were silenced and segregated on what now numbers 800 reservations across the country. Social–cultural oppression and blanket beliefs called stereotypes limit the quality of life for these female Americans. Their story is the American story. American practices have entrapped them into female roles and into the roles of unprivileged people of color.

## MYTHS AND STEREOTYPES AS A RESULT OF CONQUEST

This holocaust could only have happened because of racism, but it continues because of lack of knowledge and the denial that it even took place. This deficit on behalf of the American public limits the knowledge base and the richness of the world in which most U.S. citizens live. It robs the citizenry of their true history and the ability to make a situation right, and it robs the country of alternative perspectives in solving its social, economic, and political problems, and in achieving scientific advancement, artistic creation, and spiritual advancement. In this time of what many see as a world under terrorist attack, it is imperative that we heal from the defamations and atrocities committed against Indians and other people of color. It is important that we move quickly toward the feminization of racism and against discrimination against women and men and children of color in order to strengthen our country by cementing our unity as one nation.

What Europeans did to indigenous people, the land, the air, the sky, the animals, and other resources was to colonize them. Colonization imposed devastating changes on indigenous women. It slaughtered them by the hundreds, infected their immune systems, and created camps concentrating them on remote reservations. The severe social consequence of the reservation system cannot be understated. Because of this system Indian people were not allowed to leave the reservations without passes and written permission from white officials (Nabokov 1991). When Indians would not cooperate, the military and Indian agents held back food and starved them until they complied.

However, indigenous women can teach us how to survive under attack. They can teach us about resistance and maintaining humanity plus balance in a diverse world. These women have been conquered economically and politically, but not spiritually. And in spite of all efforts, they have maintained their culture and have succeeded in passing it on to further generations. They have persevered against white American attempts at genocide, including germ warfare, and they continue to live with a history of constant terrorist attack (Ethnic NewsWatch 1999). We will see that many of them have even gained notoriety in Anglo society.

Attention to the discovery of America was brought to the forefront by the observance of the quincentennial in the Americas. This 500-year anniversary of European exploration provided a new nonelectoral political platform and increased publication on critical perspectives regarding the presence of white people in this hemisphere. The quincentennial lay to rest the outdated contentions that white men "discovered" the Indians and the New World; in fact, the Americas were very old and very well discovered by indigenous populations before the Europeans arrived. Prior to the coming of the first male Europeans, the Spanish, there were entire civilizations, like the ancient Inca, Olmec, Maya, and later the Aztec.

Unfortunately, the resurgence in interest and publication during the quincentennial did little to remove stereotypes about the original women on this continent. U.S. citizens still prefer to think of males as representing indigenous people. In their minds the male is the noble savage of the last century, ignorant, trading everything away cheaply, but inherently vicious, especially when full of liquor.

With a thought that manifests linguistically, the stereotyped native woman begins with her being called a squaw. The term "squaw" is always insulting to indigenous women and should never be used. It is as racist as the word "nigger." In American movies and literature native women are most frequently stereotyped as being fat and ugly on one extreme or extraordinarily beautiful and all loving of the white man on the other. With regard to Indian men, squaws were and are stereotyped as all-pleasing beasts of burden, walking three paces behind an untamed male and his horse. Today, native women are rarely thought about as contemporary women, in contemporary dress, and in various high-ranking professions. Nevertheless, they are very present. Some have lifestyles rooted in their indigenousness, others reject this, and some know they are "Indian" but do not know anything about their indigenousness. Nevertheless, they exist and have much to teach.

In preparation for, during, and after the quincentennial, U.S. American Indians, activist scholars, and writers continued their tradition of drawing into question the stereotypes of indigenous people, how history, the media, and so on have presented them, and the idea of male-centered cultures. They exposed the stereotype of Indians as bloodthirsty barbarians seeking to prevent the civilization of an untamed wilderness, later to be referred to as "Indian Territory," by white people. This action gave way to the fact that North America once had fewer and different territorial boundaries that are not acknowledged today, and the fact that many cultures were matrilineal, female dominant, and very peaceful.

This "setting the record straight" about "Indians" translated into popular culture and in some arenas is becoming more evident. Attempts are manifesting in stories about indigenous women like Pocahontas and Sacajawea. One of the first attempts at humanizing Pocahontas was by Jean Fritz (1983). The demand for the stereotype is overwhelming. One only needs to look at what has been done to trivialize, romanticize, and corrupt the story of Pocahontas. Contrary to the popular media image, Pocahontas was a very young girl betrayed by the errors, lack of appreciation, and lack of cultural sensitivity on the part of the ambitious John Smith (Morenus 2002).

Sacajawea, on the other hand, has not been as badly maligned in the media as Pocahontas because she is missing. The lack of animated film for the sake of "family" entertainment has spared her the slim, sexy, white-male-obsessed image of Pocahontas. She has been more accurately portrayed in documentaries and biographies as the woman who nurtured a newborn child while traveling with her French "husband," Meriwether Lewis, and William Clark while exploring the Louisiana Purchase. Unfortunately, for the sake of public education and accurate historical celebration, Lewis and Clark received all the credit, and Sacajawea still reveals an alluring portrait as she gazes at us from the one-dollar American coin.

When the average U.S. citizen scans the country's history for an indigenous female presence, little surfaces. If contemporary "Indians" are mentioned, they tend to be extraordinary like the World War II code talkers or assimilated men, like the honorable Senator Ben Night Horse Campbell from Colorado, or R. C. Gorman, the famous artist. I am still surprised when young feminists do not know the plight of Indian women. Perhaps the most well-known indigenous women are Wilma Mankiller, the first female principal chief of the Cherokee Nation, lecturer, consultant, and author; and Marilyn Whirlwind, an actress in the no longer shown television program *Northern Exposure*. Although there have been some criticisms, Whirlwind's role was one of an intelligent, not easily taken-in female who would not allow others to control her worldview, or her vacation, when she took a weekend to visit Seattle. Wilma Mankiller made American history when she led the Cherokee Nation in participating in national public policy and human rights. Indigenous women's contributions are not limited to these two women. Among them live numerous writers, including poets and scholars like Rayna Green, Joy Harjo, Beverely Hungry Wolf, Brooke Medicine Eagle, and Mary Summer Rain. These women render women's experiences of reservation life, insights into the boarding school system, family hardships, spirituality, and their personal failures and successes while tribal traditions were on the decline.

## BEFORE THE CONQUEST

When Columbus arrived in 1492 an estimated 10 million people with some 300 distinct cultures who spoke over 200 different languages lived in North America alone. They were concentrated on the West Coast, now known as California, about fifty-six people every fifty square miles. The Southwest was the second most populated region, with nearly fourteen inhabitants per fifty square miles. Those east of the Mississippi lived an average of nine persons per fifty square miles (Nabokov 1991, 4). There is no estimate of how many of these people were women. In some tribes women were supreme. They certainly ranked higher, and with more power, than in most European societies of the same time. Women of native societies voted long before any other women of the world. It was not until 1924 that Indians acquired voting privileges in the United States. Early women, however, were equals of men as warriors, and many women were just as famous (Gridley 1974).

Most tribal and clan designations were imposed upon the indigenous by outsiders. Prior to the arrival of the white man, people divided themselves according to the regions they occupied. With the arrival of Europeans, maps were drawn, lines separated regions, and the original inhabitants were given names according to European worldviews. The Chumash of the south-central coast of California and the Channel Islands are named from a Spanish corruption of *mitcumac* or *tcuma*, terms used by coastal people to describe the occupants of Santa Cruz and the Santa Rosa Islands. In other instances Spanish tribal names were not rooted in the native language and referred to the regions where people lived: Serrano for mountain people, Costanoan for coast dwellers. After the arrival of European males, a few Indian women "married" the Spanish, and incorporated some Spanish traditions into their lives via food, dance, costumes, and language. Today, American Indians and Alaskan natives speak more than 300 distinct languages. This results in dialects more diverse than the entire Indo-European language family. Spanish rape of Indian women and intermarriage between indigenous women and Spanish males also produced the mestizo, a mixture of Indian and Spanish people who dominate what we now know as the Americas. In the United States, most mestizo Chicanas see themselves as indigenous, and identify with their mother culture.

Even during this time in history, indigenous people defined regions in a way that had little to do with white settlement patterns or boundaries drawn on maps. When white man, and later a few women, came into the area, they named it according to their conceptions of boundaries and imposed the tradition of private property. The early Spanish gave coastal people names like Gabrielino or Luiseno after the Spanish missions they were associated with (Time-Life Books 1994). On the West Coast there were roughly thirty-four autonomous Pomo bands, whose Hokan-derived dialects were as different from one another as English and German. Each group had their own housing style, favorite foods, art, material needs.

There is a contemporary false assumption by racists that indigenous people do not produce "high art," and that they in fact are artless and indolent. This has provided outsiders with a rationale for imposing on them and exploiting their resources, including their artistic ability. Spanish friars and military confined tens of thousands to build and decorate missions in an effort to convert them to Christianity and make them "more productive." The tragic effect was the disruption of the subsistence patterns and the exposure of Indians to the ravages of European-borne diseases. By the 1800s the missions declined and those who followed regarded the indigenous people as property to be used up and discarded, or as pests to be exterminated.

In the tribes there has been a division of labor with equal value. Males were hunters and protectors of the village. When they were home from hunting or making war, they worked at keeping fit via physical activity and athletic games. They made their own weapons and built their own traps, canoes, and/or dugouts. The male constructed his tools. If he were a Plains Indian, he would raid and take the horses of his enemy. This was the mark of a good warrior; it granted him status and prestige. Meanwhile, the women maintained the stability of the village. She made her own tools and had her own games.

Some indigenous tribes were fierce enemies of the Spanish and Anglos. During Spanish rule, Mexico wanted to end the freedom of Indians, who resisted in accordance with the threat to their lifestyle. Attempts were made to protect women from the soldiers' advances, but threats of rape were constant. A report written in the late 1770s testified that soldiers at the San Gabriel Archangel and San Juan Capistrano missions went out at night to the nearby villages to assault Indian women (Nabokov 1991). If the women were hidden, the soldiers beat the men to learn their location. Father Serra castigated the civil authorities for ignoring the shameful conduct. Some Indian women entered the missions to gain protection from sexual predators. Sexual violence, harassment, and rape continued. After 1800 troops pursuing runaways or fresh recruits even claimed women as prizes during clashes with villagers in the Central Valley. Some of the women became pregnant after being raped or abducted. Many reacted by aborting their fetuses or killing their newborns via strangulation or suffocation. Conceiving and killing a child under these conditions was perceived as either a vulgar degrading consequence of a desecrating act, or an act of mercy. Life as an Indian was too painful.

Children as well as women were abducted into slavery. Most white men considered Indian women and girls unattractive but necessary. Many purchased women and kept them as servants and concubines against their will. A girl considered suitable for this purpose could bring $200 or more on the slave market. In the 1800s, indigenous territories were flooded with unattached white males. They and white settlers rapidly multiplied, taxing the natural food sources. The food supply began to diminish among all Indians who had contact with Anglo settlers who tended to be Protestant and spoke only English. Indian women and girls were the first to feel it, because they were the ones with the most immediate relationship to food.

Peter Nabokov (1991) renders extraordinary insight into Indian relationships with whites. During the gold rush, white men raped Indian women, and newspapers referred to it as obtaining a "squaw." Some of the Indian attacks against whites were retaliations for rape, a crime native groups abhorred among themselves. In one instance, a Nisenan woman was raped and abducted by a miner named Big Tom. Her people demanded her return. When Big Tom refused to return the woman, a group of Nisenan warriors attacked his camp, rescued the woman, killed Tom's companions, and chopped the rapist huimself into pieces. However, not all interracial unions were forced upon Indian women, or devoid of affection. A few native women welcomed relationships with white men who treated them kindly and shielded them from hunger and abuse. Anglos scorned white men who entered into such relationships as "squaw men" and called their offspring "half-breeds."

To try to survive in a changing world, native people had to be "good Indians" (Hale 1993), and a few women turned to prostitution (Nabokov 1991). A prostitute's life was, and is, short and bitter. They aged quickly and became diseased. Many of the women contracted venereal diseases from white men. These diseases spread devastation among the tribes, but numerous other germs (such as cholera, typhoid, malaria, smallpox, whooping cough, and measles) were unconsciously and sometimes purposefully communicated to Indians by whites as they settled or passed through Indian country. Blankets infested with measles and smallpox were given to Indians with the intent to annihilate entire tribes.

When Europeans encountered indigenous people, they were ill equipped to relate to them and to their environment. This is why the story of the Pilgrims is so pervasive. It deals with fundamental, universal, human concerns of food and survival. Many myths must be laid to rest with regard to Indian history, particularly the Thanksgiving story. Contrary to popular belief, the first Thanksgiving did not take place on the East Coast among white Pilgrims and Indians. It took place in New Mexico between the Spanish and the Pueblo people, and it was not a single event. Many shared dinners of thanks took place throughout the year (New Mexico Spanish Genealogy Society 2001).

Most readers are aware that the natives were not prepared for their encounter with European men, much less European women. The result for the Indians was exploitation, violence, germ warfare, cultural and physical genocide, purposeful lies, broken treaties, and poverty. Continued subjugation in the form of high incarceration rates and alcohol and drug addiction has made most indigenous people distrustful of whites and many have come to regret that Indian people fed the Europeans, taught them how to live on the land, and even married them.

## BUFFALO WOMEN OF WAR

Today's Native American scholars and authors are descendants of long suffering and creative women. Buffalo women who watched the buffalo being slaughtered by white men for fun and profit mark a distinctive era. They are a generation that was murdered, imprisoned, and forced to march hundreds of miles across the country during the white man's effort to "round them up," relocate, and thereby control them if they could not kill them. Stories of the "longest walk" or the "trial of tears" abound.

Indian men within and outside tribes disagreed about how to react to American relocation efforts of the mid to late 1800s. Some chose to fight, to resist, and women and children resisted along with men. Only a few of them get mentioned. For example, Huera, sometimes called Francesca by the Mexicans but always referred to as Mangas's (Apache) second wife, was one of them. Her Chiricahua name was Tze-gu-juni or Pretty Mouth, and throughout her life she had much influence upon Mangas's and Geronimo's decisions (Nabokov 1991).

Successful Apache hunters and warriors like Mangas often had several wives, each bearing children. Warriors of lesser status might marry only one woman. Promiscuity was rare. Promiscuous women were disfigured by knife slits that made their indiscretions clear. Many Apache raiders captured young women in Mexico. These women were often slaves that might be taken by the men on dangerous treks considered too risky for the real wife, especially if she had a child. Usually, captured females were accepted as being Apache and joined the households of wives.

Sometimes the presence of new women created domestic strife (Nabokov 1991). While newly acquired women might serve as bedmates, they bore the stigma of "non-spouse." This now makes it difficulty to conduct genealogy. Many names of women and children of this status have disappeared, but among most tribes childhood laughter was tolerated when no enemy was near. Children, however, learned silence as a precaution against the unknown, and were often sequestered in a well-hidden camp while the men rode away to look for the white soldiers who sought to capture the tribe and place them in detention camps or on reservations.

Nabokov introduces us to another woman, Lozen. Some called her "Dexterous Horse Thief," and others referred to her as "Warrior Woman." She was the younger sister of Victorio, the chief of the Warm Springs Apache band. Lozen was a healer, and had the seer's power of discernment. She traveled with Victorio and he took full advantage of her extraordinary skills of prediction. She attended each war ceremony, where her name was called along with other warriors (Nabokov 1991). But Lozen was not unusual. Other women went into war. They fought ferociously. Some were messengers and emissaries between Apache warriors and Anglo military men. Women also served as sentinels. They were magnificent horsepersons and handled rifles and knives well. Some were good runners and excellent at living off the land, sometimes armed with one blanket and a knife.

During the government relocation of Indians, many tribes were mixed with others whose languages they did not understand. Some of them were enemies. Because they were thrown together, some mixed out of the need to survive. White men mistook some tribes for being another tribe or for harboring a specific warrior. Generally they were all killed. To escape these atrocities many went across the international borders of Canada and Mexico, where American jurisdiction ended at the border (Hale 1993).

Janet Campbell Hale (1993) lent insight into intertribal relationships in her book *Bloodlines*. During the relocation, inter- and intratribal quarrels among the captured became fights resulting in homicides. A few Mexican friends, shepherds, and small rancheros gave or traded or sold the resistor's arms and supplies. Several Anglo men engaged in the illegal sales of weapons to Indians.

My grandmother told me stories of how some of the women on the long marches gave birth to babies, some of them in winter. The marches did not stop and the women had to catch up. Most of them carried their babies in their arms or on cradle boards for well over three hundred miles. They often killed their babies or gave them away to Mexican women in order to prevent them from growing up under genocidal conditions.

When Indian resistance was subdued and "resettlement" was an institution, a few Indians wanted personal peace and settled by themselves. Some settled in groups. Most settled in villages, clustered with others of their own background and tried to revive what had been lost. Some acculturated to reservation life. Some became urban Indians (Simon 1996), trading reservation poverty for urban poverty and isolation. In both cases women were frequently embarrassed by their poverty. They were angry at how they had been humiliated and depressed by their traumatic experience. Nevertheless they remained "strong of heart" and moved beyond the atrocities to create yet another life.

Women had to decide about following the "Jesus road," Christianity. They anguished over questioning their own spirituality, being forced to convert to Christianity, and the consequences of holding onto traditional values. Some joined invented religions, like Silas John and the Four Cross Cult, which blended old and new ways. As there is today, there was spiritual diversity on the reservation. There was also distrust of white men.

There have been so many other difficult periods in U.S. and Indian relationships. Therefore, it is difficult to select the most difficult, but the horrific experience of relocation has to rank among the highest, and Indian women were present every step of the long march, the journey into "civilization." There are several publications on the subject, but for a more thorough discussion on buffalo women see *Apache Mothers and Daughters* (McDonald Boyer and Duffy Gayton 1992) and read any number of publications on the subject written from the Indian perspective.

## STRONG-HEARTED WOMEN

Contemporary women struggle daily to raise children that are assets to both Indian and white society, and they are succeeding. They are women, like those that work at the Native Women's Health Education Resource Center (2002), who work with the drug and alcohol addicted, in social welfare service agencies, in hospitals, in their churches, on reservations, in urban slums, and in their homes. They struggle to send their children to universities. The unsung heroines include those who help organize powwows and health conferences, write novels and poetry, sing, produce film and video, and in the process advocate for their people, the rightful respect of women. They are educators, politicians, businesspersons, clergy, attorneys, senior citizens, community center directors, and government administrators. They know their history and resist by surviving, living to tell the story.

Some Americans believe the stereotype that indigenous women are quiet, unassuming women, accustomed to working like animals, under miserable conditions, with so little value they were traded, "in the old days," to white men for guns and trinkets. Implied in this stereotype is the idea that white men had the means by which to acquire or violently access women, and that indigenous women had little defense or interest in whom they served.

The truth is that women were necessary and powerful forces. With little effort, in museums, encyclopedias, even on the Internet, it is easy to encounter pictures of women of the nineteenth century posing next to men, building houses, obtaining food, cooking, holding babies on cradle boards, gathering materials to make their houses, and actually constructing those homes. One can find pictures of women gathering acorns or pinon nuts to be ground in preparation for food (Time-Life Books 1994). To document diversity, there are pictures of women's lives in their regional and tribal dress.

Because of indigenous female scholarship, native women are beginning to take on a sharper academic focus, but this focus is not filtering down into the masses because female scholarship has not been integrated into the mainstream curriculum. One must ask why. I contend that focus on indigenous people of past centuries makes it easier to place emotional distance between what has happened to "Indians" and what is happening today. By separating realities, one can be repentant, sorry, for the indignities and even the violence of over 100 years ago, but one does not have to involve them today to correct an injustice. More simply, Americans will not place their energy and their resources "on the line" to solve the mistrust of racism and sexism.

If North American children were lucky, they learned in school that corn was sustenance for "Indians." They often learned that the pilgrims fed the Indians in celebration of their first harvest, and that the head of an Indian was on a five-cent coin. Little or no mention was paid of the fact that the Pilgrims were starving to death when the Indians fed them. Further, acorn and pinon nuts were essential sustenance acquired, stored, and prepared by women. Turkey was part of the diet, but certainly not the substance. Children were also not taught that some indigenous people lived in the mountains and the foothills, that others were desert people, and some lived near the ocean (Time-Life Books 1994).

The impact of conquest on women was that many Indian women disappeared. They were driven off, enslaved, felled by disease, or murdered by intruders. The transitional period is most highly evident in what is referred to as the period of the buffalo women, women who lived during the time of the killing of the all-important buffalo. This period has no definite beginning and ending dates. Their daughters and granddaughters are considered contemporary, but they live with the history of their mothers and grandmothers.

As I participate in conferences, "sweats," and general conversation with them, I have come to know that the four directions—north, south, east, west—were not sacred to white men. To most indigenous people the four directions are sacred and exist in this order: east, south, west, and north. For many, no matter where one stands on Mother Earth one is at the center (Schaef 1995). Because the Earth is the medium by which sustenance is provided, it is called Mother Earth. It is female. For the Apache and other indigenous people, especially the pueblos, everything was matrilineal, followed the mother line. As a rule, today children belonged to their mothers' clan, and the line of descent is traced through the mother. In the past a newly married man moved into his wife's home, and left that home if she wished him to leave. She simply placed his belongings outside the door. Today divorce is common.

White men contended that Indians could not write. This is not true. Even during the long marches they left a record. The lie about illiteracy diminished and discredited the indigenous. The truth is that Indians had no use for the written English language before contact with Europeans. Most people had a record-keeping system written in what English speakers call drawings or petroglyphs. The information simply was not written in English, in a form whites could understand.

Indigenous populations had social–political systems specific to the nations, tribes, and regions. The land and their relationship to it dictated much of how they conceptualized reality.

An indigenous women's feminist perspective incorporates this, and although there is much diversity, Indian people have many similarities, and this is one of them. Cultural blending, however, is highly evident. For example, the Supreme Being is referred to as the Great Spirit, but some refer to it as Grandfather, the creator and giver of life. For some these beings are god. In order for cultural blending to have occurred, there had to be a transition period.

The transition period is a colonizing process, a procedure for subjugating people by devaluing their knowledge and resources. Shortly before the arrival of Europeans in the Western Hemisphere, there were premonitions and prophecies of the terrible consequences of their coming (Nabokov 1991). Foremost among them was the root of what the Mexicans call La Llorona, the wailing spirit woman who warned of their arrival and the hardships that would follow. The ability to believe in spirits lingers on for indigenous women. Many, however, question whether spirits are real.

Although there is much diversity, Indian people have many similarities, and cultural blending is highly evident. In the Southwest La Llorona is a blend of Spanish and Indian tradition. In addition, the Supreme Being is referred to as the Great Spirit, but some refer to it as Grandfather, the creator and giver of life. In order for this to have occurred, there had to be a transition period.

Among the Dine, Changing Woman was and is a great spiritual and historical entity. Traditional indigenous people do not separate everyday life from spirituality. It is not something that is engaged in once a week or twice a day. It permeated their existence. Changing Woman was the most sacred of them all. She was instrumental in creating the people of the Earth and teaching them how to live in harmony with other living beings. These beings included humans, the mountains, air, water, plants, trees, and animals. Changing Woman was kind and friendly. Her story is kept alive today in the centuries-old religious ceremony called the Blessing Way (Nabokov 1991).

Once again, I refer you to Nabokov (1991) to read how, among eastern tribes, Sky Woman had two sons who are often reported as symbolizing good and evil. Sky Woman created the Earth. Mary Brave Bird lectures on how Sky Woman's sons brought to the Earth both good and evil things.

Georgianna Sanchez (2002) notes in her university lectures how among the Iroquois that lived in the general area now known as the state of New York, women had extremely important roles. They had tremendous power. They did not vote in council, but they selected the males who served on it. When the Europeans arrived, they were the ones who interpreted the council, because it was full of men, as the leadership. Women could overrule the decisions of the council, but were never considered in the leadership by white men.

Brave Bird, Sanchez, and many other Indian women note how women figure largely in Indian creation stories which helps to explain how indigenous people came to originate on the land. Beliefs about the oldest residents of the hemisphere do not include the popular migration theory so prevalent among nonnatives. This theory contends that early man (note how the word man also stands for women) trekked in small bands from Siberia to Alaska through the Bering Straights and migrated south. The idea that humans could have evolved in several places is outside the white paradigm demanding that one idea is supreme. This idea is so far removed that some refuse to render credit for vast and varied civilizations built by a bunch of "natives." So far removed is this idea that credit for vast monuments, like those of the Inca and Maya, are even attributed to extraterrestials. Indians certainly could not have performed such deeds. UFOs, unidentified flying objects, brought the creators of immense civilizations and their cities, medicine, astronomy, pyramids, and temples.

Throughout my fifty-six years of life there has been little emphasis on the theory that humans evolved from Africa, where the oldest human remains have been discovered. Those remains are female. This discreditation, via neglect and sometimes purposeful omission, emphasizes a lack of contributions by non-European cultures. This leads us to conclude that only white people ever did anything exciting, brave, or important; only the white god is all-powerful; only Europeans tell the truth; only European writing, language, and history are good. Only white men are the good guys. Indian children are powerless to question this. This becomes their inheritance, their reality.

Prior to the imposition of white society, the indigenous had no understanding of royalty or titles. It was the European who insisted on recognizing one leader, preferably male. Titles such as king, queen, prince, or princess were imposed upon indigenous people by Anglo-Saxon European colonists. Because women were the creators of life, they were connected with things related to creativity, such as tending crops, harvesting, and storing food. Today there rarely are crops to tend. Women and children no longer work in the fields together. Few make wide use of many wild plants because so many of the plants have disappeared due to the environmental impact of "civilization." Plants once served as both food and medicine.

Unlike the Pueblos, who tended to stay in one place, the nomadic tribes were on the move. It was the women who took care of the loading and unloading of household goods. My visits to Lakota homes reveal that today these women live in square concrete government houses. The women of the plains took down and put up the tipis, but life was not only about work. Women engaged in socializing, having fun, especially at social events that were theirs alone. They danced and had sewing circles to make new clothing, blankets, or coverings for the house. They chatted, teased, and strategized on their food-gathering expeditions. Today jealousy and competition live on the reservation, usually over men. Dances are still engaged in, but mostly at powwows. Women had their own games. Younger women played an exhilarating ball game and the seasons were celebrated with special feasts and ceremonies. Today women play basketball and soccer.

Before the white man came to the frontier, there was a rhythm and pattern of joy, sorrow, and times in-between. Today poverty, pain, and struggle impact both urban and reservation Indians, and this is what most people think of when they think of Indians, but they are much more than this. The white man wanted land, silver, and gold. They took it and now Indians strive to gain and use the white man's currency.

## WOMEN AS CULTURAL WARRIORS

Historically, indigenous women have resisted colonization and the problems it brought to them. This dedication to resistance sometimes bestows the title of "cultural warrior" upon a person, male or female. AIM brought the term into popularity and it is now used throughout the Southwest to refer to an advocate from within the victimized population. The term warrior generally is applied to males, but as assimilation has occurred, as well as the need to empower the process of resistance, new meanings for words have been invented, and a woman can also be a cultural warrior.

Most indigenous people on reservations throughout the country still have use for axes, guns, and horses the Spanish introduced. These articles were not first used to make war. They were used to chop down trees, supply firewood, and build log houses and dugout canoes. Later they were utilized to defend against enslavement by colonizing populations. Slavery among Indians had a different connotation. It was frequently an act of retaliation and engaged in solely for the purpose of acquiring cheap labor. The acquisition of cheap labor was secondary to the retaliation for perceived wrongs among nations. It is true that after initial capture captives were traded, but many, especially women, were incorporated into the tribe. When the white man came they were traded to whites as commodities to be used primarily as cheap labor. Foremost among these captives were women. Once frontier white (Anglo) women were rare, but they did exist. Interaction with these women will be discussed later, but for now suffice it to note that both Spanish-speaking and English-speaking women were condescending of Indian women.

White men, like Kit Carson (Quaife 1935), however, took Indian wives and had children referred to as "half-breeds." Indian women acted primarily as domestics and provided sexual services. These slaves are frequently referred to as "wives" in historical literature, but more often than not there was little sentiment attached to most of these women and marriage did not mean the male took the female to church or before a judge, signed papers, and became incorporated in a community. Indian women had no legal rights in American frontier society. Their rights were within their tribe and nation. Today, intermarriage does not exist too often among white men and Indian women, but it does exist. Now most of those relationships are based on love and other human needs. However, as Lakota community advocate Corrine Kills Pretty Enemy revealed, it is interesting to note that more Indian women marry white men, and fewer Indian men marry white women.

Although the frontier was culturally diverse (Blea 2002), Indian women most frequently saw Spanish women on ranchos, where servitude sometimes was less intense. They saw Anglo or "American" women at the fortresses designed by whites to protect whites and/or trade. In military forts, they saw white women growing flowers and exhibiting other strange ways, like eating with a spoon and fork and dressing in tight uncomfortable clothing. It was at the forts that indigenous women were introduced to the tin can, which they learned to cut and shape into jingles for ceremonial dress.

During the 1900s Indians who accepted forced religious conversion and white education experienced more success. Conversion made them more "civilized." Marion Gridley (1974) was among the first to give us a glimpse of the political consciousness of Indian women of the nineteenth century. Although she does not provide an analysis of feminist consciousness, she does provide a review balancing two cultures. She also leads us to ask some interesting questions about assimilation and acculturation, the processes that allow people to participate in a culture; in this case these were the social vehicles that allowed Indians to participate in white culture.

I have done extensive research on the U.S. war with Mexico. After the U.S. war with Mexico, racism and sexism became more intense (Blea 1995, 1988). During the U.S. war with Mexico, Indian males were sometimes recruited to guide the U.S. military. This heightened the conflict between Mexicans and Indians, and women were caught up in the male fighting. The war ended in 1848 with the signing of the Treaty of Guadalupe Hidalgo. The United States not only acquired the vast amount of Mexican territory now known as the Southwest; it acquired a large Mexican and Indian population, some of which was intermarried, especially among the Pueblos. The resulting society did not value white women. It valued Mexican and Indian women much less and resulted in a social toxicity that exists to this day.

However, women's resistance to extermination policies led many women to advocate on behalf of their people. These women, however, are not adequately documented, but their descriptions reveal how complex the lives of native women have become. Some women in need of more research include Nancy Ward, Sarah Winnemucca, E. Pauline Johnson, Susan La Flesche Picotte, Wilma L. Victor, Elaine Abraham Ramos, Gertrude Simmons Bonnin, Maria and Marjorie Tallchief, and Esther Burnett Horne. These women were bilingual. Now many women are now at least trilingual. They speak Spanish and English, plus their own language. A review of women's history reveals that there were several forms of race and gender consciousness. Some women would not have anything to do with Europeans and they intensely disliked

Indian agents who monitored their incarceration (Gridley 1974). Some Indian women became firmly indoctrinated in white ways at Indian schools. There, their hair was cut and their dress was changed. They learned to eat with forks and knives, speak the white language, sleep in and make the white man's style of bed, wash his dishes, scrub his floors, and play his games. At these schools children contracted strange diseases and odd methods of treatment, which consisted of steam baths or washing in cold streams to cure whooping cough or measles. Many children died, but some women stressed that it was important to be able to receive and absorb all that whites had to offer and to weave it into opportunity. Among this ideal was that without education Indians would never be able to think and act for themselves; they would be dependent upon the white man. Today, many would disagree and claim that white education robs Indians of indigenousness. Many Indian-school-educated women became nurses working for federal agencies that supervised Indian affairs. Nurses of the late 1800s and the early twentieth century were instrumental in establishing health aid programs. During the first half of the 1900s tuberculosis ravaged the reservations. There was not an Indian or Eskimo family in all of what is now Alaska that was not touched by it. Today, the greatest health problem is alcoholism and diabetes.

My conversations with native women while conducting research for this book reveal that assimilated Indian women were, and still are, thought of as progressive by some whites and traitors by some Indians. These women had racial and gender ideas of their own, and they experienced rejection and discrimination while having to prove themselves to both whites and Indians alike. They often laid the foundation for many reforms in the white-controlled Bureau of Indian Affairs (BIA). The efforts of these women were not isolated. Some, like Roberta Campbell Lawson, an Alluwe born in Indian Territory in 1878, headed large organizations such as the 3-million-member General Federation of Women's Clubs (Sonneborn 1998). Campbell Lawson married a white man. Intermarriage is still a questionable action, not only among Indians and but also among whites. Implied in taking this action is an abandonment of native culture, a selling out, in order to acquire acceptance and economic security from whites. Intermarriage is seen by most Indians as false consciousness; one cannot be fully accepted by those who have historically oppressed Indians.

The color of a person's skin matters (Sukiennik 2002). Even if a person of color is treated well, this does not translate into treatment of the entire group. Getting treated well is interpreted as "acceptance" only when the number of people of color is very small in white groups. With regard to African Americans, this opinion was rendered as recently as April 28, 1999, at the National Conference of Black Mayors and was viewed on C-SPAN across the nation. The belief is that one cannot look to the system that enslaved or oppressed people to free them.

Some Pueblo women came to the forefront in the arts and there has been much written about them. Women like New Mexico artists Pablita Velarde

(http://www.ipl.org.cai/ref/native; http://www.amazon.com; http://www.living
treasures.kxx.com; http://www.heard.org) and Maria Montoya Martinez (http://
/www.pueblopottery.com/sans; http://www.sanildefouso.com/maria) rank
among the highest. They demonstrate how delicate the need for balance is in
the life of an Indian female professional. Both artists incorporated traditional
methodology and technology in creating masterpieces that sell for thousands
of dollars. Velarde drew from Pueblo folklore to render her images. The more
she painted, and the more whites bought her images, the more she felt separated from her people. During her lifetime painting was a task reserved for
men, and Velarde was looked upon as a rebel "selling out" to white society.

Velarde and Martinez both lived for many years off the reservation. Velarde
returned there to nurture her art, but also because her husband could no longer
tolerate the importance of her artistic success in their marriage outside the
reservation. Upon returning to the reservation both the marriage and the art
flourished. Montoya Martinez, on the other hand, was more traditional. She
did not like living off the reservation. Montoya Martinez was tricultural and
preferred the natural environment of her home. She had a Spanish background
and interacted extensively with whites. Unlike other women, Montoya Martinez
and her husband Julian worked together to create great works of art known
around the world and purchased for extraordinary amounts of money. Montoya
Martinez and her husband made decorating pottery acceptable to men, thus opening up new employment for them. The couple was so famous for their signature
black pottery that it has brought economic stability for the Pueblo and created
an environment for the continuation of the tradition (Fleet 1997). After the
death of Julian, Montoya Martinez's son, Popovi Da, worked alongside his
mother until his death in 1972. From Maria Montoya Martinez we learn that it
is possible to have great success and still be true to oneself and one's culture.
Generally, professional women of color do not have an easy time managing
career and marriage, as well as the historical transitions and radical shifts in
public policies, but in spite of this they continue in contemporary society.

## SURVIVING COLONIZATION

Today most Indians want to govern themselves. Even those who have complied with U.S. government intervention realize that the white system does
not work for them. By the mid-1880s nearly every reservation had its own
reservation council, police force, and system of trial courts. To Indians, ac-
commodating whites does not mean abandoning culture. The Northwest Indians continued to fish and incorporated new ideas and materials brought by the
white man (Deloria 1977) to engage in what today is a thriving business, and
now American education is not as fervently opposed as were the Indian schools,
and cultural transition is as important as the trading posts and the materials
they brought to Indian women. They brought cotton cloth that is still used to

make clothing and quilts. The introduction of cloth was followed by the presence of sewing machines and creating cultural goods for tourist consumption in order to purchase cars and trucks.

Some tribes have become extinct. Some informally dissolved and then were reorganized, but there are currently 558 federally recognized tribes (Gover 1999). Unrecognized tribes exist and are fighting for recognition. A total of 1.2 million people live on reservations in thirty-two states in the union. Reservation schools educate roughly 53,000 students. Dams are deteriorating and irrigation systems are falling apart, making it difficult to farm. The current generation of Indians suffers obesity from store-bought food. Yet there are attorneys, doctors, and politicians. Some of them are women, and some of them are in coalition with other indigenous people, Chicano–Latino human rights activists, and environmentalists.

Most of these accomplishments are the outcome of the Native American struggle that in the 1960s exposed and criticized failed Indian policy that never asked the Indians what they wanted or needed. Foremost, the Native American movement brought attention to the need to break the cycle of poverty: poor education, poor political representation, poor housing and health, the lack of economic power, the high rate of male incarceration, and both male and female alcoholism. In fact, assimilation and federal policy is seen as cruel and inconsistent with regard to indigenous populations. This causes severe stress, which leads to illness. These policies have been administered by the Bureau of Indian Affairs and compared to the ethnic cleansing of Kosovo. The push–pull policies have caused highly strained relationships between the Bureau and Indians (Gover 1999). The BIA monitors the only group that has a federal agency appointed to govern or supervise its affairs. The reservation-system policies have also been likened to South Africa's apartheid laws, and include not only ethnic cleansing, but also treaty making, treaty breaking, warfare, and crooked Indian agents. These policies include assimilation efforts and the allotment of 90 million acres of land to individual Indian control.

There were reorganization efforts between the 1930s and 1950s, which included rebuilding tribal governments and the withdrawal of federal support, and then the rebuilding of tribes in an effort to allow them to self-determine which programs they wanted and which they did not. Although the goal for some of the tribes is to become self-sufficient, others desire federal help. Some of the tribes, like the Dine in New Mexico and Arizona, are huge. Others are very small. The biggest problem between the Bureau of Indian Affairs and Indians is that Indians do not trust the bureau, white people, and other agencies whites have established. According to Kevin Gover, assistant secretary for Indian Affairs (1999), Indians do not trust them to keep their promises and to extend offers that better the quality of life for indigenous people.

To resist "being taken," exploited again, they are always on guard. To resist cultural genocide a few new cultural beliefs have been developed; but for the most part, old ones persist and work very well. Even today, it has been my experience that most Lakota women believe that four days after giving birth women are considered to be equal to menstruating, being on their "moon." Several friends, like Corrine Kills Pretty Enemy, observe that during this time they cannot take part in certain ceremonies or rituals. During this time of her cycle, her power is strongest and they might upset the intent of the ritual or ceremony. Aside from the demand to practice their cultures and the return of Indian land, medical care is still a primary concern. Many young white doctors and nurses take their first caseload on Indian reservations. There they practice on "real" patients in order to gain confidence to start their own practices or join an ongoing practice. These doctors and nurses do not remain long. Reservations are often far from large cities, which tend to produce the doctors. Thus, health care is inconsistent, and some say not very good (Brave Bird 1993).

Forced conversion, religion, and spirituality is a primary issue for the indigenous. Native Americans can be found in several of the most prominent religious organization in the United States, most notably in the Catholic Church in the Southwest, but few women are ordained ministers and none are priests. In the Catholic Church, drums, songs, and native dress have been incorporated into Sunday mass. Some no longer are familiar with their traditional religion. They do not practice it, and condemn others for doing so. Yet others, like those in the Native American Church, have had to fight for the right to harvest hallucinogenic peyote for religious purposes, and to practice the Sun Dance (Brave Bird 1993).

Although there are women who are highly active in Indian communities and in native spirituality, it is not apparent that they are feminist. Their brand of feminism, like that of other women of color, is embedded in their activism to empower women as they empower their people (Kills Pretty Enemy 1997). Like those feminists of color, and unlike white women, most indigenous are more holistic in their approach to controlling their own bodies, minds, and spirits. In their activism they advocate for the health and balance of the environment, animal rights, and human rights. A contemporary problem for Indian women is exposure and this is especially true if they are artists. White men control the art world. All women who participate generally have the same issues. Indian women, however, have more layers of racism and sexism to overcome when trying to excel. Indian men generally get the most attention and the most money, but not without a price. For most artists, the loss of Indian control of Indian art is a heated issue.

Somewhat akin to concerns in the art community is the appropriation of Indian relics by white-controlled museums. For years the tribes have tried to gain possession of the relics and bones of ancestors. There is no regulation of this trade and no protection of the productions of what in some cases are groups of endangered human beings. The nation has an endangered species act protecting nearly extinct animals, but it does not regard, nor protect, Indian people and their cultural productions. To safeguard against this, some of the tribes are building cultural arts centers controlled by Indian people. Art assists in being human and self-defining. Colonized people often internalize their oppression and manifest it in self-destructive ways. Among Indians themselves the issue of blood frequently divides cooperative efforts. Some full-blood Indians rank themselves higher than mixed blood or half blood. The last U.S. Census (2001) estimated that life expectancy is fifty-six years for women and forty-eight years for men. This was well under the average age expectancy in the 1970s for white Americans. There are only one and a half million tribally affiliated indigenous citizens left in the United States, but that number appears to be growing, and some activist women and men see childbirth as a way of resisting extermination and strengthening the number of people and the culture. For them it is a matter of perseverance, proof that in spite of overwhelming odds they have survived (see Table 2.1).

Although many Indian men have internalized white male ways, among American Indians women commonly have had more equality with men. They are seen as partners in the life process, and are consulted in decision making. Since contact with European societies, the role of women has steadily diminished in value. Christianity and its male-centeredness did much to erode the role by promoting the view that men were superior to women. Broken Indian treaties and resettlement programs were tools in the disempowerment of Indian women because white men only wanted to dialog and negotiate with men. White policy regarding Indians also did away with traditional decision-

**Table 2.1**
**Total U.S. American Indian, Eskimo,**
**and Aleut Resident Population**
**Estimate by Percentage and Gender**

| | |
|---|---|
| Population | 2,448 |
| Percentage of total | 0.9 |
| Median age (years | 27.8 |
| Mean age (years) | 30.7 |
| Male population | 1,211 |
| Female population | 1,236 |

*Source*: Population Estimates Program, Population Division, U.S. Census Bureau, Washington, D.C. (Internet release date January 2, 2001).

*Note*: Projection to November 1, 2000. Numbers in thousands.

making processes that included women. In some tribes they had the final say in who would be the leaders or whether to go to war. Formal and informal policies stripped Indian women of identity and the right to marry who they wanted. Formally, they ceased to be considered Indian if they married a Native American outside a federally recognized tribe. Women could lose or hide their Indian status if they married a white man, but the couple did not escape the social attitude that intermarriage was not a positive thing.

U.S. government policy and Christian tradition denied native women the right to pass their heritage on to their children. Mestizas lost their mother's maiden name as part of their full name. This promoted identity crises, and the ostracism of women from their community and their culture. It also abandoned a matrilineal legacy by destroying dual family identity, and it cemented patriarchy. Nevertheless, elderly women's roles have retained some power, but older women are expected to fill the role of unpaid babysitter and homemaker to the rest of the family unit, especially when all the adults are working or otherwise occupied. Thus, women have internalized the caregiver role from a very young age to old age. When a woman chooses to do this, she become instrumental in cultural transmission, but most women do not have a choice about this.

## INTERNALIZED COLONIALISM

My fifty-six-year experience relating to Indian women's issues reveals that Indian women do not have a choice about several things, including their priorities. They, including me, continuously have to make mental adjustments for at least two sets of cultural practices. For example, over time whites have declared bartering and trading to be unacceptable means of exchange. This devalued the practices, but Indians continued them among themselves. However, bartering and trading have moved from a primary way of life to a secondary economy. Many have little or nothing to barter, and they have become more dependent on money. Today money is absolutely necessary, and the internalization of its worth has increased in the lives of Native American women.

Perhaps personal women's traditions have survived best. Most notably are the womanhood ceremonies. According to Ines Talamantes (Apache) and Ines Hernandez (Nez-Pez), both indigenous women and feminists plus Native American scholars, when a girl menstruates she becomes a woman and must practice modesty. She usually dresses in beautiful buckskin. Womanhood rituals of various tribes demand long preparation. Those who attend the celebration are fed and housed well, sometimes for several days.

Perhaps the Navajo, the Dine, are best studied among the indigenous people of the United States. By the 1700s Dine children assumed the clan affiliation of their mother. If their mother was not Dine, a new clan was created (Grimes 1992). Among some of them no other individual, with the possible exception of the mother's mother or mother's sister, had the right to scold children that were not theirs. Rude or naughty children are insulting. Girls are taught to be generous, to share in burdensome tasks, and some are expected to bring in extra income. In the 1940s and 1950s cars and trucks replaced wagons (Grimes 1992) but some very elderly people still preferred the floor for eating and sleeping. It is my experience that ghost sickness is still real to many tribes. Among the Dine, when a person dies, the living are not to speak the name of the dead because doinf so might bring illness. Although this custom is not generally practiced as strictly as before, there was a time when all of the dead person's belongings were burned, broken, or thrown away, and if the deceased was a woman's husband, she would be left impoverished. Among the Cheyenne, her brother-in-law would take her in.

As I live among my native sisters, I note that a very popular belief lies in the burning of sage, a traditional defense against ghosts, bad energy, and other unknown dangers. It is also used for cleansing homes, buildings, and the atmosphere in which meetings take place. A handprint on the inside wall above the door of a house and windowsills and door frames painted turquoise also protect against evil spirits and bad intentions. As in the past, a specialist in fumigation with sage or greasewood is sometimes required, especially when someone dies. Death is considered a natural part of the life cycle, but how one lives on Earth is still a health concern, part of well-being. Fumigation varies among indigenous cultures, and other natural elements like dry cedar, tree resin, or sweet grass are used. Indians do not die in the sense that they are gone forever. In some tribes the person joins with environmental forces and returns in the form of rain or snow. In others they join the ancestors.

Most indigenous people now bury the dead in a fashion whites insist upon, underground. However, within the acceptable manner they interject their traditional beliefs. Taos Pueblo people wrap the body in a blanket. A few who have accepted mainstream ways have even prospered. Interracial and intertribal marriages have increased, especially among Navaho men and Apache women. These former enemies have cultural ways consistent with one another. Some of the elder women have refused to become fluent in English. The younger ones had no choice. As indigenous women are more frequently confronted with assimilation and acculturate, their alcohol and drug abuse increases (National Women's Health Information Center 2002). Indians are still being sold liquor by whites, and alcoholism is still seen as a criminal offense instead of a health concern.

Other health concerns include pulmonary disorders. Tuberculosis caused a high rate of death from the mid to late 1800s into the twentieth century. Today one of the leading killers is diabetes. According to my inquiries at the National Women's Health Information Center (NWHIC), a project of the U.S. Public Health Service's Office on Women's Health Department of Health and Human Services, poverty and unemployment have fostered welfare dependency and diets replete with government commodity foods that are high in fat and calories. The malnutrition that was a problem among American Indians and Alaska natives two generations ago has been replaced by obesity. Sixty percent of both male and female urban American Indians and Alaska natives are reported to be overweight and therefore at risk for diabetes and other illnesses. Nationally, approximately 20 percent of American Indians have diabetes, a rate twice that of the general U.S. population. Non-insulin-dependent diabetes mellitus has reached epidemic proportions among some tribes. Although it remains less of a problem for Alaska natives than for American Indians, the prevalence of diabetes mellitus among Alaska natives has increased tenfold in the past thirty years.

To resist and redirect indigenous poverty and internalized destruction, the American Indian civil rights movement has gained national and international support, ranging from Hollywood actors to human rights activists in Japan, Latin America, and Central America. They have especially gained support from Mexico among the Yaqui and Huichol. AIM also has alliances that link them to the black and Chicano civil rights movements. Intertribal partnerships have moved on to become second-generation relationships. Sometimes there is blatant hatred of whites, and some indigenous people still fear African Americans, but many have broken the color line and now associate freely with critical members of other groups to question whether to fight in wars with foreign countries.

Most women, regardless of culture, have a difficult time dealing with war. Some Pueblo women have had difficulty with men listening to them when expressing their concern to tribal councils, not only about war, but also about drug and alcohol abuse. Conversations with Bernie (mother) and Michelle (daughter) Issues (2002) reveal that some Pueblo women provide for the home and the children and are dependent on the good nature of their spouses for assistance. Sometimes acculturated men interpret the traditional role of women to mean that any money he earns is his. This happens because men have internalized that they should have some priority because they are men. Because money defines men in the dominant society, Indian men who cannot obtain employment are subjected to a variety of stresses. Suicide is paramount among Indian youth, especially males, who often intentionally cause their own deaths by strangulation, alcohol poisoning, or from inhaling household cleaners. Some youth do not hesitate to disrespect their elders. More than ever before, Indian women are at high risk of losing children to drug and alcohol abuse, alcohol- and drug-related accidental death, and suicide.

There may be a number of reasons why indigenous women are not seeking treatment at rates comparable with men. These include that most drug and alcohol counselors and programs are directed toward males and that there are few Native American women involved in treatment, but more often there are traditional taboos against cross-gender counseling. As for all women, fewer indigenous women are identified as having alcohol problems and fewer are referred to treatment. In addition, male partners may be reluctant to allow their female partners to obtain treatment, especially if they are still involved in alcohol abuse, and women may be reluctant to seek treatment if their male partners are still abusing. Added to this is the lack of childcare, which is a barrier to women seeking treatment.

Women react differently than men to alcohol consumption. Females have higher rates of cirrhotic problems and complications than do men, and are more likely to die due to liver injuries brought on by alcohol consumption (National Women's Health Information Center 2002a). Women are also more vulnerable to neurological problems and are more likely to die from alcoholism then men. Women who abuse alcohol and other drugs are also more likely to suffer from low self-esteem and depression. They are more likely to blame themselves for their alcoholism than are men. Indian men believe they have less control over their alcohol consumption than Indian women, and women alcoholics, like other women, are more likely to attempt suicide while men are more likely to succeed. Women who abuse alcohol are also three times more likely to attempt suicide than nonalcoholic women, and many U.S. studies have found that sexual abuse is a major contributing factor to alcoholism in women (National Women's Health Information Center 2002b).

In researching this chapter I have found that reliable statistics on contemporary U.S. Indian women are difficult to find. I also know (because I have visited there) that in Gallup, New Mexico, the city called "Drunk City" by a national television news program, has a rape rate of intoxicated Indian women that is high. One thing is clear: In order for the United States to heal from several of its social problems, special attention must be paid to the development of alcohol and drug treatment centers specifically for Indian women, and for the development of indigenous women treatment models in existing facilities.

## RESISTING DESTRUCTION AND
## MAINTAINING HARMONY

Maintaining harmony and balance as humans walk their earth journey is one goal of indigenous women. The Dine strive to walk the path of beauty. They and other native people are dealing with 500 years of things going wrong. Their paths are narrow and crooked; and many have taken the wrong path. They have internalized white values and these values are killing them. White food and drink are foreign to their bodies, their minds, and their spirits and it will take more than a few years to correct these problems. Parents cannot do it by themselves; the broader white community must get involved in a cross-generational effort. Abuse is not a native characteristic. Children are sacred. Sexual abuse dishonors women, the bearers of human beings.

In most tribes there are ceremonies and rituals to support establishing and maintaining balance. But some white man's sicknesses, like diabetes, require white medicine in white establishments. To restore harmony while being hospitalized, the indigenous sneak articles and perform rituals clandestinely in the facility and at home. Healers exist both in the cities and on the reservation, and they generally are not heavily concerned with money, but a gift, sometimes money, is generally presented. Money, lots of it, is required to obtain white medical treatment and it is scarce among Indian people.

In most traditional indigenous cultures, illness and disability are often understood as a manifestation of the supernatural, the result of an evil spell, a sin or an unnamed wrong (Indian Health Services of New Mexico 2002). Native women often see illness and disability as an imbalance or lack of harmony with oneself and one's environment, but they do not neglect the fact that the person simply became ill in the sense that whites see it. While indigenous people go to Western medical doctors to deal with acute illnesses, many also adhere to religious and cultural beliefs. Even though most native people continue to use holistic approaches to health care, traditional white medicine generally renders little support. In fact, traditional Euro-centered cultures draw distinct lines between the spiritual and the medical. The medical is deemed by them to be worthier because it is "science." When I was a mental health worker in the 1970s and 1980s, I saw that in very few cases, shamen and curanderas found support from administrators and doctors; the clergy was generally furious, but this is changing. Still, to some of them, indigenous practices are unscientific, witchcraft, the work of the devil. Indigenous practices that heal the spirit, the mind, and the body at the same time threaten the scientific and Christian social and political base. This is contrary to white medicine, which seeks to isolate the illness and patient for treatment. Health activists have long maintained that family plays a significant role in determining rehabilitation outcomes for persons with beliefs based in other cultures. Families very often are close knit and reflective of the extended family system. When the disabled fails in their efforts at independence, families are rarely judgmental. Instead, they welcome the member back into the family and encourage them to make their next attempt at self-sufficiency.

Some feminists believe that in the general society, men with disabilities are treated better than women, even in their own homes. People may feel sorry for the men, but a woman is resented because she can no longer perform the free services she once rendered. Rural cultures, especially among indigenous people, place a heavy reliance on physical labor. Both men and women may be involved in household repairs, removing debris, hunting, or fishing, plus performing wage work. These physically demanding tasks place native women at risk for many disabling conditions, including arthritis. Because whole families may be dependent upon her work for a living, the role these women fulfill is critical. Any disability that hinders her involvement causes severe economic hardship for her family. A disability that reduces her ability to fulfill these functions can severely restrict self-sufficiency, her quality of life, and her contribution to the collective well-being of the family unit and tribe.

Advocates for urban Indians know that urbanites have a more distant relationship with their traditional culture than nonurban or reservation Indians (Parker 1996). Many leave the reservation and return to the city. Moving is a way of life for many. Some tribes have found that gambling supplies money to address some of the housing, health, and economic needs. In fact, one of the most heated political issues is the economics of Indian gaming. Even Las Vegas protests its legalization. The Indian Gaming Information Center notes that Indian gaming now exists in twenty-six states, but that not all states allow Las Vegas–style gambling. Indian gaming centers provide entertainment to patrons, but provide jobs for Indians. They also provide money for health clinics and schools that incorporate Indian traditions. Many white Americans resent this. As I live and travel around my home state of New Mexico, I hear negativism on the subject of Indian gaming by whites. They feel Indians have received special treatment on reservations and that gaming, and the money it generates, is but an additional privilege.

The quincentennial of Columbus's experience in the Western Hemisphere was a great opportunity for healing and reconciliation of our racism and sexism. It was but a small step in a humane direction. The lessons that could have and should have been learned were not incorporated into our general ideology of America patriotism and this is now international knowledge. More Americans should join the global environmental movement. It strives for harmony and balance. European colonialists and their descendents have destroyed so much of the continent's original life forms, and created so much waste, that it is no longer safe to live in some places. This waste is supported by world views that include the use of technology in promoting profit, upward mobility, individualism, and power mongering, attributes that have brought some indigenous people to the brink of extinction and threaten the survival of others.

I have taken note that the United States has no cultural policy. Efforts to protect cultures from destruction have been those made by endangered cultures on their own behalf. Those outside these cultures rarely see how cultural destruction impacts them. This lends credence to the charge that white Americans appear to place little value on human worth unless their niche in the life cycle contributes to white empowerment. Our history, our wars, have given witness to this, and other countries have noticed this. The recent war efforts demonstrate that there is little respect or tolerance for a god that is not Christian. The role of American Indian women in creation beliefs with indigenous roots are just as strong as the Adam and Eve story of Christianity, but only indigenous people seem to know them, and only they seem to respect and value them. If anybody who is nonindigenous does care, we have not yet heard their voices loud and clear. They must speak up because they are being "lumped" together with racist sexists, who seem to have a louder voice.

One tactic taken by indigenous people to protect their cultures is using treaties with the United States in the U.S. court system. This experience points out the contradictions of these legal agreements and some white people deeply resent this (American Indian Law Students 2002). They feel the "Indian" is trying to cheat them, and that they do not have responsibility for something done in the past by their ancestors. Yet they live on colonized land and allow cultural genocide to take place. Americans cannot heal from racism and sexism until they acknowledge the fact that they profit from their ancestors' colonization of Indians. In order to heal the nation, we must also make retribution, somehow correct history, and engage in another way of thinking about the world. To Indians this means noting that whites have a responsibility to pay for the privileges they have gained at the expense of Indians.

## RECONCILIATION AND RETRIBUTION
## FOR WHITE PRIVILEGE

In accepting the responsibility for white privilege, whites and Indians can move toward balanced lives. This helps whites teach and learn morals, ethics, responsibility, and truth, and will bring forth international respect. This is especially important for children, who grow up believing in distorted "truths," thinking they know right from wrong and then finding out that they have learned a thought system that is misleading and full of lies. Because this has not been corrected, American children sometimes grow up confused, without a solid base for their identity. Their discovery of historical lies or half truths leads them to distrust adults and authority. It fosters a lack of a sense of civic duty. For many children of color it kills interest in education and in the political and economic structures of the United States. In my opinion, the most secure route to achieving social continuity is not patriotism; it is truth. Truth in a historical context is essential for building the future and for teaching youth pride and responsibility into the next generation. However, struggle against the dual effects of sexism coupled with racism has advanced very little in spite of the September 11 attacks and over forty years of civil rights activism.

In establishing their equilibrium, indigenous women concern themselves with the past and how it shapes the future. They reconcile this and focus upon the survival of their people and culture. According to Kills Pretty Enemy (2000), president of Tokata International in Alexandria, Virginia, for some Indian women survival has been stifling culture to build a career with the federal government. This is especially true if one works for the Bureau of Indian Affairs within the U.S. Department of Interior and the Indian Health Service (IHS) or the Public Health Service (PHS) and has to live near Washington, D.C., where indigenous people are rare.

Promoting the privatization of treatment services (Hart 1995) and entrepreneurship among indigenous people does not work because of a distaste for individualism, private business is rarely an economic option for Indian women, but many Indian women have been nurses. Such entities as the Women's Educational Equity Act (WEAA) Leadership Training Program, directed primarily at native women, attempts to sustain women in the field. However, ingrained native patterns of behavior, fear, and lack of self-confidence and self-esteem when functioning in the "white man's world" prevents indigenous women from becoming entrepreneurs when women-owned businesses are increasing.

Indigenous women often have difficulty balancing the goals of being in business and profit with their spirituality, generosity, and communal nature. Most Indian beliefs at one time or another are in contradiction with the goals of business, profit, and upward mobility. Indigenous cultures hold people who share their material resources, especially with the less fortunate, in high esteem. Often those who work for government entities or who are in business are considered "apples": white on the inside, red on the outside; traitors.

Reconciling these differences or inventing another way for indigenous people to become self-sustaining is imperative to ending one of America's biggest embarrassments—that of Indian oppression and colonization. One thing is clear: We must get away from a description of the United States as monocultural. The notion of a single society with one cultural norm must be abandoned. There are many societies that make up the United States, and there are several cultural models and modes of human relations, and this is America's strength. It has a huge talent pool, but it is not being utilized.

September 11, 2001, offered the United States a great opportunity for healing and reconciliation. It drew our attention to our nation's people and its need for unity, but unity does not mean homogenity. The quincentennial cemeted the notion of one people for Indians in the Americas. It promoted the recognition of the violation of human rights throughout the hemisphere, the destruction of the environment, our dependence upon one another and nature, and the inhumanity of racism and sexism. If Americans can combine the two lessons we can move toward forgiveness and regain trust and interaction. This requires women in order to establish the harmony of the physical, psychological, and spiritual requirements of the environment and of humans.

Several authors like those represented in *Native American Testimony* (Nabokov 1991) lament that there is no recognition that within half a millennium Europeans destroyed entire groups of people and created so much waste it is impossible to live in some places. Those people and those places are extinct, gone forever. This waste is supported by white world views that include the use of technology in obtaining profit, upward mobility, individualism, and power for a few men, not women. These are attributes that have brought some indigenous people to the brink of near extinction. Sanchez and members of her family are trying to revive and relearn their native Barbareño-Chumash language. What is ironic is that so many people take political action to save endangered species of animals and plants, but these same people will not put the same energy into saving endangered humans and their cultures.

Thus, in order to gain international respect, America must engage in some house cleaning and take responsibility for the white male privilege a few men have tried to impose on other countries. U.S. citizens forget that whites profit immensely from colonization. In order to heal the nation, we must make retribution and correct our historical errors. Retribution can be as simple as revising school history books and teaching some "American" literature as examples of racism and sexism.

Correcting history means revising it and congratulating those who fought bravely for their homeland and still lost the wars. It means taking pride for having chosen to engage in a difficult task and that there is honor in it. It also means understanding that making retribution does not always involve a great deal of money. An example of this is in the renaming of Custer Battlefield or the Little Big Horn Battlefield National Monument (National Park and Conservation Association 1998) to the Washita Battlefield National Historic Site in Cheyenne, Oklahoma. The Washita Battlefield National Historic Site name change is holistic; it is inclusive and demonstrates how justice can be achieved. However, this struggle against the effects of racism did little to heal the effects of sexism combined with racism. For indigenous women the need to become physically, emotionally, spiritually, and politically self-sustaining is immediate. Reconciling this requires the feminization of racism, putting a female face on racism and ascertaining how age, income, politics, religion, and the criminal justice system affects or excludes women in the decision-making process. Putting a female face on survival teaches us that women have survived by cooperating with patriarchy. They have made necessary adjustments. Some have accepted and internalized their oppression but many more have resisted and have become bicultural. Indian women are tricultural.

## REFERENCES

Blea, Irene I. 2002. *Maria Josefa Jaramillo: Spanish Frontier Wife of Kit Carson.* Unpublished manuscript. Albequerque, New Mexico.

Blea, Irene I. 1995. *Researching Chicano Communities.* Westport, Conn.: Praeger.

Blea, Irene I. 1988. *Toward a Chicano Social Science.* New York: Praeger.

Brave Bird, Mary, with Richard Erdoes. 1993. *Ohitika Woman.* New York: Grove Press.

Deloria, Vine. 1977. *Indians of the Pacific Northwest: From the Coming of the White Man to the Present Day.* New York: Doubleday.

Ethnic NewsWatch. 1999. SoftLine Information. Available at: <http://www.ethnicnews.com>.

Fleet, Cameron, ed. 1997. *First Nations—First Hand.* Seacaucus, N.J.: Chartwell Books.

Fritz, Jean. 1983. *The Double Life of Pocahontas.* New York: G. P. Putnam's Sons.

Gridley, Marion E. 1974. *American Indian Women.* New York: Hawthorn Books.

Grimes, Joel. 1992. *Navaho: Portrait of a Nation.* Englewood, Colo. Westcliff.

Gover, Kevin. 1999. "American Indians." Assistant Secretary for Indian Affairs, testimony as televised on C-SPAN, April 13.

Hale, Janet Campbell. 1993. *Bloodlines: Odyssey of a Native Daughter.* New York: Harper Perennial.

Hart, George. 1995. "U.S. Should Try Turning Juvenile Corrections into Private Enterprise System." *Ojibwe News,* September 26. Available at: <http://www.presson.net>.

Indian Health Services of New Mexico. 2002. Telephone interview with Madeline Clines, May 10.

Issues, Bernie, and Michelle Issues. 2002. Interview, University of New Mexico, January 21.

Kills Pretty Enemy, Corrine S. 2000. Interview with author.

———. 1997. *Business Tips for Women*. Alexandria, Va.: Tokata International.

Mankiller, Willma. 1993. *Mankiller: A Chief and Her People*. 1993. New York: St. Martin's Press.

Martinez, Maria. 2002. Available at: <http://www.amazon.com>, <http://www.maria pottery.com>, and <http://www.pueblopottery.com/sans~1.htm>. (Information about pottery.)

McDonald Boyer, Ruth, and Narcisus Duffy Gayton. 1992. *Apache Mothers and Daughters*. Norman: University of Oklahoma Press.

Morenus, David. 2002. *The Real Pocahontas*. Available at: <http://www.geocities.com/ Broadway/1001/poca.h>.

Nabokov, Peter. 1991. *Native American Testimony: A Chronicle of Indian–White Relations from Prophecy to the Present, 1492–1992*. New York: Penguin Books.

National Conference of Black Mayors. 1999. C-SPAN, April 28. (Broadcast of panel dsicussion.)

National Parks and Conservation Association. 1998. "Custer Battlefield or Little Big Horn." *National Parks* 72, no.1–2: 1.

National Women's Health Information Center. 2002a. "Chronic Illness among Indian Women." Available at: <hhttp://www.4women.com>.

National Women's Health Information Center. 2002b. "Actions for Health Professionals— Making Prevention Work." Available at: <http://www.4women/Alcoholism>. Last visited July 2002.

Native Women's Health Education Resource Center. 2002. Lake Andes, South Dakota. Available at: <http://www.4women.com/index/cfm>.

New Mexico Spanish Genealogy Society. 2001. Available at: <http://www.nmgene alogy.org>.

Parker, Sara C. 1999. "Urban Natives and Urban Issues." *The Circle* 17, no. 4: 22.

Public Broadcasting System. 2001. *The West Project*. WETA.

Quaife, M. 1935. *Kit Carson's Autobiography*. Lincoln: University of Nebraska Press.

Sanchez, Georgianna. 2002. Telephone interview, June 24. American Indian Studies, California Satat University–Northridge.

Schaef, Anne Wilson. 1995. *Native Wisdom for White Minds*. New York: Ballantine Books.

Simon, Naomi A. 1996. "Suburban Natives Strive to Keep Culture Alive." *The Circle* 17, no. 4: 23–28.

Sonneborn, Liz. 1998. *Encyclopedia of Women: A to Z of Native American Women*. Available at: <http://www.Goodminds.com>.

Stillwel, Maxine. 2002. Telephone interview by American Indian Law Students. January 12. Indian Pueblo Cultural Center.

Sukiennik, Greg. 2002. "Study Treats Skin Tone Stereotypes." Boston: Associated Press.

Time-Life Books. 1994. *The Indians of California*. Alexandria, Va.: Time Warner.

U.S. Bureau of the Census. 2001. "Characteristics of American Indians." Public Information Office memo, March 17.

Velarde, Pablita. 2002. Available at: <www.amazon.com>, <http://www.livingtreasures. kxx.com/bios/pabl>, and <http://www.friendsbandelier.com/shop.asp>.

# CHAPTER 3

# Chicanas and Immigrant Latinas Inherit and Internalize Colonialism

One thing that was made perfectly clear during the war with Afghanistan was that the Taliban did not want American influence in their culture. Middle East countries have told us this since the taking of U.S. hostages by Iran. Most immediate was the Taliban need to keep women from Western influences. To resist, women met clandestinely to do such revolutionary things as lift the burqa and put on makeup (Revolutionary Association of Women of Afghanistan 2000). This may seem a trivial exercise, but for a male-dominant power that wants to keep women "in their place" and keep out Western influence, it is not. Like many Middle Easterners, Chicana feminists know that the key to keeping traditional culture from being wiped out by a dominant culture is to keep the dominant culture's influence out. With the imposition of internal colonialism, conquest on their own land in 1848 (at the end of the U.S. war with Mexico), they saw their culture and people destroyed or changed dramatically. They have survived social, cultural, economic, and political transitions and they have persevered against attempts that cannot be referred to as anything other than cultural genocide as a result of hate and greed. Immigrant Latinas are unprepared for the social dynamics of combined racism, class discrimination, and sexism when they enter the country and have an extraordinary challenge to their new country.

## CHICANAS AS INDIGENOUS WOMEN

Some Chicanas prefer to be recognized as indigenous, but some indigenous people do not see them this way because they are the descendents of the oppressive Spanish European. Chicana feminist have researched the indigenousness they claim, and in several other publications I have detailed the part Spanish, part Indian heritage of the mestiza (Blea 1992a). For now, let us continue the discussion of how Indian women were and are essential to the survival of their communities and to the survival of the early Spanish explorers who came to in the Americas (Blea 1992b, 1997). Indigenous American women had lifestyles very unlike the women of Spain. Their physical features were darker in color. Their straight hair was coarser, and their attire and lifestyle were casual and colorful. The native women of this civilization had the distinct norms and cultural values of long existences in different regions. How and when language was used was very important to them. For example, Aztec women celebrated the approaching birth of a child with poetry, naming and presentation rituals that incorporated the new mother and child in sacred ceremony. The mother spoke to the unborn child in Nahuatl. They praised it and told it of her hopes for its future. Herbs and teas were used in doctoring, a profession open to women. Upon a child's birth, it was presented to the gods, thereby incorporating it into a physical as well as a spiritual world where women had power.

Colonialism is malleable and cruel. It twists and turns to get what it wants. The Spanish, who came to the "New World" in the name of the monarchy and Christianity, immediately appropriated indigenous feminine power by combining it with the power of the Virgin Mary, who was adored by Spanish men as an abnegated, nurturing, all-forgiving woman. They destroyed the icons and beautiful temples and religious sites of the Indians and with the rubble built churches to their blessed "mother." The mother of Christ was also used in the conquest as a symbol to the Indians that the Spanish god was more powerful than Indian gods were. They forced the Indians to accept their one god or to be killed, and taught the women, like those in Spain, to model their lives after the Virgin Mary, who was secondary to Jesus Christ, the Son of God. The Indians were intelligent. They knew that mothers are more powerful than sons are, and combined Spanish and indigenous icons, feast days, and spiritual sites. Their version of the Virgin Mary became the patron saint of most of the Americas. From this cultural blending appeared a brown-skinned, Indian-looking virgin in Mexico. La Virgin de Guadalupe appeared to the Indian Juan Diego on the hilltop of Tepeyac, a place where Indians worshiped the Nahuatl goddess Tonatizin, the protector of pregnant women. Today she, not Jesus Christ, is the leading deity, not only in Mexico, where she is most popular, but also among Mexican immigrants and most Chicanos. La Virgin de Guadalupe is also recognized all over the world.

While the new virgin provided a great deal of the basis by which the Spanish were able to impose and maintain colonization, *la bruja* was seen in alliance with the devil, the Spanish European deity of the underworld. The categorization and dichotomization of Heaven and Earth, good and bad, became a cementing element for women. The Catholic Church was already hierarchical and in tight alliance with the queen and king of Spain. Prior to the rule of Queen Isabela, the power of the church had been concentrated in the hands of men for hundreds of years.

In the 1800s various Central and South American countries sought to liberate themselves from Spain. During this time a male's reputation was translated into the family's reputation, even if he was poor. Family reputation also controlled women. Women conformed to strict forms of conduct that demanded they be accompanied and discrete at all times. The majority of the men who came to the Americas were at best working class. Only a few officers had any resources. When they brought women, the Spanish females were shocked and repulsed at how bronze-colored women wore loose clothing and how men had easy access to them. Social stratification was not only based upon race, but also rooted in class and place of origin. Upper-class Spanish women born to Spanish parents in Spain, and who remained in Spain, were esteemed most highly, but were isolated and sheltered. Those who came to the Americas held secondary social positions. Those who were born in the Americas but had Spanish parents held third place. Below them were women of mixed Spanish and indigenous blood, followed by those with Spanish and African blood. The lowest-ranked women ranked under Indian and African men. They were the women with two Indian parents or two African parents. Spanish men had taken Indian women as slaves, lovers, and even wives. They brought slavery to the Americas, and the offspring of Spanish men and Indian women became known as mestizos, the mixed Spanish and Indian gene pool consisting of contemporary Chicanas, Hispanas, and Latinas.

Two women emerged during the Spanish colonial time. Foremost was the queen of Spain, Isabela, who forwarded declarations to the "New World" condemning the foul treatment of the Indians. There is no mention of the treatment of the Africans. The other woman was Sor Juana Ines de la Cruz, a colonial nun in Mexico who not only criticized the church, but also the state for its treatment of Indians, and protested the role of women in both the church and secular society. For this she endured severe consequences that, in my opinion, led to her demise. Church officials took away the means by which she did her work and studied.

Primarily women have documented women's lives. In academia Chicanas asserted themselves as activist feminist scholars as early as the late 1960s. They documented the experiences of women in Meso-American and pre-Columbian culture. Some learned pre-European languages, poetry, and other art forms. They critiqued U.S. history and recorded women's lives during the

U.S. imposition on Mexican territory. They also researched the racism that followed it, the growth of the railroads, labor movements, and the impact of two world wars. In the process they taught the United States about women like Sor Juana Ines de la Cruz. They taught about Josefa Dominguez (an upper-class woman who defied her husband to assist the liberation of Mexico), las Adelitas, and labor activists like Emma Tenayuca, Luisa Moreno, Josefina Fiero, and Lucy Parsons.

Some early Chicana feminists abandoned their Anglo names, which had been changed from Spanish names when they entered Anglo-dominated schools. Others wanted nothing to do with either Spanish or Anglo oppressors and changed their names to Indian names. They did all this while monitoring and criticizing the Chicano movement when incidents of sexism arose. In fact, the movement's major problem was intolerance of women. It failed to adequately address the issues of gender imbalance, and it weakened its own foundation by male infighting to fit the dominant hierarchical structure that they had internalized. Chicano males simply fought over who was going to be the leader, but the movement had other failures. It called for decolonization but lacked a strategy for it. It did not provide a plan for casting off social, political, religious, gender, class, and psychological oppression. It lacked the incorporation of female leadership and the world view of women and their ideas, and failed to take advantage of female coping and creative mechanisms. These coping skills included physical, linguistic, psychological, and spiritual survival, much of which was rooted in their indigenousness.

## CONQUERED, CONQUERORS, AND COLONIZED

Immigrant Latinas tend to view Chicanas as highly Americanized, sometimes even unfriendly to them. This, however, wears away when social contact is increased and immigrants move into Chicano communities. Although Chicanas are a group of women who overtly and covertly have resisted U.S. imposition upon their bodies, land, and culture, they have in fact internalized some of the conquering culture.

Chicanas, who are primarily U.S. born, are distinguished from Latinas, who are generally considered recent immigrant women. Not only were they born outside the United States less than three generations ago, they still have ties to their mother countries. There is controversy among Chicanas as to whether or not to identify as Latinas, and there is controversy among a few Latinas, who sometimes want to be identified as Chicanas.

Chicanisma, Chicana feminism, involves a political orientation that violates the white need to simplify racial and ethnic groups and place them into hierarchical categories. This is not only related to their need to attribute value to people and things, but also to maintain a hierarchical structure in which women are subservient for the purpose of control and to insure privileges for men, especially white men. I believe that white women gain only secondary privilege, but they at least have more than most men of color. Although Chicano men are ferociously victimized by this system, they at least can cling to being rated higher than their own women. Thus, Chicana and Latina feminists are sometimes confusing to those who seek to simplify the world. These women simply do not fit the social mold created for them. Thus, they are frequently ignored. Although patriarchy and the male-dominated white world view create many problems for Chicanas, from them we can learn about the struggle to persevere, to create, to balance individual spirituality in a frequently hostile world.

The development of a political consciousness came quickly for Chicanas. Their brand of feminism embraces the understanding of the intersection of gender, race, and class upon their lives, but also upon other groups of people both within the national borders and internationally. Not only do they understand this; they seek to do something about it. How they go about this is based upon the complex foundation of their identity.

The complexity is rooted in the fact that Chicanas' European ancestors are from Spain. The Spanish conquered Indians in the Americans, and from this fact comes a very tiny bit of white privilege. France ruled Mexico for a short while, but Chicanas generally do not identify with that. They are indigenous and because of Mexican rule over their homeland are referred to by some as Mexicans. By the mid-1800s Mexicans were conquered by the United States, and as conquered women Chicanas had to learn to speak English. They tend to speak at least two languages, interact fluently in at least two cultures, and some of them are international women with friends and family in Mexico and other countries. This makes Chicanas uniquely talented. Nevertheless, their uniqueness warrants little social reward.

Primary to the consciousness of the Chicana is the nature of a colonial existence, war, and the struggle to maintain an indigenous and Spanish European ancestry in balance with the influence of Anglo-American culture. Since the imposition of European culture as law, the Chicana's life has been characterized by contradiction and the need for inventiveness in maintaining the balance of self within a disempowered and continually victimized minority community. Chicanisma advocates for the civil and human rights of women and men in an attempt to escape colonialism. They also extend their human rights philosophy to countries outside the United States. In doing this, they dichotomize in addressing gender bigotry and subjugation; but not when addressing racism. Here, they share the impact of gender prejudice with white women, but experience it at the same time they experience prejudice and injustice from them. Several U.S. feminists have tried to address racial intolerance, but this means giving up power and power is a nonnegotiable item.

Chicanas recognize the colonial atrocities the Spanish committed against the indigenous side of their identity and still feel the pain of the experience, but they also comprehend that Anglo-American men raped, hanged, and killed them. Even though feminism sometimes appears to take second place in their lives, it does not. Chicana and Latina feminism is only sometimes embedded in the needs and desires of Chicano and Latino men. Their brand of feminism is aligned with discussion and actions to end racial injustice because for them it is impossible to separate that they are women and persons of color at the same time.

To live like this requires physical, emotional, and spiritual strength. To outsiders these women sometimes appear unpatriotic or ungrateful for the privilege of living in the United States. Because of their international experience, they know that sometimes life is better in the United States, but their emotional ties to relatives and friends in Central and South America prevent them from taking full pride in being "American." They know how "Americans" treat these relatives and friends and people of color in their own country. They are also offended by the treatment of Mother Earth, who gives them life. They detest the atrocities committed by profiteers against the entire Earth and the sacredness of the environment.

To address these brutalities they claim their U.S. constitutional right to assemble and advocate for themselves and for their people. They criticize how life is lived under an oppressive government that has historically terrorized their people. They analyze how ethnic-cleansing policies were developed, and how their young men were taken to fight wars under a flag representing the rhetoric of democracy. Nevertheless, they are comfortable not having to experience the savageness experienced by women under Taliban rule. There is no pride, no patriotism, in this, only hard work striving to keep a balance, a symmetry that can keep them physically, emotionally, and spiritually healthy.

It has been my experience that one of the things that affects Chicanas and other women of color in a country where the emphasis is placed on youth and beauty is their inability to reach that ideal. The ideal is Anglo European. Some have come to hate their bodies and their skin color. If they are tall and lean then they are too dark. If they are light skinned their own people tease them and call them *huera*, blond. Implied in this is the abandonment of identifying with their culture and striving to get accepted by the dominant culture. Today, Chicanas, like other women, spend thousands of dollars on beauty products, and like other women some Chicana and Latina feminists are trying to teach others that those who won the war dictate the ideal of beauty.

The most devastating result of the U.S. war with Mexico was the loss of land and political powerlessness. The society revolved around land and the respect accorded to large landowners. The land not only gave them a means of exchange; it rendered self-identity and spirituality. After the U.S. war with Mexico ended in 1848, the conquered Mexican people had a choice: to move south of the new international boundary or remain where they were and become U.S. citizens. Because people were not told they had a choice, and because they were on their homeland, they remained where they were (Blea 1988). Some lived in cities like Los Angeles, San Antonio, and Santa Fe. Others were more rural, but by the 1950s many of those who were rural had lost their land through various land schemes constructed by whites and had moved to the cities, generally to work as laborers or to live in poverty. The families who remained rural exist there today in various states of poverty.

The layers of contradictions, resentment, and distrust make it difficult for most Chicanas to know their history, the experience of their culture and people in American, and their own language. These have been suppressed to the point that many do not know what indigenous genetic and social influence still exists in their lives. To produce this phenomenon, the dominant criminal justice system, politics, religion, and the health and educational systems all play a role. The interaction of these social institutions in defining the quality of life for Chicanas and their people is the target of U.S. Chicana feminists.

## CATHOLIC PATRIARCHY AND SPIRITUAL REFORM

A feminist perspective poses that periods of significance for men are not as significant, nor significant in the same manner, for women. This holds true especially in American Catholic Church history. For Chicanas and Latinas, surviving in America means a loss of control of their spirituality that has manifested in a loss of identity and a connection to a larger sense of being. Yet only a few Chicanas have openly called for an entirely different religious structure, one based in indigenousness; often one that abandons Christianity but for the most part integrates indigenous belief systems with Christian beliefs.

Because of an inability to conform to church doctrine, many have left the church. Change in it is too slow and too small. The women who have chosen to work within the Catholic Church have focused upon liberation theology as an ideological framework for social and religious change at the same time. Liberation theology is generally associated with Central and Latin America. There, priests and church members have striven to interpret the theories governing Christianity as a form of social politics seeking to get the world power of the Catholic Church involved in promoting human rights. Progress has been slow there also.

Thus, Christianity is seen as a male-dominated religion superimposed upon Chicana and Latina indigenous ancestors as an instrument of colonization geared toward stripping them of their identity, their world view, and their means of resistance or liberation. Only men can be priests in the Catholic Church, and only a male can become Pope. There is generally a contradiction between the teachings of Christianity and the behavior of its proponents. Christians have tolerated gender and racial intolerance founded in male politics and women know this. These contradictions have been imposed upon women and some women have supported them. If they do not, they are told they are committing a sin and going against God's representative on Earth.

Male advocates of liberation theology believe there is room for Chicana–Latina liberation within the context of liberation theology; after all, it is about liberating people. But admitting that Christianity is a tool used to maintain control,, one that has flourished on conquered land, and that this is wrong is contradictory to male domination. Thus, women cannot even begin to discuss with men whether women can become priests, especially when they are desperately trying to recuperate from the rape of their female ancestors and the savagery committed against Mother Earth.

Mostly, Chicanas and Latinas want to make the church more responsive to their people's concerns by basing their arguments on the need for viable representation in ongoing religious rites, direct social services for Chicano–Latino poor, having services in Spanish, and requesting more Spanish-speaking priests. Very few have questioned and confronted the power of the Pope and the Vatican's antifemale policies on female deities, female leadership, birth control, and abortion. Fewer note that Chicana nuns tend to do domestic chores and work more with the poor than Anglo nuns, who tend to teach school, have administrative duties, and have more influence over orders or convents dictated by men.

While conducting research for *Bessemer* (Blea 1992a) and again for a book entitled *Researching Chicano Communities* (Blea 1995) I discovered that in protest, many Chicanas and Latinas have quietly converted to other more fundamentalist religions. Those who have converted cite contradictions between teaching and acting in the Catholic Church and an inability to have a direct relationship with God as major reasons for leaving. They resent going through a priest and the Pope in directing their lives, and note that there is much ceremony and ritual and that the priest and the church structure interfere or buffer what people want. The fundamentalist religions, on the other hand, hold entire services in Spanish. They have Spanish prayers, teachings, music, and songs. Women feel a more integral part of the services because they are more than part of the audience. Fundamentalist religions are not only more expressive, but women can be ministers. They can testify at microphones before the congregation and gain some leadership skills. They stand in or in front of an audience, lead prayers, preach, cite passages from the Bible, sing, and generally feel more fully connected to God. They can ask questions, clap their hands and dance, cry and pray out loud or in silence. They ask for prayer and offer to pray for one another. They touch one another and visit one another in their homes. In these churches women are called sisters and the men are their brothers. There is much less hierarchy. It has been my experience that in born-again churches social and political awareness sometimes manifests in female testimonies, but much control over their own lives is frequently rendered to a male God. The vehement belief in God being in control, however, renders minimal potential for feminist action. It does not change the structure of the society.

It has been my experience that very few Chicanas and Latinas know the Catholic Church's history and its political nature in the United States and/or in their country of origin. If they have some information, most ignore indigenous spiritual suppression. In fact, most do not claim being Indian. They know that identifying with oppressed people brings additional discrimination. Thus, they turn against their own indigenous history and by neglect they denigrate and discriminate against Indians.

To counter this, Catholic Chicana and Latina church activists call for the implementation of liberation theology. They contrast the tremendous wealth of the church and the poverty of Chicano and Latino people, and note that the church engages in noncontroversial activities such as adoption, marriage counseling, food, and lodging for the poor. Chicanas and Latinas have called for a lifting of the burden of racial oppression from church structure, but have not demanded the removal of male-dominated church privilege rooted in its history of American atrocities and neglect. Relief from oppression may mean removing the church from occupied land, and this is unthinkable to most.

For Chicanas and Latinas who have taken control of their own spirituality, religion and spirituality have become a system of shared Christian and Indian beliefs and practices built around the idea of harmony between human, natural, and supernatural forces. Characteristic of the manifestation of spirituality is the notion of the power of being female, the nature of life-giving forces on Earth, in the water, the sky, the trees, the animals, and the afterlife. For some this may involve sweats, prayer, and other rituals of a physical, psychological, and spiritual nature. This is a population that believes in ghosts, that there is evil, and that one can be hexed by *brujas* (witches), but that individuals have power to counteract this. Chicanas, Hispanas, and Latinas simply want their interpretation of the American dream. Some demand cultural sovereignty and/ or the right to learn, keep, nurture, and teach their culture without any form of retribution.

In linking spirituality to the history of Chicanas in America, one would think that society was shaped by the call of rugged white individuals who responded to the pull of vacant and virgin land (Schlissel 1988). What called the Spanish to the homeland of Chicanas was the Spanish and then the Anglo-American government's need for gold and the Catholic Church's need for converts. For Chicanas this goes beyond defining what is the frontier and the shaping of its society by the male need to defend themselves against the barbarians of Indians. It also goes beyond the pull of imperialist economic expansion to the subjugation of Mexicans. As with Native Americans, the social–historical experiences of white men and women that created the myth of the American frontier and the foundation of the American dream have not transferred to Mexican women. However, Mexican men related to the dominant structure primarily out of necessity, and in their peripheral involvement at the lowest level of the American social–economic ladder they felt they had more power than women did.

The Americanization of Chicanos and Latinos has produced Latino men who have participated in American wars in order to sustain masculinity and prove they are "real" Americans. After World War II some obtained education, but they continued to conceptualize the world according to their male experience in it. When a few recognized that American society was and is hierarchically stratified, compartmentalized, and dichotomized, they also realized they could contribute to their own oppression or react to expose it. When women joined the dialogue, they demonstrated how internal colonialism and patriarchy produces a low worth attached to Mexican women. This is difficult for some men to accept because sometimes they play a role in it. They gain male privilege when things are put into good and bad categories, where being a woman is considered bad (Blea 1997, 1992a, 1992b). Most Latino men fear being associated with anything that is considered female. Some still manage to prevent "their women" from exposure to feminist perspectives, and in their homophobia and male prerogative dictate that if a woman does not meet their standard of beauty, is old, bisexual, or lesbian, mentally or physically impaired, or a feminist, she further deteriorates in worth.

Even under these conditions, however, Chicanas and Latinas create poetry, plays, songs, music, paintings, dances, and careers. Within the stresses imposed by Catholic patriarchy, which is dominated by white males in the United States and in other countries, they grow up, have lovers, get married, birth or adopt children, get divorced, write books, teach classes, advocate for their people, and die. In this context, discriminatory practices are ever present in both formal and informal rules and in the form of a need for money and other capital, the mode of exchange imposed by European colonialism.

Capital and private property are contingent upon one another. If one does not possess capital, one quickly becomes private property. Policies and cultural practices like the tradition of taking a male's last name when a woman marries tag women as belonging to someone. Even in marriage, one of the Catholic holy sacraments, the husband's status does not transfer to the woman. If his worth is positive, she is secondary, identified as the "wife." If it is negative, however, women are perceived as partly to blame. This practice produces women with low self-esteem, something women of color always guard against, especially if they chose to have intimate relationships with other women.

If one is not heterosexual there are punishments. The social consequences of being bisexual or lesbian manifest in sin according to the Catholic Church (http://ww.ReligiousTolerance.org), which declares that homosexuals go to hell when they die (Anzaldua 1999). When a woman chooses not to have sex with men, she is punished, even victimized by hate crimes manifested in beatings, rape, and exorcisms. In most Chicano and Latino cities and villages it is taboo to have sex with a person of the same gender. Women who do are ostracized by the Catholic Church and by their families. They may not adopt children, have their loved one's picture on their desk at work (if they can get work), take their partner to family celebrations, or be a minister or priest.

As noted, I have written about how colonialism, patriarchy, capital, and private property produce major contradictions for Spanish-speaking and other women of color (Moraga 1981). In my experience, at the same time they desire upward mobility, they have been victimized by class discrimination and resent the discriminating class. These contradictions produce self-conflicts, frustration, anger, sadness, depression, various acting-out behaviors, suicidal tendencies, and alternative perspectives on how it is possible to live a life. Although some of these tendencies are destructive, some are truly gifts that Chicanas and Latinas give the world.

Most accounts of la Chicana include a summary of the four strongest spiritual cultural beings: *la Virgen de Gualalupe* (the Virgin Mary), *la Llorona* (the wailing women), *la bruja* (the witch), and *la curandera* (the healer). It is interesting to note that these beings are women and extremely powerful, and that their power is not to be taken lightly. The cultural presence of these figures also demonstrates that attempts at cultural genocide have not been successful. I have concentrated upon these cultural figures before (Blea 1997, 1995, 1992b, 1988), and will not go into detail here. It suffices to say that female presence symbolizes the strength and spirituality of Aztlan, the land of origin for the Aztec ancestors of Chicanas, and embodies the identity of Chicanas and the entire Latino culture.

*La Virgen de Guadalupe* and *curanderas* are "good" women. Some people do not believe in the spiritual and herbal healing power of the women noted here. Others see *curanderismo* as the work of the devil and his earthly representatives, *brujas*. The dichotomous nature of these entities has not only exposed Chicanas and Latinas to contradicting role models; it has led to negative stereotypes that entrap women into gender and spiritual roles not created by women. More important, the dichotomies fail to teach women the light and dark power of the goddess, and the fact that Chicanas and Latinas have tremendous positive and negative power available to them for good or for evil. This frightens men.

Spiritual suppression combined with racial and gender discrimination plus the stereotypes found in white society about the powerlessness of women places Chicanas and Latinas in struggle against overwhelming odds. Yet some have resisted entrapment and have lunged forward to create their own worlds, their own realities, and their particular sense of spirituality. But because not all Latinas have evolved at the same time in the same direction, Chicana feminists are stereotyped as radical, unhappy women who do not trust men and have lesbian tendencies (Blea 1997).

## CHICANA POWER

It was not until the 1960s that Chicanos organized on a massive scale to address the problems they had as conquered persons who were severely discriminated against in education, employment, health, the criminal justice system, politics, and religious institutions. In a short time a few brave pioneer women stood up and demanded an end to sexism that translated into Chicana power.

Many of these women are still living and tell of the resistance they encountered from both men and women in the movement. In spite of this they persisted in drawing attention to what was then called "minority female" concerns.

The battles were heated. Chicanas continuously explained to Chicanos that gender intolerance and injustice was like racism. It functions to the disadvantage of everyone by dividing groups of people and fragmenting efforts to promote social change. Chicanas were not alone. They soon learned that other women in the civil rights movement, the black civil rights movement, and the American Indian movement were facing the same dilemmas. Knowing this served to encourage them further.

The 1960s were loud, hostile times that also consisted of dissatisfied white youth protesting the Vietnam War, seeking flower power, sex, drugs, and rock and roll. These elements crept into the civil rights movements, where there were boycotts against agricultural harvesters of grapes and lettuce and educational and criminal justice institutions. Demonstrators demanded Chicano Studies. Men appropriated female work, cited credit for themselves, and insisted upon a male-dominated movement. Soon, a few isolated women demanded Chicana Studies. These Chicanas continued to take part in the boycotts, sit-ins, and pickets. They analyzed their roles, their role models, and even their mothers' roles for their structure and function. Revolutionary songs, like "Las Adelitas" from the Mexican Revolution in 1910, were revitalized. Chicana poetry was popular; art and theater flourished. At the same time, Chicanas walked every step, fought every battle, and encountered the same violence experienced by men.

Chicana feminism was still resisted by men and some women. Parents were embarrassed that their daughters wore serapes, headbands, and Emiliano Zapata or Che Guevera T-shirts and talked "that way" about realities that were unmentionable: racism and sexism. These activities were the markings of poorly socialized females and they reflected on the family, especially the male head of it. Most fathers felt it was bad enough they were poor; they did not want their children flaunting it, and the mother's thought it was not ladylike. Slowly, a few men, some parents, and even grandparents realized the importance of what was happening and joined in the struggle for human rights. Eventually they came to see Chicana feminist issues as concern for their people, *la raza*. Lest the reader be mislead, the subject is still controversial in Latino and Chicano communities. Sensitivity for Chicana feminism was short lived. The minimal commitment males made to it clustered around the rhetoric of movement participants, and few males ever took action to openly support women's issues.

Men were more interested in the relaxing sexuality of the 1960s. For the first time in history interracial sexual relationships were engaged in and discussed openly. While active in the civil rights movement, I noted that many Chicano men had sex with their first Anglo female. To some men, it became a revolutionary objective to "f—" a white man's woman. Some Chicanas engaged in sexual relationships with white men, but it did not mean the same thing. Males interpreted it as an action proving their personal victory over the white man. Chicanas were considered to be betraying the movement. Most movement activist had sex with opposite genders of their own culture. Whatever the rationalization, sex outside the culture became a heated topic dividing the sexes in the movement until the issue of immigration took priority.

Women who experienced the Chicana movement of the 1960s and 1970s wanted a better country. They accomplished much by claiming their homeland, Aztlan; they empowered an entire culture and made the world for other Chicanas, Chicanos, and Latinos in general better. More recent immigrants do not know this part of American history. It is not a part of the naturalization exam. Those few who have taken the time to learn it struggle, along with Chicanas, to diminish the points of conflict between the immigrant and the native born, but those conflicts exist.

There is an ongoing debate over how persons of Spanish-speaking origin prefer to identify themselves. Some prefer to be called Hispanic. Others reject this and use Hispano as a government-imposed label and prefer a self-identity embedded in the Spanish language. Some prefer the label to be Spanish; others cling to Chicano. The most recent term is the all-inclusive Latino. Its homogeneity is rejected by many. Whatever the preference, the variance causes fragmentation among the population, and organizational efforts are condensed.

Some people want desperately to fit into the dominant society, others reject it and those who seek to assimilate outright. Some Latinos want to live in the United States and maintain their mother culture, and others want to earn higher incomes in the dominant society but have their personal lives exclusively Latino. Some Latinos strive to interact with everyone at the same time and for everyone to get along. The big question is whether the dominant culture will accept them. For the most part no, but it may be changing as a result of September 11.

Recent immigration has served to empower Chicanas by increasing their numbers when combined with immigrant Latinas. Most Americans are not aware that Latino immigration is encouraged when there is a need for cheap labor power and discouraged when there is an economic recession (Suaro 1998). In fact, many rich people encourage immigration because it renders them profit. When it comes to U.S. Latinos' power relationships and U.S. labor needs the push–pull has resulted in U.S. immigration policy that is geared to meet the needs of profiteers. Generally, this relationship is focused upon when discussing Mexican immigrant workers who come to the United States. However, an example of another push–pull policy can be found in the experience of Cubans. The Cuban Information Archives revealed that by the mid-1980s, about 129,000 Cuban immigrants arrived in the United States in boats from the port of Mariel (Cuban Information Archives 2001). U.S. officials delivered them to "refugee centers" to live in what some described as concentration camps. U.S. officials estimated that 2,746 of the refugees were reported to be criminals and mental patients. Fidel Castro, president of Cuba, claimed they were not, but took them back in 1984.

Chicana feminists do not see Cuban Americans as supporting feminism. They tend to be middle-class conservative Republicans, while Puerto Ricans lean Democratic and are working class (Arango 2000). It is that diversity that causes confusion for the Census Bureau over race classifications in Hispanic–Latino communities. It was reported to me that physically, most census takers cannot tell Cubans apart from Puerto Ricans. Even other Latinos have difficulty with them. All they know is that Cubans and Puerto Ricans speak faster Spanish and I have heard jokes about this. Some of them have learned to hate Fidel Castro, also known as El General, because he kicked conservatives with higher resources and American sympathies out of the country in the 1950s. The exiles in turn have launched a campaign in the United States against the otherwise charismatic leader, and U.S. officials use this push–pull history to disrupt Cubans from the island. This is a heated controversy, and Cuban Americans are divided in their loyalties to Cuba, the island, the land, and U.S. policy that affects Cuba.

Constant Mexican, Cuban, and Puerto Rican immigration and migration makes it difficult to count the increasing number of Latinos, but it also makes it difficult to promote feminism. For example, the U.S. Commission on Immigration Reform (1999) says most Mexican female immigrants come from the poorest parts of Mexico. They leave their country and live at a subsistence level. In this search to meet basic human needs for food, clothing, and shelter, most lack feminist consciousness.

## CHICANO AND LATINO NUMBERS
## THREATEN OTHER AMERICANS

Other factors concerning U.S. citizens is how the large number of poor immigrants, and how most Americans perceive them, will affect the power distribution in the country and the lives of private citizens. According to the U.S. Bureau of the Census (2000), the government managed to get a better Latino count in the 2000 census because it was the first time the survey allowed people to classify themselves as belonging to more than a single race. For about 14.9 million Americans of Hispanic ethnicity, however, responding to the survey was confusing. The number of race options increased from five in 1990 to sixty-three in 2000, and in totality, 15.4 million Americans checked only the "some other race" box; about 97 percent of them were Hispanic. Much of the confusion stems from how the federal government views the category "Hispanic." It views it as an ethnic group instead of a race; races are much larger groups of people, like American Indians. Ethnicities are cultural subgroups. Chicanos and Latinos are mixed-race, highly diverse people with a potential for social and political power that is yet unrealized, and self-identity is primary among the fragmenting factors.

Some Hispanics do not see themselves in racial terms. When they answered the census race question, they felt the question did not apply to them. One question asked if a respondent was "Hispanic" or "non-Hispanic." A person of "Hispanic" ethnicity can be of any race. Another question inquiring about race allowed people to check one or more of six different race categories, including "some other race." Nearly half of the country's 35.3 million Hispanics chose only "white" as their race. As I live and travel among Latinos a growing number want "Hispanic" to be officially considered its own race, rather than an ethnicity. A race is larger, therefore more powerful, in the minds of their advocates. One has to ask why it is so important to the U.S. government to know the race of its citizens. The answer lies in negative race relations.

Nevertheless, the number of Hispanics increased 58 percent between 1990 and 2000. It is unclear how much of that gain was due to undocumented immigration. Many undocumented women (workers who are in the United States illegally, or without going through the legal process and acquiring proper documentation that allows them to work in the United States) do not respond to the census for fear of being separated from their families and being deported. This does not empower the Chicano–Latino community. The Census Bureau launched a big push to count everyone but did not ask the respondents' their legal status due primarily to pressure from Hispanos. Various estimates before the 2000 census placed the number of undocumented immigrants at 6 million. The Population Division of the Ethnic and Hispanic Statistics Branch of the U.S. Bureau of the Census is reviewing that number after the total U.S. population of 281 million was 3 million higher than a previous census estimate. The figures vary, but many service providers and advocates feel the total number of undocumented immigrants in the country could have climbed to between 8.5 million and 9 million in 2000 (see Table 3.1).

**Table 3.1**
**Total U.S. Hispanic Origin (of any race) Resident Population Estimate by Percentage and Gender**

| | |
|---|---|
| Population | 32,832 |
| Percent of total | 11.9 |
| Median age (years) | 26.6 |
| Mean age (years) | 29.1 |
| Male population | 16,489 |
| Female population | 16,343 |

*Source*: Population Estimates Program, Population Division, U.S. Census Bureau, Washington, D.C. (Internet release date January 2, 2001).

*Note*: Projection to November 1, 2000. Numbers in thousands.

The Census Bureau plans to continue with the current race classification system for the 2010 count, but that may change as the government studies the latest results, which continue to be tabulated and then reworked. Many organizations are watching what the U.S. Bureau of the Census will do. Among them are social scientists in Chicano Studies departments in the nation's universities, member organizations such as the Mexican American Legal Defense and Education Fund, and the National Council of La Raza. These organizations also monitor immigration policy and other population issues. Hispanics rival non-Hispanic blacks as the country's leading minority group. Hispanic data were the first nationwide race data release from Census 2000. The Hispanic population dramatically increased by about 58 percent over the past decade (from 22.4 million in 1990 to 35.3 million in 2000). The number of non-Hispanic blacks, meanwhile, may have increased to as much as 21 percent from a decade ago, to 35.4 million. The non-Hispanic Asian population surged as much as 74 percent, to 11.6 million, and the population of American Indians and Alaska natives who were not Hispanic nearly doubled, up as much as 92 percent to 3.4 million. The growth rate for non-Hispanic whites, meanwhile, lagged behind (up no more than 5.3 percent) to 198.2 million (U.S. Bureau of the Census 2002).

Some feel the increasing presence of Hispanics means African Americans have a better partner in terms of shared political and socioeconomic issues, but some African Americans have internalized mainstream hierarchy and competition and feel that Hispanics are a threat by being serious competition for limited government resources. Social concerns like poverty, education, and urban development are issues that African Americans and Hispanics have in common. Other shared issues can be even more threatening than competing for the disbursement of $185 billion in federal funds. For example, the census data will be used to redraw some electoral boundary lines. People of color fear redistricting, an old colonizing trick. It fragments large Hispanic voting blocks and keeps the population disempowered. Figures compiled on race and ethnicity are also important for enforcement of a wide array of civil rights laws, including voting rights and workplace regulations.

There is U.S. territory beyond the mainland. In U.S. colonies such as the U.S Virgin Islands and Puerto Rico, there are a large number of undeclared residents. There are an estimated 4 million Puerto Ricans, plus there are roughly 4 million illegal immigrants from various countries that are not usually counted in the census. The U.S. Census 2000 did count 28.4 million foreign-born people, who represent nearly 10.4 percent of the total U.S. population. Those foreign born in Latin America comprise approximately 51 percent of the total U.S. foreign born. A total of 39.9 percent of the Latino foreign born live in the western part of the United States, where the highest number of Chicanos live, and 26.8 percent live in the South, 22.6 percent live in the Northeast, and 10.7 percent live in the Midwest. The foreign born from Latin America are especially more likely to live in the West (42.1 percent) and in the South (32.6 percent). Foreign born from Central America, who represent two-thirds of the foreign born from Latin America, are also concentrated in the West (58.5 percent) and in the South (27.4 percent). For politicians, the large potential voting block, especially in the West, has become very important. Latin American foreign born, those from the Caribbean and those from South America, are concentrated in the Northeast (45.5 percent) and the South (48.7 percent), respectively.

In 2001 the Immigration and Naturalization Service (INS) estimates that at least 3.6 million out of the 5 million illegal immigrants are Hispanic or Latino, and 38.9 percent were women. The total number is expected to rise to about 50 million by the year 2005. This estimate is threatening to some members of U.S. society, especially to the dominant white population. Not only is there fear of loss of white privilege and social control; there is fear of retaliation by the oppressed "minority" group, which is sure to foster social and cultural change. Thus, several pieces of legislation limiting immigrant rights emerged. These efforts, however, are historical. Chicanas and Mexican women, some of them with 500-year-old homeland histories on U.S. territory, have experienced selective immigration legislation targeting Mexicans and its violent consequences. Most important, and even more threatening to some, is the fact that Latinos and the immigrant populations are not crossing over into mainstream culture (Larmer 1999). They prefer their own cultural productions, heroines and heroes, and entertainers. Further, immigrants to the United States truly reflect the face of the Americas, North, Central, and South, which forces the United States to redefine its position in the hemisphere.

The large number and the working class ethics of U.S. Latinos have brought purchasing power. In discussions with members of the entertainment business, I found that Hollywood is looking to expand its market to take advantage of the billions of dollars Latinos have to spend (MarketResearch.com 2001a, 2001b). Celia Cruz, Rita Moreno, Carmen Zapata, Gloria Esteven, and Christina Aguillara demonstrate that Latinos are a mixture of many of the world's races, cultures, and religions with European, African, Native American, Arabic, and Jewish backgrounds. They are "old world" and "New World," traditional, and ultra modern. Only in the Americas has there been such a mix of races and cultures. Only in the United States do Latinos share this with others. They demonstrate to the world a common heritage and destiny rooted in humanity and in their example that traditional concepts of race can be transcended and humans can produce wonderful things.

In 2000 the U.S. Bureau of the Census recorded that the Latino population on the U.S. mainland was composed of the following groups: Mexican American, 66.1 percent; Puerto Rican, 9.0 percent; Cuban, 4.0 percent; Central and South American, 14.5 percent; and "Other Hispanic," 6.4 percent. Some data on Hispanos and Latinos exclude residents of Puerto Rico because it is a territory and not a state. However, it too has a long history of native people, immigration, and colonialism. Data on this U.S. Hispanic population reveal that Puerto Ricans are somewhat similar to those on the U.S. mainland. The 2000 census estimates that the Puerto Rican population was 3.9 million, representing a 10.4-percent increase since 1990. According to the 1990 Census (which is the most recent data available for Puerto Rico), 90.9 percent of residents were born on the island. With regard to socioeconomic status, fewer than one-half (49.7%) of island Puerto Ricans twenty-five years and older were high school graduates, although one in seven (14.3%) was a college graduate, a figure higher than that for mainland Latinos. Poverty rates in Puerto Rico are quite high relative to those of both mainland Latinos and the United States in general: Over one-half (57.3%) of the island population lived below the poverty level, as did two-thirds (66.7%) of Puerto Rican children. Finally, while one-fifth (20.4%) of the island residents were unemployed at the time of the 1990 census, that figure declined to approximately 14 percent in 2001.

What also accounts for the rapid growth of the Hispanic population is increased birth rates between 1995 and 2000. The National Center for Health Statistics notes that in 1998 Hispanic women had the highest fertility rate among all racial and national origin groups. There were 84 births per 1,000 for Latina women ages fifteen to forty-four years old. In comparison, the fertility rate for white women was much lower, with 57.2 births per 1,000 white women. The age breakdown of the Latino population shows that Hispanics are much younger than non-Hispanics, with a large proportion of children. In 2000 more than one-third (35.7%) of Latinos were less than eighteen years old, compared to over one-fifth (23.5%) of whites and more than one-third (32.4%) of blacks. In contrast, relatively few Latinos were age sixty-five and older (5.3%), while whites had more than twice that amount (14%) and blacks had a similar rate (7.8%).

As a former member of the National Association of Chicana/Chicano Studies (2002), I know that Hispanics have a much smaller percentage of graduates than whites or blacks. In 2000, one of two (57%) Hispanics twenty-five years old and over had graduated from high school and 10.6 percent had graduated from college. In contrast, over seven of eight (88.4%) whites and almost three of four (79%) blacks twenty-five years old and over had completed high school in 2000, and 28.1 percent of whites and 17 percent of blacks completed college that same year. However, high portions of Hispanics are participating in the labor force. In 2000, 67.7 percent of the Hispanic population sixteen years old and over, or 21 million persons, was employed, which was comparable to the figure for whites (67.3%) and slightly higher than the level for blacks (65.8%). Despite the fact that a comparable percentage of Hispanics, whites, and blacks were employed at the end of the last decade, the unemployment rate for Hispanics was 6.4 percent, compared to 3.7 percent for white workers and 8 percent for black workers. It appears that the darker the skin, the less employment opportunities are forthcoming.

Hispanics are generally employed in manual labor, service occupations, and support. In 2000 Hispanics were almost twice as likely as whites to work in service occupations (19.4% and 11.8%, respectively) and as operators and laborers (22% and 11.6%, respectively). Moreover, 14 percent of Latinos were in managerial or professional occupations, compared to 33.2 percent of whites. The data may indicate that the higher status and salary and cleaner the job is, the fewer Hispanics. The lower status and salary and dirtier, the more Hispanic males are represented. This has severe consequences for women with partners. They not only live on less money; they have to clean the clothes, the bathrooms, and the utility room, if they have them and do not have to cart clothes off to the laundry.

## UNDOCUMENTED WOMEN

In 2000 almost one-half (46.9%) of Hispanic men fifteen years old and over were employed—some in precision production, craft, and repair occupations (18.6%); others as executives, administrators, and managers (14.9%); and some in professional specialties (13.4%) (U.S. Bureau of the Census 2000). The majority (58.2%) of Hispanic women were employed in administrative support, including clerical (23.7%), professional specialty (17.8%), or service occupations, except in private households (16.7%) in 1999. In comparison, white men were concentrated in managerial and professional specialty occupations (29.1%), white females concentrated in technical, sales, and administrative support (40.6%), and black men and women were employed in occupations similar to those of Hispanic men and women.

Although the Census Bureau (2000) Hispanic median family income remains well below that of white families, it has increased since the end of the last decade. Real median household income for Hispanic married-couple families was $37,132 in 1999, compared to $59,697 for white non-Hispanic families and $50,656 for black families. Between 1998 and 1999, real median family income levels increased 4.3 percent for Hispanic families, 2.5 percent for white non-Hispanic families, and 4.6 percent for black families. Combined, black and Hispanic men and women are making significant contributions to the overall economy.

The number of Hispanic-owned businesses is rising dramatically, and the projected buying power of the total Hispanic population was $452.4 billion in 2001 (U.S. Bureau of the Census 2001a), an increase of 118 percent since 1990. However, poverty rates for Hispanic families, working Hispanic families, and Hispanic children remain disproportionately high. At the turn of this century, more than one-quarter of both Hispanic and black families lived in poverty, while the poverty rate for white non-Hispanic families was relatively low. Moreover, the data show that poverty is three to four times as common among Hispanics as among non-Hispanic whites. People of Hispanic origin represented about 24 percent of all people living in poverty. Finally, one-third of Hispanic children were poor when the last census was taken, compared to 9.4 percent of white non-Hispanic children and one-third (33.1%) of black children who were impoverished. Not only is there a low regard for women and men of color; children of color are highly victimized by discrimination.

The majority of Hispanic households are married-couple families, but a significant proportion are also female-headed families (U.S. Bureau of the Census 2001). In 1999 over two-thirds (68%) of Hispanic households were married-couple family households; however, nearly one-quarter (23.7%) of Hispanic households were female-headed family households. In comparison, 82.2 percent of white households were married-couple family households in 1999, and 13 percent were female-headed family households.

The majority of the Hispanic population lives in five key electoral states: California, with a Hispanic population estimated at 10.1 million (32% of the total U.S. Hispanic population); Texas, 5.8 million (18.4%); New York, 2.6 million (8.2%); Florida, 2.2 million (7%); and Illinois, 1.2 million (3.8%). However, the percentages vary from period to period in various regions, and states with historically smaller Latino populations have also experienced significant growth in the last several years.

In February 2000 President George W. Bush mentioned in his State of the Union address that home ownership by "minorities" needed to increase in the United States. He was referring to the fact that most Latinos are renters, with relatively low home ownership rates overall, much lower than the national average of 65.7 percent of all households (Bush 2001). By comparison, 72 percent of white households were home owners, compared to 45.4 percent of blacks. Hispanics are also less likely than non-Hispanics to participate in federal low-income housing programs. During the last five years, approximately 19 percent of public housing renters were Hispanic, 30 percent were non-Hispanic white, and 48 percent were non-Hispanic black; similarly, roughly 15 percent of Section 8 tenant-based renters and 11 percent of Section 8 project-based renters were Hispanic, while 44 percent and 54 percent, respectively, were non-Hispanic white, and 37 percent and 32 percent, respectively, were non-Hispanic black.

There are both hopeful and disturbing signs with regard to Hispanic health. On the positive side, smoking, drinking, and illicit drug use are less prevalent among Hispanics than among non-Hispanics. At the end of the last decade, 27.4 percent of Hispanics twelve years old and over smoked. This compared to 30.5 percent of whites and 29.8 percent of blacks; 42.4 percent of Hispanics twelve years old and over used alcohol, compared to 55.1 percent of whites and 40.4 percent of blacks; and 5.9 percent of Hispanics twelve years old and over used illicit drugs, compared to 6.4 percent of whites and 7.5 percent of blacks. However, the infant mortality rate for Hispanics was relatively low. The infant mortality rate was 6.3 per 1,000 live births for Latinos, compared to 6 per 1,000 for white infants and the astonishingly high rate of 14.2 per

1,000 for black infants. However, HIV/AIDS and diabetes are two serious health threats affecting the Latino population. On average, Hispanic Americans are almost twice as likely to have diabetes as non-Hispanic whites of similar age, and are disproportionately represented among reported cases of AIDS. Hispanic children accounted for about one-fourth of all pediatric AIDS cases in 2000. Further, a large percentage of Hispanics, especially Hispanics who are poor and children, lack health insurance coverage. Over one-quarter (30%) of Hispanic children lacked any form of health insurance, a rate higher than that of either white (14.4%) or black (19.7%) children.

Brief national and international attention to immigrant Latina domestic workers appeared in the news in January 1993. Zoe Baird was nominated to President William "Bill" Clinton's cabinet. Baird's appointment was blocked when it was discovered that she had hired an undocumented female worker to provide her with childcare services. The charges were that Baird knew the woman was in the country illegally. Baird maintained that she hired the woman out of concern for her children. Somehow the reply made no sense. Some felt Baird did it out of concern for her pocketbook. They also questioned why a woman with Baird's economic means would not provide licensed daycare for her children. She retreated from further discussion of the cabinet appointment and the issues were not addressed. Needless to say, Zoe Baird seemed to disappear from politics. In her case, there were no charges filed against the father of her children. To be fair, he may have lost the benefit of Zoe's potential income.

Yet immigrant women are generally the scapegoats. Undocumented women have been providing cheap childcare for white women and men for years. They are relatively powerless in the United States. They cannot demand the minimum wage, medical benefits, vacation pay, social security, workers compensation, or unemployment benefits, and are at the mercy of their employers not to turn them in to immigration authorities before paying them their earned wages.

Other Latinas do not begrudge the undocumented woman employment. Those few with resources often hire them also. Chicana feminists, however, are generally disgruntled with the low wages paid to undocumented workers, and have spent years trying to remedy the problem. In addition, Chicana and Latina feminist have been critical of the fact that it is generally white men who gain profit by employing undocumented women. In addition, the case of Kathie Lee Gifford and how she was underpaying women in underdeveloped countries who constructed her lucrative clothing line lent even more attention to the issue. It is a class, gender, and race issue for Chicana and Latina feminists. They object to the victim being blamed for working illegally. Undocumented women are simply trying to escape poverty, not trying to increases exorbitant wealth that has to be hidden from the United States by rich people who do not want to pay taxes.

According to my conversation Jorge Bustamantes (2000), director and researcher at el Cologio de la Frontera Norte, an independent institution dedicated to studying immigration, the patterns of immigration are different for women. More urban than rural females and more males migrate to the United States. The more highly educated women tend to immigrate more frequently because of the need to exercise their talents and skills, and often they immigrate to get away from men who harass them at work or in their personal lives. Some want out of their abusive marriages, or to get away from the embarrassment of having their fiancées marry others. Further, immigrant Latinas tend to have different labor markets in the United States than men do. They frequently discover that they cannot use their talents and skills without furthering their education or gaining training. If they have degrees, most institutions will not accept them. Many educated immigrant women have had to take lower positions. Immigrant women generally tend to concentrate in light textile work, food service, home and hotel–motel maid service, and home childcare.

Regardless of whether they are undocumented or documented, immigrant Latinas and U.S.–born Chicanas must contend with *machismo*. This brand of *machismo* is different from the mainstream, tall, and handsome white man who can fight off his enemy and get all the "girls." It changes when the *macho* is brown. Tall, dark, and handsome lovers are considered full of a false sense of power that is exercised upon women, children, and weaker men. Few feminists realize how racist the use of this word has become. English appropriation of the word has vulgarized it and taken away the meaning that it once had. It once meant honor. A man gained status, power, and prestige by being honest and keeping true to his word. The sexist version of what Spanish-speaking males consist of neglects their diversity. The majority of Latinos are not tall, but some are, and they come in various skin colors and are heterosexual, bisexual, and homosexual. They are rich, poor, middle income, educated, illiterate, gang members, drug addicts, in and out of prisons, and high-ranking members of corporations. Most important, they come with various political, ethnic, and racial consciousnesses. They are generally seen as powerless by white men, and some white women see the tall, dark, and handsome stereotype as sexy.

Concentration on immigration concerns masks the fact that many Latinos and Hispanos have been in this country since before it was a country. No mention is made of the fact that they are often typical "American" success stories, but that for most opportunity has been limited. Even when discussing the Catholic Church, mestizos are an enormous group in the hemisphere, over 50 percent of all Catholics (Aguinaco 2002), but they are by no means represented in proportion to their population in the theology and in the Catholic Church leadership, or in any other segment of society (Aguinaco 2002). One factor that can unite the large female Latino population and bring them together with feminists groups to promote the feminization of racism is their shared issues as women, and the fact that most of them share cultures or blood lines with at least one other culture.

## CHICANA AND LATINA FEMINISM
## AS CULTURAL SOVEREIGNTY

Unless there is complete revolution (an overthrow of a social structure and the construction of an alternative), there is, at best, social reform. Many Chicanas wanted a complete revolution during the 1960s. With no resources to support revolution, reform won out, and other strategies were incorporated. Most became part of institutions and systems and now promote reform from within. Other things changed, however. Not only did women and men stop wearing strong gender-typed clothing; Vatican II instituted more liberal changes in the church. Nuns and priests wore street clothes and head coverings were no longer necessary so those women could attend mass. More secular Chicanas took off their bras. They wanted control of their own bodies, and this included the right to use birth control and, for many, to obtain abortions without fear of sin, going to hell, and abandonment by their loved ones.

Many young women experimented with drugs and sex in the 1960s. Even though the Chicano and Chicana movement was cross-generational, the movement created great emotional distances between some young feminist women and their mothers. *Verguenza*, shame, was a factor, but it was more than this for Chicanas. Out of respect, many moved out of the house and did not subject their mothers to their lifestyles, but like other women they were also struggling with sexuality and their male counterparts. When differences entered into close relationships, discussions were heated. There was much arguing with men over being called a girl, a bitch, a whore, a broad, a squeeze, or a chick. Feminists demanded to be called women. Their fathers thought of them as forever childlike.

Some young women were "kicked out" of their homes. Many went to universities. Some ended up on the streets. A few Chicanas graduated from universities and became attorneys, elementary school principals, professors, and politicians. Since the movement, Chicanas and Latinas have become highly visible in meetings, walking on the streets, in schools, in stores, in the media, in the government, on university campuses, and even a few can be found in the boardrooms of the United States. Most Latinas under thirty-five do not know they did not have these freedoms in the 1960s. Women all over the world have fought for these freedoms.

There is but one feminist movement in the world and women of color are the largest population taking part in it, and it manifests differently in different countries. At the height of social criticism in the United States, Anglo feminists and their issues received the most attention. Chicanas related well to most concerns, but they saw the issues via their own experience as poor people of color. They experienced sexism within their own cultures and they could not separate this from the racism and poverty they experienced in the dominant society. Some early feminist concerns included equal pay for equal work.

For Chicanas this did not mean breaking the glass ceiling, the invisible barrier to upward mobility that some white middle-class women experienced in corporations and institutions of higher education. For them, equal pay meant escaping poverty, but poverty was nowhere near the top of the white middle-class-controlled feminist agenda in the United States. This took some time to change. Many poor white women and women of color struggled long to feminize it, to make it a feminist-movement concern.

Women of color were called "minority women" in the 1970s and 1980s, and the white feminist movement was unsuccessful in addressing internal concerns. There were a few successful coalitions, but women of color withdrew into their own feminist movements within their racial or ethnic groups. From time to time women of color met and talked and worked with one another. They discovered they were having the same experiences, both with the Anglo feminist movement and in their own civil rights movements. These women formed coalitions at meetings and conferences, and were among the first coalition builders of the American civil rights movement. Even though they never banded together, they developed an ideology of equality that strengthened their movements. This ideology, however, has yet to be fully recognized.

In the 1970s women of color still conceived themselves as "minority women." In the 1980s they were identified as "Third World women." This label meant to convey a message that they had more in common with underdeveloped countries than with white women in the United States. In the 1990s a new way of spelling Chicana arose: Xicana. This spelling denoted the link between being Spanish and Indian in heritage. Like other women of color, Chicanas never abandoned their people. The strategy was more easily understood as the intersection of race, ethnicity, class, and gender, intersecting variables. The analysis primarily developed on university campuses. Neither the white feminist nor men in the civil rights movements paid much attention to it until they saw it in publication.

Many Anglo feminists are trying to deal effectively with their white privilege, but much has yet to be resolved. Recent attacks on affirmative action did not solidify the feminist movement with other elements of the civil rights movement beyond the immediacy of the issue. Somehow the groups see themselves as individual groups, unable to see social change in a much larger context. They have internalized individualism and competition, and compartmentalized to the extent that it creates boundaries between groups. Many maintain that white women have gained the most from affirmative action.

Reclaiming the homeland is important to Chicanos. For the most part the reclamation is symbolic and linked to the struggle to be recognized as indigenous. To be from Aztlan is to be political, to claim cultural sovereignty as a North American Indian. In Aztlan the war against man-made, not woman-made, boundaries takes place. Aztlan is a place in which to exist; it is a spiritual place, where physical, psychological, and spiritual strength is drawn. Some feel there is no room here for gender differentiation, but there is. To be Chicana is to have a relationship to Chicano–Latino history as a woman who has been physically, socially, spiritually, and psychologically violated. The homeland is feminine. Mother Earth nurtures and renders identity, dignity, and roots. It is a place and an idea, and it demands behavior that fights to protect it and its people. Immigrant Latinos do not always share this ideology. Their homelands and their indigenous roots are elsewhere.

Empowering women has been engaged in by offering university and college courses on Chicanas and Latinas. Another strategy is to provide upward mobility. This is the bottom-up approach to solving problems, an example of hierarchical European thinking that attempts to end the stereotype of Chicanas and Latinas as ignorant, sexually charged, good dancers, and willing to be home taking care of their men, who often wander into the beds of other women. These stereotypes are not much different from those of other women of color, who are also stereotyped as "welfare queens" and baby machines. There is no movement urging women not to marry, not to have children, to have a career, to adopt and adapt to a lesbian lifestyle, and to invest in one's own body and quality of life without a man.

Men are being challenged in several arenas. On July 29, 1998, I was watching a popular television program entitled *Unsolved Mysteries*. Toward the end of the program was an update on a story about a young Puerto Rican woman who sought and gained the capture of her Puerto Rican rapist. The young woman had met her predator in school and had dated him. When he became much too demanding and possessive, she (with the support of her mother) decided to break up the relationship. The young man could not or would not accept her decision to disassociate herself from him. He abducted and raped her, saying something to the effect that she then belonged to him. This incident was bothersome to me for several reasons. The conscious or unconscious cultural value in the early 1960s was that a young woman was "spoiled," damaged goods, and unworthy of any other man if she was not a virgin. If the boyfriend was her rapist, she might as well marry her rapist because no one else would "want" her. In addition, her family would be shamed.

This Puerto Rican female's experience also reminded of a Mexican woman I met 1995 while attending the U.N. Fourth World Women's Conference in China. The same thing happened to her in the 1950s, and to many other women generations before her. Their mothers and fathers also did not protest. They also were forced to marry their rapists, and they paid for "their" mistakes. It was not until the late 1990s that anyone reconceptualized and concluded that the women were victims and not responsible for male sexual behavior, that they had been kidnapped and raped and this was a crime, one that violated their human right to be safe from such an atrocity.

According to the frightening cultural stories told to me by my university colleagues and Asian contacts, this ancient tradition of "spoiling" women, insulting families, and forcing them into marriage is not solely a Latino phenomenon. Sometimes these traditions clash with the law. It has happened for centuries in various countries. In the United States in the early 1990s it happened to a young Vietnamese woman in southern California. Her boyfriend kidnapped her. Certain members of the two families got involved and the conflict escalated into the newspapers and on the television news programs. The newspeople noted that the young woman's family was pressing kidnapping charges, and that the members of the young man's family could not understand why the male was being charged with a crime.

The young Puerto Rican woman featured in the *Unsolved Mysteries* program was effective in having her rapist captured and brought to trial. The program gave no details on the results of the trial. In the past, too many women did not have the support of a feminist culture; neither did their parents, who they depended on for help. I do not know what happened to the Vietnamese woman. I moved from California and the incident did not make national news, but I did know women in the 1960s that experienced what the Puerto Rican and Vietnamese women experienced. These women symbolize the many young women who were and are victimized by young men seeking to fulfill personal agendas at their expense.

Yet the power of the appropriation of the word *machismo* has been so profound that even Latinas and Latinos want to believe and live out the stereotype. Therefore, there is a tendency for men to want to be "macho man," to have the kind of body always in demand by women, to have a certain way of talking, walking, and general presentation that makes them sexual conquerors. These are the men who stare right through women, undress them as they walk by. It is a comical image in search of power and dominance. Foremost among these characteristics is the message that real men do not cry. This encouragement not to reveal vulnerability is damaging. It does not allow men to claim their cultural right to be honorable men, but it also victimizes women and places males at a risk by encouraging male predators. It also hurts Chicano and Latino communities by promoting stereotypes and negative role models for children.

## THE LATIN EXPLOSION

Contemporary stereotypes and myths are always in the making. The latest U.S. rage is the "Latin explosion." This attention to Latinos is evidenced by several factors, including the July 12, 1999, issue of *Newsweek*, which notes that Hispanics are hip, hot, and making history. It is also fueled by the fact that by 2005 one-quarter of the U.S. population will be Latino. Chicanas and Latinas figure prominently. In each there are those who strive to empower their culture. One witnesses this when looking at their daily activity as workers, small-business owners, corporate executives, street vendors, artists, writers, wives, religious women, sisters, mothers, daughters, and older women. The first generation of activist Chicanas are, for the most part, now in their fifties and sixties, but there are still stereotypes. Discrimination is fluid. The stereotype of the kind and generous *abuelita* (grandmother) must advance to include women of action who are helping other aging women preserve their health and economic status. These older women are viable family and community members. In fact, it is elderly women who display the most cultural saliency. They contribute continuity and stability to traditions, to family units and to communities. Chicana feminists have done much to honor older women. They have integrated them into their art, poetry, plays, and even academic writing. Both in theory and in practice they have focused on them to promote discussions on cultural saliency, multiculturalism, and how some women have totally broken barriers consistent with their history. For many women tradition has created barriers, but the perseverance of senior women has made it possible for younger women to define their roles as doctors, academics, attorneys, and social activists.

U.S. Chicanas and Latinas are active in a global context, traveling across international borders and time zones, exchanging money, and getting educated and transforming social institutions. They know that when women change, men change, relationships change, and society changes. Most important, culture changes. For activist Chicanas and Latinas, social change is placed in the context of liberation from the oppression and domination of a Eurocentric culture. This is more easily understood as a need for cultural sovereignty. Cultural sovereignty is the freedom to practice the unique blend that constitutes Chicano and Latino culture without the imposition of Anglo attitudes, laws, or policy. The assumption here is that Chicanas and Latinas in the United States live in occupied territory and are restrained or otherwise limited in the their ability to occupy space that is at best controlled by them and at least represented by them.

Since gender and racial injustice are social characteristics in the dominant culture, Chicanas and Latinas have to deal with it. Not all have reacted in the same way. Some women have internalized negative messages and have very low and unmotivated self-esteem. Others are stuck in anger and violently resist the elements that disempower them, while others are well rooted in their identity and are self-defined women. For most, defining themselves within the context of negativity is the rule. In addition, women have not all developed the same and with the same consciousness. Some still think they do not want liberation because it means they have to go to work and give up their husbands. Others seek cultural sovereignty via education. They chose to go to school to earn a degree and return to resist the impact of colonialism by working with their people. This is not true sovereignty. Chicanos and Latinos cannot gain sovereignty because there are too many competing interests. There is a delicate balance on this topic, however. It is gained via limiting personal interest, adopting the internal colonial model, and balancing a sense of being. These are but three of the factors that explains uneven development in feminist consciousness among Chicanas and Latinas.

Some feel it has limited cultural sovereignty; others feel it can support it, but that it needs reform. A *Los Angeles Times* article (O'Connor 1998) reported that a Mexican-born mother feared that if she left her three U.S.–born children in public schools they would end up like her: poor in a barrio housing project surrounded by gangs and drug dealers. What was implied was that public schools were not educating Chicano and Latino youth in such a way that they could escape some of the trappings of inner-city poverty and cultural deterioration. The *Times* article reported that more wealthy parents put their children in suburban private schools, away from low-income immigrants from Latin America and Asia. Parents with more resources have turned to inner-city Catholic schools where a host of national studies say disadvantaged African American and Latino students are outperforming their public school counterparts.

At the time of the *Times* article nearly three in ten Latinos were dropping out of school. An official of the Tomas Rivera Policy Institute, a prestigious research organization, maintained that given the right opportunity, low-income children, regardless of culture, can live up to their potential. Catholic schools, through a combination of factors, appear to be providing those opportunities. Enrollment in nationwide Catholic schools has grown more slowly than in public schools. A total of 46 percent of the county's 92,500 Catholic school-children are Latino, but Latino Catholic school enrollment has jumped 60 percent in the Los Angeles archdiocese since 1970. The influx of Latinos has helped buoy California Catholic schools to their highest enrollment since 1965.

It has been my experience that some Latino students emerge from the large Chicano and Latino middle-income groups, but many more are from poor families who are among the recipients of $11 million in financial aid. My California State University students were often teachers. They reported that inner-city students, especially in the lower grades, enroll speaking Spanish or with limited English. California Catholic schools have a much higher number of immigrants and low-income students than other states in the country. However, they appear to be getting the same high achievement results. The Los Angeles teacher's union, however, says it is wrong to compare public and Catholic schools. Catholic schools can easily expel drug users, gang members, and disruptive students. They do not take severely handicapped children, and they benefit from the "self-selection" effect of parents willing to commit resources to send their children to private schools.

Many public school teachers would like to adopt some Catholic school features, except the notoriously low pay scale of Catholic teachers, who earn an average of $21,882 annually (Pino 2002). Catholic schools provide safer environments, demand parental involvement, possess strict discipline codes, and students appear to receive more attention. There are many parents of public school children willing to try anything to keep their children in school so they can graduate and go to prestigious universities.

Feminists are worried about the low quality of education and some even feel children are being hurt by public schools. It could be that Catholic schools are meeting the spiritual needs of children, thereby rooting them in self-identities built upon a powerful foundation that makes them part of a larger whole. But public and Catholic schools are socialization agencies. They indoctrinate children into mainstream cultural values and objectives, and some parents send their children to school reluctantly. Legally, parents have to send their children to school. There are no accredited schools rooted in Chicano and Latino culture they can send them to, and the study of sexism is not a priority at any institution.

To feminists, cultural sovereignty means possessing and controlling a social, historical, spiritual, and emotional space. For women this means being free from fear or intimidation for not having a man in one's life and the freedom to be herself with no fear of losing him if one is in her life. It means securing services, time, and space for herself that do not threaten her culture, her family, or her career. She must be free not to subordinate herself and her own feelings and desires, especially with regard to controlling her own body. One of the times this comes into play is when deciding about birth control.

When the birth control pill was first introduced, it was tested on Puerto Rican women (Blea 1992a, 1992b; Snider 1990). Some members of the population were suspicious of limiting the reproduction of Chicanos and Latinos and urged women not to participate. It is therefore not surprising that a few women of color still declare that both birth control and abortion are forms of genocide, devices to eliminate people of color: ethnic cleansing. Some feel they are immoral or a sin. Therefore, trust, the need for acceptance, and fear of sin are issues of contemporary concern to service providers and for feminist cultural activists.

Because I was raised Catholic, I know adult women and men, the Catholic Church, and several other aspects of the culture put pressure on newly married women to have babies. Higher-educated Chicanas and Latinas are postponing marriage and birthing children at a later age. At this time this is not threatening family values in Chicano and Latino communities, but it is changing family relations and child-rearing practices. Because more women are working than ever before, grandmothers, aunts, and sisters are finding themselves providing childcare for a family member in what is perceived by the child's mother as a more hostile world. The mothers, quite frankly, do not trust anyone who is not family to care for their children. What it means to Chicana and Latina feminists is that women are experiencing the stresses that all working mothers experience, plus the overwhelming burden of racism, and I feel most Chicanas and Latinas do not appear to be thinking more of their self-interest, their self-realization, or even their careers. They, like a great deal of women of color, work because maintaining a household (even at the lower levels) requires it. They have babies because they value the extended family, and they work to better the quality of life for their families.

As in many countries, the first born should be a male. Unmarried women, and even girls, receive the message that marriage and bearing children is what will fulfill them. Even though Hispanics have the highest marriage rate in the nation (U.S. Bureau of the Census 1993b), the high rate of divorce indicates that it is not as fulfilling as it is marketed to be. Divorce in U.S. society soared to 69 percent over the previous decade (U.S. Bureau of the Census 2001). The average marriage lasted 6.6 years, and 40 percent of children born will spend some of their youth in a one-parent household. Belief in marriage, Catholic beliefs about birth control, and the need to feel worthy are reasons why there is such a high teen pregnancy rate. It is my opinion that another reason is that girls do not receive enough affirmation. They look for it on the arm of a boy. Oftentimes these are cases of statutory rape (Blea 1992b). A young man eighteen to twenty-one years old seduces an underaged girl, gets her pregnant, and walks away. This person is rarely prosecuted. Motherhood as a result of early seduction upheld by institutional patriarchy, male supremacy, and *machismo* is reactionary and brutal to girls and women who do not want children or who do not want to marry and cannot be good mothers. The early seduction effect on girls is just as traumatic, but girls will not admit it because they believe they have done wrong and deserve punishment.

Cultural sovereignty has to do with a community's need for self-determination and the population's right to make decisions for itself in its self-interest. This right to social space has been denied Chicanos and other Latinos, who are forced to abandon culture in order to scratch out a living in the United States. Many have to engage in competition when they do not like it in order to earn more money. The prevailing assumption is that those who are uncomfortable competing are weak, and that social space is severely limited. There are very few jobs, other resources, classrooms, courses, parking spaces, or even members of the opposite sex to go around. In order to gain the prize, criteria for access is established. Those who "qualify" can have access, but have to compete in order to keep their place. This is especially sad when fifth grade girls feel they have to have a boyfriend, and when teenagers hurt one another over a boy.

Since much social space is hierarchical and was never created for women, especially women of color, in the first place, those who created the structure, white men, rate highest and get the best places on the socioeconomic ladder. According to tradition, the top ranked receive the most benefits because they are the best, the most qualified, the most worthy. To those socialized in this way of thinking, this behavior appears to be logical. Those at the bottom should be at the bottom because they do not meet the criteria as well as those at the top. This mentality supports girls and young women to "get a man." They do not want to be "losers."

Until the 1960s few Chicanas questioned who developed the criteria in the first place. Today, activist Chicanas and Latinas understand that racial and gender inequities limit competition. Some of those who cannot compete, or who cannot compete well, have been selected out of the process via training and tests that take place prior to the final selection. Thus far, not many Chicanas have been allowed to compete.

## HEALING AND DECOLONIZING
## OF THE FEMALE MIND

Healing Chicanas and Latinas from discrimination means decolonizing the female mind, body, and spirit. This is difficult to do because those who are not selected into the social process, those who question or criticize it, do not get the benefits of passing the tests. Nor do they receive social rewards in the form of better jobs, better housing, and the ability to take more courses at better institutions to continue "succeeding." My twenty-seven years of experience as a professor on college and university campuses has taught me that because Chicanas and other women of color do not design the tests, they rank lower than their men do. It is the objective of some Chicanas to help define and design the tests, the test-taking process, and the rewards. Those in control do not want to give up their positions, and some of them are white women. Their primary strategy is to allow a few on selections committees, but never enough to carry a vote. This places Anglo-identified women in leadership, and bowls over feminism and cultural retention.

Most Latinas and Chicanas engage in personal acts of resistance, which are less visible, less organized, and more difficult to document. The forms of personal acts of resistance vary by site and situation. With regard to white feminism, they simply walked away. This form of resistance in community advocacy includes providing spiritual, moral, and economic support for undocumented workers, speaking Spanish in public places, preserving it in the family, and listening and sharing Spanish music, art, and literature with others (Ochoa 1999). These acts are often quiet and include sharing money, food, and information; advocating on behalf of individuals and families in the courts, in school, at the social services, and at the immigration office; praying for someone; and linking them to individuals and information. Sometimes these acts require more energy, like defending *raza* (Latino and Chicano people) from racial slurs, physically defending women from abusers, and advocating for women's rights in discussions with men and other women.

Those who are more organized, such as women in the United Farm Workers Union (UFW) and women in the National Association of Latino Arts and Culture (NALAC), are generally referred to as part of "the left." For many this implies "un-American." There are women in more conservative groups, such as the League of United Latino American Citizens (LULAC), and the GI Forum. There are even what some consider conservative women's organizations, like the Mexican American National Women's Association (MANA). Nevertheless, they all want the same thing: the empowerment of Chicano and Latino people within the structure of the dominant society. They do not accept arguments that were or are given to justify keeping Chicanas and Latinas in a low place in society. The women in organizations that have men in them look for any signs of sexism in an attempt to establish and preserve the sovereignty of women.

Persons who are violent to others are violent to themselves. Their acts disturb the delicate balance of being in harmony. Some will tell you that violence is part of nature, that it is natural and an inherit characteristic of being human. One thing is more generally agreed upon: Violence is caused by frustration and need. A frustrated individual can easily be spurred to anger, suicide, self-hate, and open acts of aggression against the oppressor (the source of frustration) and themselves. This is especially true when the promise of a society is so drastically different from the reality for some of its citizens. When equality, freedom, and justice are the major promises and these guarantees are not delivered, people seek change. Social change is especially demanded when social members observe that there are repeated patterns distinguishing those who have a better quality of life. In short, from oppression and frustration comes resistance, and that resistance can be violent, such as in the form of riots. Not many women have engaged in violent attempts to bring about social change. They are generally the victims, and their anger takes the form of depression.

However, there is no need to think that Chicanas–Latinas are depressed: Far from it. Most develop political leadership in the trenches. They are committed to public service, to changing laws that institutionalize the notion that some people naturally deserve less from democracy. Chicanas and Latinas are aware of the hate movements against immigrants, bilingual education, and affirmative action. These movements have invigorated activists and have promoted assertive leadership among them across the country. Several note that democracy should be conceived from the bottom up, with emphasis on the most disenfranchised. It should include activist politicians who are willing to take a moral stand. It is not about building a political career. It is about doing a job. These goals are idealistic and remnants of a true democracy, where activists perceive themselves as the conscience of government.

Traditionally, there has been reticence by some community activists to run for office. They see a fundamental contradiction between holding political office and having moral leadership grounded in popularity and the need to be reelected. This is spiritually unacceptable. For Chicanas spirituality is rooted in the land, the ocean, the forest, and the air. When those things are destroyed, blasted, dug up, scrapped, flooded, or drained to house museums, establish ski resorts, construct false rivers and bodies of water to adorn new housing, play golf, or simply amuse, the Chicana and Latina sense of spirituality is desecrated.

The same happens when a man abuses a woman. It leaves her bruised, broken, and left with open physical, emotional, and spiritual wounds. The sense of sacredness of self has been disturbed, damaged, even ruined. Reconstructing it is expensive. It takes much time, and in this country time is money. It takes much counseling and support and requires the assistance of a trained professional, and this especially costs money. Healing a population from violence committed against itself via the feminization of racism is being advocated here as an absolute necessity, one that requires the support of those involved in human rights.

Basically, there are two kinds of change: revolution and reform. Revolution requires resources, is violent, and is quicker. Reform requires fewer resources, is said to be less violent, and takes a much longer time. Reform is both violent and slow for Chicanas and Latinas, but a few changes have occurred since 1970. Engaging in social change manifests for them in symptoms of frustration and burnout. But even after generations of oppression, most do not lose their patience. Women with political consciousness do not act out their rage and pain in the form of gang violence, teen pregnancy, school dropout rates, nonparticipation in electoral politics, alcohol and drug abuse, suicide, and dependence on the welfare system. Some members of society see the reaction to the frustrations of colonization as ignorance and laziness, but feminists see it as powerlessness and false consciousness.

Women have been turned into superconsumers of everything that will make them more attractive to men and that will make men more money. Most of them have been taught to love their oppressors, accept their lowly position, and spend their hard-earned money on seductive clothing, lipstick, foundation, feminine hygiene deodorant, hair remover, panty shields, and pantyhose. Resistance has come hard for women. Most will not even entertain the notion. Some simply do not have the ability. They are fearful and have created a way of living around male power.

It has been my observation that although many white women in the feminist movement have changed, the spokespersons generally remain white. This and the unequal rate of racial-consciousness development within the movement keeps most women of color out of it. In addition, the lack of a loud and clear message that is moving toward placing a female face on racial injustice leaves most women of color with the idea that the feminist movement does not include them and does not include their interests. I frequently get asked why people of color have not banded together, taken up arms, or block voted to defeat their oppressors. The answer lies in the internalization of the colonization process. It is an intense enough process of indoctrinating people that most feel that if they work hard enough and wait long enough, things will change and they can evolve to live in a powerful position. If this does not happen, it is their fault. They made bad decisions or they had bad luck. Most women dream of marrying power, not of creating their own. Most women of color are nonviolent; confrontation is not the preferred form of conflict resolution. Instead, they exhibit their anger and frustration in art, theater, poetry, music, and spirituality. This is a quiet revolution.

Although most were raised Catholic, they generally do not practice their religion by going to church every Sunday and on all holy days of obligation, saying daily prayers, confessing, receiving holy communion, tithing, and abstaining from sex, birth control, or abortion. Some women baptize their children, get married, and are buried in the church. They construct and maintain home altars with images of the saints and indigenous icons, both in and outside of their homes. They use Catholic prayer at the same time they use indigenous herbs. They pray with the same rhythm that some indigenous people chant, and burn incense while meditating or to cleanse and environment.

Chicana feminist diets consist of indigenous foods, like cilantro, avocado, tortillas, corn, beans, squash, dried meats, salsa, potatoes, spinach, vanilla, chocolate, various chilies, salt, pepper, fish and shellfish, various meats, and juices made from fruits like mangos, pineapple, bananas, and papaya. Food preparation has been in the women's domain, but more men are learning to cook. The conquistadors and the women who later came with them brought goats, cows, pigs, wheat, and fruit trees (peaches, pears, cherries, apples). To add to the diet and to facilitate labor and travel they also brought the sheep, horses, oxen, and chickens. Indian women used all of this to prepare *tamales, empanada* (turnovers), and *sopas* (soups) on their *molcajetes* (grinding stones), on their *comal* (cooking implement), and in their *cazuela* (pans). Of course, there are regional differences to the food; in some areas it is more Indian, in others it is more Spanish. In most places it is a mixture of the two, plus an African influence.

Other female practices vary from region to region. For example, some New Mexicans and inhabitants of Arizona point with their lips and communicate with their eyes. These women, however, can easily engage in discussions about their Indian and Spanish traditions of child rearing, balancing *la Virgin de Guadalupe, brujeria* (what we now recognize as witchcraft), the healing art of *curanderismo, baptismo,* confirmation, and beliefs in *la Llorona,* ghosts, *duendes* (elves), and spirits. They know the balance and harmony in their system of health and healing, the good and evil elements of being human. This constitutes a worldview sometimes inconsistent with that of white Americans.

Increasingly, Chicana and Latina knowledge and ways of doing things has been appropriated, violated, bastardized, discredited, challenged, diluted, separated, and channeled into institutions rooted in the dominant society that exploits them for profit. One sees this in Taco Bell commercials, Cinco de Mayo sales at the local furniture stores or restaurant, and mariachi masses sponsored by the Catholic Church, and when white women write about Latinas they get published and Chicanas and Latinas do not. This appropriation takes the form of whites burning sage, hosting sweats, and selling native herbs. The behaviors are insulting, another form of colonialism.

Chicana and Latina communities, *barrios,* are adaptations to colonialism. They have cultural symbols, sights, sounds, and smells that are not found in other communities. Most evident is the use of Spanish, the spoken and written word as a shared community experience, the balancing of two very strong Indian and Spanish cultures, and a distinct sense of spirituality.

Some can name their Indian heritage. Most cannot. This is more than political ideology. It is the belief in something larger than what is experienced on earth, something larger than is explained by science or religion. It is a belief in a Supreme Being, or beings, that permeate the social conscious to influence creativity, hope, charity, and life pursuits.

The spiritual component is evident in the forms of *la Virgin de Guadalupe*, Jesus Christ, the saints, the holy family, the burning of incense, and chanting. It is evident in the celebrations, *fiestas*, and the names of towns and cities, streets, and rivers. It plays a role during major rites of passage, in birth, baptism, *quincenieras* (coming-out rituals at age fifteen), marriage, and death; in the art of the muralist, the studio painter, poets, and novelists; and in low riders, tattoos, and T-shirts.

The biggest fear is that children will be absorbed by dominant U.S. values and that talented individuals with material resources will be lost to the community. The biggest hope is that talented individuals will stay and the community will become economically stable, that bigotry will end, and that Chicanos and Latinos will be allowed to fully participate in the ongoing society without having to give up their culture. This may be impossible. Their integration is based upon their loss of culture.

Sociologists, psychologists, and anthropologists affirm that culture sustains people. This does not mean it is static and never changing. It is shared knowledge granting direction for sustaining a population. Without culture, people are empty, lost, and confused. Without cultural references, individuals become disoriented and depressed, even suicidal. The person without culture is not rooted. That person is alienated, disenfranchised, and has a difficult time relating beyond the surface. Culture is insulation against oppressive forces. It includes rites of passage from one phase of life to another. Times in a person's life that are symbolic of having gone from one status to another inform people how to live and how to act. Chicana and Latina culture is rapidly changing from within.

Latino men relate to their culture and their changes differently. They generally are not the ones conducting intimate socialization of children, especially girls. In women's studies in university programs around the country, it is understood that most men do not teach culture in the same direct manner in which women do. U.S. society socializes females to grow up with intentions to preserve culture by getting married, having children, and living happily ever after on a salary a man will earn. It socializes them to objectify and dehumanize men, but to make them a priority, a social and economic asset.

As a sociologist and mental health worker, I believe that decolonization and healing means abandoning the American dream that was never meant for Chicanas and other women of color. It means teaching and analyzing its assumptions and its promises of "the good life" for racism and sexism. Adaptation, even if it is to colonialism, is a creative process. On university campuses, their low number keeps Chicanas and Latinas isolated and struggling against discrimination, even in Chicano and Latino studies departments.

Decolonization requires freeing the mind from the belief that the colonizer and his institutions will free the colonized. Decolonizing the female mind requires freeing Chicanas and Latinas from attempting to adhere to the Anglo beauty and physical norm that few women, regardless of culture, can meet, plus the belief that having a man makes them more worthwhile. Some women do not believe this. They have changed; thus the culture will change because these women serve as role models for future generations. Their actions define a paradigm shift, a change in worldview, one gaining support not only among Chicanas and Latinas, but in such places like Hawaii, where indigenous women struggle toward the return of the islands and the decolonization of indigenous people's thoughts and behaviors.

Both men and women value family and home life (Blea 1995, 1992a). As in other cultures, more and more men are becoming involved in child rearing. Chicanos and Latinos are the youngest U.S. population, and even though some men have adapted to feminism, the majority of them have not. Chicana and Latina feminists tolerate those men. They know that men have sustained preferential treatment at the expense of women, but have endured severe hardship in their interactions with white men and women in the dominant society. These men are simply grasping for male identity and are finding out it is a weak grasp.

After almost thirty years of working with students, it has been my experience that if the mother is a teen and unwed, her parents still raise the two children, and most teen fathers simply walk away, all too frequently to impregnate another teen girl. Society still expects women of color to live down to a standard. Feminist struggle to redefine this expectation and celebrate their fluency in at least two cultures and two languages, and frequently in more than one social class. Many Chicanas and Latinas have excelled within the dominant system. They have been rewarded for being gifted in adapting to dominant norms, but the larger U.S. population does not hear much about these people because good news about people of color does not sell newspapers or consumer products. In fact, it threatens the status quo.

## REFERENCES

Anzaldua, Gloria. 1999. *Making Face, Making Soul/Haciendo Caras, Creative and Critical Perspectives by Women of Color.* San Francisco: Aunt Lute Books.

Arango, Raul. 2000. "Candidates Seek Cuban Vote." *USA Today.* Available at: <http://www.usatoday.com.news>.

Auinaco, Paul. 2002. U.S. Conference of Catholic Bishops, Telephone interview, May 21.

Blea, Irene I. 1997. *U.S. Chicanas and Latinas in a Global Context.* Westport, Conn.: Praeger.

———. 1995. *Researching Chicano Communities.* Westport, Conn.: Praeger.

———. 1992a. *Bessemer: A Sociological Perspective of a Chicano Barrio.* New York: AMS Press.

———. 1992b. *La Chicana and the Intersection of Race, Class and Gender.* New York: Praeger.

————. 1988. *Toward a Chicano Social Science*. New York: Praeger.

Bush, George W. 2001. "State of the Union." Public address by the President of the United States, televised nationwide, February.

Bustamantes, Jorge. 2000. Interview, San Antonio, Texas, University of Texas Campus, May 21.

Chambers, Veronica, and John Leland. 1999. "Lovin' la Vida Loca." *Newsweek*, May 31. Available at: <http://www.thunder.search.com/JenniferLopez>.

Cuban Information Archives. 2001. "Cuban Immigration." Available at: <http://www. cuban-exile.com>. Last visited May 2002.

Gonzales, Patrisia, and Roberto Rodriguez. 1999. "Getting into Political Trenches Brings Results." Universal Press Syndicate, Monthly internet newsletter, August 19. Available at: <http://www.amuniversal.com>.

Hale, Janet Campbell. *Bloodlines: Odyssey of a Native Daughter*. New York: Harper Perennial.

Haubegger, Christy. "The Latino Century." *Newsweek*, July 12, p. 61.

Larmer, Brook. 1999. "Latino America." *Newsweek*, July 12, pp. 48–51.

Leland, John, and Veronica Chambers. "Generation ~N." *Newsweek*, July 12, pp. 52–58.

MarketResearch.com. 2001a. "Hollywood Looking to Expand Its Market," April 24. Available at: <http://www.MarketResearch.com>.

MarketResearch.com. 2001b. "The U.S. Hispanic Market," April 24. Available at: <http://www.Market Research.com/ProductID=234615>.

Moraga, Cherrie. 1981. *This Bridge Called My Back: Writings by Radical Women of Color*. Delhi, N.Y.: Persephone Press.

National Association of Chicana/Chicano Studies. 2002. San Jose, California.

National Center for Health Statistics. 2000. "America's Racial and Ethnic Minorities." Hyattsville, Md.: Population Reference Bureau, Population Bulletin.

New Mexico Spanish Genealogy Society. 2001. "400 Years of New Mexico History, 1585–1998." Available at: <http://www.nmgenealogy.org>. Last visited May 23, 2002.

Ochoa, Gilda Laura. 1999. "Everyday Ways of Resistance and Cooperation: Mexican American Women Building Puentes with Immigrants." *Frontiers: A Journal of Women Studies* 20, no. 1: 1–20.

O'Connor, Anne-Marie. 1998. "Many Latinos Fare Better in Catholic Schools." *Los Angeles Times*, August 3, p. 1.

Pino, MaryHellen. 2002. Catholic Archdiocese without Boundaries. Interview, May 12, Santa Fe, New Mexico.

Revolutionary Association of Women of Afghanistan. 2001. "Some Restrictions Imposed by the Taliban on Women in Afghanistan." Available at: <http://www.rawa. org>. Visited April 21, 2002.

Schlissel, Arthur, Lillian Schlissel, and Vicki Ruiz. 1988. *Western Women: Their Land and Their Lives*. Albuquerque: University of New Mexico Press.

Snider, Sharon. 1990. "The Pill: 30 Years of Safety Concerns." Available at: <http://www. fda.gov/bbs/topics/CONSUM/CON00009.htm>. Visited November 16, 2002.

Suaro, R. 1998. *Strangers Among Us: How Latino Immigration Is Transforming America*. New York: Alfred Knopf. Available at: <www.pbs.org/newshour/bb/ race-relations>.

Tomas Rivera Policy Institute. 2002. Interview with Clare Lucero, research assistant, Claremont College, California.

U.S. Bureau of the Census. 2001a. "Minority-Owned Firms Grow Four Times Faster."
    Public Information Office. Report by Eddie Salyers and Valerie Strong, July
    12. Washington, D.C.: U.S. Government Printing Office.
————. 2001b. "The Nation's Nuclear Family Rebounds." Public Information Office.
    Report by Jason Fields, April 13. Washington, D.C.: U.S. Government Print-
    ing Office. Available at: <http://www.census.gov/hispanic>.
————. 2001c. Slide presentation, Ethnic and Hispanic Branch, Population Division.
    Slide 3 of 22. Available at: <http://www.census.gov>. Last visited November
    16, 2002).
————. 1993a. "We Measure America: Women and Work." Washington, D.C.: U.S.
    Department of Labor Women's Bureau.
————. 1993b. "We the American . . . Hispanics." Washington, D.C.: U.S. Govern-
    ment Printing Office.
U.S. Commission on Immigration Reform. 1999. "Binational Study: Immigration be-
    tween Mexico and the United States." Available at: <http://www.utexas.edu/bj/
    uscir/binational>.
Velarde, Pablita. 2002. Much informatin available at: <http://www.amazon.com>
    (books); <http://www.livingtreasures.kxx.com/bio/pub>; <http://www.friends
    bandelier.com/shop.asp> (biography and profiles).

# CHAPTER 4

# African American Women

The black liberation struggle is well known in the United States and throughout the world. What is not as well known is the burden of the black–white dichotomy and how it affects the women of the many black communities throughout the nation. When one concentrates on these communities and these women, one gains a more clear insight into the role of color. One also gains insight into "struggle" as a way of life for women of color. Contemporary African American women have made significant gains in the areas of education and in entertainment, two areas in which they, and more recently Latinos, have utilized to escape the poverty too often associated with "minorities." In education they have surpassed black males, but they are women and persons of color at the same time, and they share the consequence of the social factors based on color that affect Native Americans, Asians, and Latinos. Nevertheless, far too many black women, like other women of color, have not had the advantages of the democratic system as defined by the American dream. Foremost among the reasons is their history of slavery and because they tend to have the darkest skin. But African American women have other histories. They come from communities victimized by violence to exercise nonviolence in their need for liberation. They have survived to write, teach, and sing about it, and they have much to teach us, especially in the areas of attainment, or retribution and reconciliation.

## CONTRARY TO THE STEREOTYPE

One finds African American women in every facet of American society; we may not find many, but they are present in various forms, and they are present in the stratified caste system that manifests itself in terms of color and class. African American women can earn lots of money, but the money of one black female does not translate into money, power, and respect for the group that she is identified with. In a stratified, hierarchical culture like that in the United States, this value is reserved for people with white skin of European descent. Black women descend from Africa. The darker one's skin color in this system, the less is the social privilege. It translates onto groups and pits people against people. Black women have much to teach us about survival, flourishing as a civilization, and healing. They and other women of color are in the ideal position to contribute to world peace. With the exception of black women they are less threatening to white male control than are men of color. Therein lies the stereotype.

Even black comedians joke about the strength of black women. Since the 1960s much work has been done on the stereotype of these women. The most recent stereotype is urban and goes something like this: Do not mess with adult black women because they will yank your balls off. True or not true, this is what it takes to survive as an urban female African American whose history is that she came into this country as a means of exchange and a sexually available beast of burden. This is what it takes to survive rape, mutilation, servitude, and escape. What is amazing is that these strong women can love so very deeply.

In no way am I attempting to prioritize oppression, for oppression takes many routes, and as we have seen in the history of American Indians, Spanish, Mexicans, and Chicanos, there are severe consequences for both the oppressor and the oppressed. However, the dehumanizing consequence is most persuasive when one is the terrorized. In fact, one of the first strategies in colonization is terrorism and taking the humanity of the victim.

As a result of Census 2000, the Commerce Department's Census Bureau has issued new information on the African American population (see Table 4.1). The data show that 79 percent of African Americans age twenty-five and over have earned at least a high school diploma and 17 percent have attained at least a bachelor's degree (Current Population Survey). Both percentages represent record levels of educational attainment. Thus, African Americans can no longer be considered ignorant, but a question that affects this and other groups of color is the quality of education and why so many drop out of school.

The March 2000 Current Population Survey (U.S. Bureau of the Census 2000a) indicates that about one-half (51%) of women fifteen years of age and over were living with their spouse; 25 percent had never married, 13 percent were divorced or separated, and 10 percent were widowed. It also estimates that there are 8.7 million African American families in the United States and that less than one-half (48%) of all African American families are married-couple families. Women maintain 44 percent of the total families with no spouse

**Table 4.1**
**Total U.S. African American Resident**
**Population Estimate by Percentage and**
**Gender**

| | |
|---|---|
| Population | 35,470 |
| Percent of total | 12.8 |
| Median age (years) | 30.4 |
| Mean age (years) | 32.3 |
| Male population | 16,857 |
| Female population | 18,613 |

*Source*: Population Estimates Program, Population Division, U.S. Census Bureau, Washington, D.C. (Internet release date January 2, 2001).

*Note*: Projection to November 1, 2000. Numbers in thousands.

present and men maintain 8 percent with no spouse present. This disproportionate number blurs other factors of significance. For example, among African American men age fifteen and over, 39 percent were currently married, 3 percent were widowed, and 10 percent were divorced. Among women, the corresponding proportions were 31 percent, 10 percent, and 12 percent. A similar proportion (42%) of African American men and women had never married.

Like other racial and ethnic groups, African American families tend to be larger than white, non-Hispanic families. A total of 21 percent of African American married-couple families had five or more members, compared with 12 percent of white, non-Hispanic families. African American women age sixteen and over were more likely than their white, non-Hispanic counterparts to participate in the labor force (64% compared with 61%). For men, the reverse was true. African American men had a participation rate of 68 percent compared with 74 percent for white, non-Hispanic men.

About 47 percent of African American householders were homeowners. In order to pay for homes, health, and other necessities, African Americans age sixteen and over who were employed, 25 percent of the women and 18 percent of the men, worked in managerial and professional specialty occupations. In 1999 the median household income was the highest ever recorded for African Americans ($27,910). Half (51%) of the African American married-couple families had incomes of $50,000 or more, compared with 60 percent of white, non-Hispanics. In that same year the poverty rate for African Americans fell to a record low of 23.6 percent. Thus, although things are getting better, there still are some residuals of discrimination against the group as a whole.

The March 2000 Current Population Survey used a series of twenty-one tables to produce a publication entitled "Black Population in the U.S.: March 2000" (U.S. Bureau of the Census 2000a). This publication, the Internet, and other Census Bureau information has been used to attempt to compose a realistic picture of African American women as they are understood by the U.S. government. As for all persons, the data are just that, data. They do not render a picture of what it is like to be an African American female on a daily basis. For this, one needs to have practical experience with African American females, their communities, and their significant others.

The economic census is taken twice a decade in years ending in 2 and 7. One was being taken at the time of the writing of this book. Thus, by time of publication the figures are sure to change, but the U.S. Bureau of the Census Public Information Office (2001) anticipates that the trends will continue. Minority-owned businesses keep growing. Although it appears that people of color are expanding entrepreneur opportunities and that small businesses are becoming more diverse, the growth estimates do not include C corporations. C corporations encompass all legally incorporated businesses except for subchapter S corporations. Subchapter S corporations are those of shareholders who elect to be taxed as individuals rather than as corporations. A total of 252,900 C corporations produce roughly 43 percent of all revenues generated by minority-owned businesses. Including C corporations, there were more than 3 million minority-owned enterprises employing 4.5 million people and generating $591.3 billion in revenues at the beginning of this decade (U.S. Bureau of the Census 2000e). Overall, minority-owned firms made up 15 percent of the nation's businesses and generated 3 percent of all receipts. This is a substantial contribution in dollars alone and does not account for the talent and time involved in creating and maintaining a business.

The vast majority of these firms, about 82 percent, were sole proprietorships, unincorporated businesses owned by individuals. California, Texas, New York, and Florida, the nation's most populous states and home to nearly half of all minority residents, had the largest number of minority-owned businesses. While Hispanics owned the largest share of firms owned by minorities, Asian- and Pacific Islander–owned firms reaped the largest share of minority-owned business revenues, about 52 percent. Men were owners of about 55 percent of the firms owned by each of the four minority groups, but African Americans had the largest percentage of firms owned by women.

Thirty-nine percent of all minority-owned firms had 1997 receipts of under $10,000; about 3 percent had sales of $1 million or more. Average receipts per firm were $194,600, compared with $410,600 for all U.S. firms excluding publicly held corporations and firms (such as mutual companies) whose owners' race or ethnicity could not be determined, but about one in five of all minority-owned firms had paid employees. More than 4,400 minority-owned firms had 100 or more employees, and 59 percent of all minority-owned firms were in the services and retail trade industries, accounting for 43 percent of all receipts.

Census 2000 and other health-related data (National Center for Health Statistics 2000b) reveal that life expectancy is increasing and that African Americans are growing older as a total population. However, the median age continues to be about six years lower than that for whites. Less than one-tenth of the population is sixty-five years old or over, and black women, like women in most groups, tend to live longer than black men do. About one-third of the population is under eighteen years of age. The median age for blacks is about twenty-eight years (U.S. Bureau of the Census 1999b). The African American voting-age population increased to 20.4 million in 1990, and the average life expectancy for a newborn baby was sixty-nine years, about six years less than that for whites.

African Americans are located in all states, and they are largely an urban people. Most live in cities and in large metropolitan areas. The majority live in the twenty largest metropolitan areas of the nation (New York, Chicago, Los Angeles, Philadelphia, Washington, D.C., Detroit, Atlanta, Houston, Baltimore, and Miami) and they are purchasing more homes, especially in the suburbs. African Americans have also made significant gains in educational attainment and college enrollment. More black women than black men have completed college, and the number of black households, especially female-headed black households, increased because of the increase in divorce and separation rates. As a result, fewer children are being reared in two-parent households across the country. Also, consistent with national trends, more African American women and men are choosing not to marry or to live alone.

A higher proportion of black women than black men are in the labor force, and there are now more black females than black males in the civilian labor force. The number of blacks employed in professional jobs, such as lawyers, doctors, and engineers, has increased, and the median income of black married-couple families also improved and grew to 83 percent of comparable white families. African American per capita income was lower than the national per capita income, and poverty levels for African American persons and families were similar at the beginning and the end of the decade (U.S. Bureau of the Census 2001). The current social circumstances of African Americans are closely tied to African American history and how they came to be part of the United States. Slavery characterizes that history; so does the struggle to survive and escape it and the social toxicity it has bestowed upon America.

## THE PERSISTENCE OF COLOR

One thing that cannot be escaped is the color of a person's skin, and in the early history of the United States color was associated with slavery and the need to escape it. Many people still associate dark skin color with low attainment and even criminal actions. Few want to acknowledge the criminal action of taking people from their native land, transporting them as animal cargo, and dumping them in a foreign land to be exploited.

As mentioned before, historical periods of significance vary by gender. From 1450 to 1750 there were enormous changes in the North American continent, and this time period affected African Americans as much as it affected Native

Americans, who first encountered European explorers and before long saw their world transformed and largely destroyed. But European explorers not only ventured to the lands and natural wealth of the Americas; they also traveled to Africa, where they began the trans-Atlantic slave trade that would bring millions of Africans to the Americas. This slave trade would, over time, lead to a new social and economic system, one where the color of one's skin could determine whether one might live as a free citizen or be enslaved for life.

It is unfortunate that women do not know their social history, the context in which they and their people's lives have developed in the United States. The lack of a social–historical context, an understanding of who they are and how their racial group functioned and continues to function in the history of the United States, limits a move toward the feminization of racism.

Until the last two decades most African American women had few options in obtaining perspectives on themselves other than those that existed in white textbooks, in the movies, and on television. Today we have an entire population of women and men who rebel against the "mammy" images they grew up watching. They do not want their children learning about Africa by watching Tarzan, Cheeta, Jane, and their superior relationship to the "natives," natives that tended to be barbaric males who could, with little provocation, become ruthlessly violent.

If U.S. African American women prior to the 1960s were lucky, they heard about Egypt watching Hollywood moves like *Land of the Pharaohs, Spartacus, Cleopatra, The Ten Commandments*, and *Gone with the Wind*, but the actresses were white unless they played slaves and servants or handmaidens. Thus, most women who matured prior to the 1960s grew up with the narrow ambition to be wives and mothers. The black civil rights movement gave them other ambitions, and the arena of entertainment was an outlet for the most talented. In fact, it was not until the late 1960s that it became general knowledge that there were numerous black producers, actresses, actors, and singers. Among them were Geraldine Baker, Dorothy Dandridge, and Mahalia Jackson. These women contributed much to the arts and blazed a trail for the existence of black entertainers outside of stereotyped roles.

By the late 1960s and early 1970s the black civil rights movement was in full swing and it became general knowledge that African Americans, including women, had made major contributions not only to literature and theater, but also to politics, education, science, and health. In black studies programs and department all over the nation, students learned about the Moorish occupation of Spain for almost 800 years, the impact of the Roman Empire on African lives, and American slavery, resistance, reconstruction, and emancipation. Those that participated in the civil rights movement, however, found that if they wanted to know their history they had to struggle for it themselves, and that there would be white resistance.

Today most U.S. citizens cannot escape the impact of the civil rights movement and the contributions of women, but until Black History Month began to be acknowledged few of us knew that black women were a huge part of the struggle to promote freedom and justice for all. During the yearly February black history celebration, we learned about the lives and contributions of Frederick Douglass, Booker T. Washington, W.E.B. DuBois, Marcus Garvey, A. Phillip Randolph, Martin Luther King, Jr., and Langston Hughes. It took awhile, but today we also learn about the work and contributions of abolitionist Harriet Tubman, Billie Holiday, and Lena Horne, plus literary greats like Zora Neal Hurston, Maya Angelou, and Toni Morrison. Thanks to the work of women, we can read, see, and hear about human rights activists Rosa Parks and Coretta Scott King, political and other national personalities like Shirley Chisholm, and even Oprah Winfrey, whose television program has enlightened the general population like few other efforts.

Yet why, after forty years of women marching and teaching and advocating for the feminization of racism, are our lives so profoundly split, isolated, and disconnected? Perhaps it is because not only white women, but also women of color have internalized sexist and racist concepts of American reality. Because white women have historically been the teachers of black women, we tend to believe that to be white is to be intelligent and sophisticated. Perhaps even African American women and other women of color see white women as manipulative and always after something. They certainly are viewed as enjoying white privilege.

Black women and other women of color are not usually canvassed for opinions that do not have to do with them as consumers. When *Essence* and *Ladies Home Journal* magazines convened a roundtable discussion on race in order to assess some of the issues that still divide black and white women, the perceptions were startling (Edwards 1998). In fact, they asked why, after a defining civil rights movement in the 1960s, a move to liberate women in the 1970s, and the push for affirmative action and diversity programs in the 1980s, did race remain such an issue? What emerged during the roundtable is that much of what distressed relationships between races in the 1990s had to do with how each perceives not only its own experience, but also the experiences of the other. White women at the roundtable said they saw black women as strong, assertive, and confident. Black women said they saw themselves as strong, assertive, and vulnerable, and that this was a burden. Black women saw white women as privileged, in control, and protected; this was an asset. White women saw themselves as privileged, guilty, and uncertain, and that was unsettling.

How we see and interact with one another is dictated not just by skin color and gender, but also by other factors, such as age and class. The problem is that U.S. citizens are compartmentalized into separate and unequal categories. These facts are incorporated into public policy and the media, and youngsters still get the false impression that contributions by African Americans are secondary to the creation of the real history and culture of the United States.

It is unfortunate that gender discrimination documents black history as dominated by male religious leaders, inventors, explorers, scientists, architects, entertainers, and trade unionists because women have contributed a great deal. They have influenced politics, health, education, law, and morals and ethics. Black artists, writers, and musicians have rendered some of the most original and distinctive art forms associated with the United States, and women, especially contemporary women, are among them.

There are other types of stratification in U.S. society. One with no name is that which places lack of value on art. For example, art has less value than science, but art is what captures and validates what it is to be human. In the arts alone, the number of African American women making cultural contributions is phenomenal. These works are exhibited, collected, and are beginning to be archived in an effort to preserve them for future generations. One fine example exists in *Bearing Witness: Contemporary Works by African American Women Artists* by Jontyle Theresa Robinson, Maya Angelou, and Tritobia H. Benjamin (1996). This publication accompanied an unprecedented exhibition of works by twenty-five African American women artists who engaged in celebration of women's artistry. There are seventy illustrations, sixty of which are in full color, featuring paintings, sculptures, prints, fabric, and mixed-media works by significant contemporary artists such as Carrie Mae Weems, Faith Ringgold, Lorna Simpson, Betye Saar, and Howardena Pindell. Included in the text are essays by scholars and curators discussing the impact of African American women on the arts, society, and culture, African American women are painting, sculpting, engaging in photography, working with mixed media, and making prints to sell for profit. They are active in their communities fostering these talents and others.

Many women, however, are doing their work in private and do not seek public attention or profit. The unglorified work of homemakers, mothers, and grandmothers does not go unnoticed by this author, who knows this nonwage work is just as important as any other work. It advances civilization when a women engages in the arts and when she engages in nurturing others and guiding them spiritually and politically in becoming good citizens in her own home.

It is my opinion that many white U.S. citizens resent the surface advancements of African Americans. Discussions with African American feminists reveal the same. Some white Americans even feel people of color are not real Americas. Real Americans are white and white history is the real, the good, and the legitimate history of the United States. They are wrong. African American females have worked hard to document the lives of black women and have taught the United States how to live up to its goal of freedom and justice for all who reside within its boundaries.

To avoid having to add an entire new body of knowledge to their intelligence base, some white people focus upon how very few Afrocentrists have made, or are making, exaggerated claims that Africans and African Americans made all the major contributions to civilization. Ethnocentrics exist in all societies, but those who do not resist valuable information on American culture build diversity, broaden their world, and enhance the quality of their lives.

Those who have not been fortunate enough to incorporate the history of African Americans and other women of color into their intelligensia are culturally illiterate and culturally deprived. Their educational system and their society has failed them, or they have failed their society.

## HOMELAND AND CIVILIZATION

All people have a homeland, a place where they originate. American Indians and Chicanos today live on their homeland, their Mother Earth. Africa is far from the United States, but contributions to the world begin with claims of the birth of humanity in Central Africa, where the earliest skeletal remains have been found to be female (Piccione 2001). But even knowledge can be colonized, or "white-washed." For example, the name of the earliest skeletal remains is Lucy. Why was a name more like that of the earliest human ancestor not chosen? Perhaps it is not only racist, but also sexist. The name is a diminished form of the full name, Lucille, which is not an African name. The early skeletal remains are often the basis of migration theory, that "man" first immigrated to other continents from Africa. According to the theory, climatic adaptation and mutation took place over thousands of years and resulted in the emergence of distinct ethnicities and races as reactions and adaptations to environmental factors. Despite differences, these ethnicities are part of the same species, Homo sapiens sapiens. According to evidence dating to about 25,000 B.C., a different species of genetically advanced groups of early Africans, Homo erectus, thrived during the period between 1.8 million and 100,000 year ago by producing tools and other necessary articles for life. Most scholars stress that "he" migrated through Europe and Palestine. However, there is evidence that entire groups, including women and children, migrated. Even in the year 2000 the word "man" is still used to distinguish "humans." We have not yet dealt effectively with how sexism manifests itself in the English language and how it inherently sees women, especially women of color, as having less value.

Like people of China and Indians of the Americans, the people in Africa refined and crystallized culture and civilization over hundreds of years. It reached a zenith along the Nile River, where most cultural attention has focused on ancient Egypt. This region has been portrayed as exotic via the movies and romanticized escapades of whites who found riches associated with pharaohs and queens. Whites have appropriated what fulfills their fantasy and represent queens and pharaohs as white persons who were considered, and considered themselves, representatives of God.

According to several colleagues who teach African American studies, because of the evolution of culture and civilization along the Nile, Africa is seen by some anthropologists as the mother of all continents. As proof of this, ecological studies of plate tectonics, the movement of the earth's surface, are cited to determine that Africa is the only continent to have maintained its basic position over the ages. Other land masses have broken apart to form what we call North America, South America, Europe, Asia, and India.

Like other civilizations, African civilization has expanded and contracted in size at different periods in its long history. Examples of a different world civilization include its concept of monarchy, medicine, religious philosophy, burial practices, mathematics, art, and architecture. There are also economic systems rooted in the vibrant trade relations in ebony, ivory, oils, animal skins, gold, and other materials.

Young African American women and men are not taught that Africa and other countries serve as examples of shared strategic alliances created by royal weddings that solidified political unions. Thus, women have a political and military history that is not interpreted as political because it does not fit into the preconceived notion of politics, the military, and contributions to civilization.

African cultural advances contributed texts and papyri to the world in which was documented African history. In African American studies courses we learn that in these records are outlined medical procedures and treatments, calendars of religion, and astronomical events such as the winter solstice and spring equinox. The winter solstice and spring equinox are commemorated throughout the world, and indigenous people did the first recording of them. These were and are periods of significance to women, who have inherited religious and philosophical and ethical teachings that were not segmented and separated into distinct entities, but instead were linked to one another to create an integrated world view. African and Native American gifts to the world have allowed clear ideas on monotheism, one god, a virgin birth, immortality, infinity, justice, and human commandments.

Note that when people native to a country speak or write about their country the term "she" is used. One would think that women would have a higher status, but in America there has evolved the contention that "man" is superior to land, to the thing upon which he lives, that which gives him life, Mother Earth. In this world view the Earth can be desecrated and treated as if it is not sacred. It can be exploited and destroyed in the name of American progress and profit. Those who seek to protect it, environmentalists, are discredited and diminished in value by contentions that render them unpatriotic, unprogressive, and tree-huggers.

Because of her military, political, and economic greatness, America has enemies. Unlike America, Africa's wars have been fought on her own territory. Africa is no stranger to colonialism, and those countries that are colonized are given lower status. Thus, Africa's ability to continue to contribute to the advancement of global civilization has been destroyed or kept secret by her conquerors. Further, this lack of knowledge about Africa makes it difficult for African Americans to have pride in their homeland. It is therefore necessary to instill that pride, and members of the African American community work hard to do this by promoting cultural celebrations like Kwanzaa, observed December 26 through January 1. Doctor Maulana Karenga, a professor at California State University, Long Beach, invented Kwanzaa in 1966. It consists of seven principles:

1. Umoja (unity): to strive for and maintain unity in the family, community, nation, and race.
2. Kujichagulia (self-determination): to define ourselves, name ourselves, create for ourselves, and speak for ourselves.
3. Ujima (collective work and responsibility): to build and maintain our community together and make our sisters' and brothers' problems our problems and to solve them together.
4. Ujamaa (cooperative economics): to build and maintain our own stores, shops, and other businesses together.
5. Nia (purpose): to make our collective vocation the building of our community to restore our people to their traditional greatness.
6. Kuumba (creativity): to do as much as we can to leave our community more beautiful and beneficial than we inherited it.
7. Imani (faith): to believe with our hearts in our people, our parents, our teachers, our leaders, and the righteousness and victory of our struggle.

## CULTURAL BLENDING

Some cultural blending has taken place among Africans and that has often been transported to America and can be seen, heard, and tasted today. For example, the Moors ruled Spain for hundreds of years. Moorish influence was transmitted to the Americas when the Spanish came to explore the hemisphere. It is evident in the architecture of southwestern Catholic churches and even in some Spanish surnames like Espinoza.

North African Moors, neighbors to Egypt and Nubia, are credited for their preservation of Egyptian scientific and literary wisdom. They translated ancient scientific works in medicine, pharmacology, astrology, the humanities, history, and law. This also was contributed during the Moorish occupation of Spain and transported to the "New World" by the Spanish conquistadores (New Mexico Spanish Genealogy Society 2001). Jews in Spain incorporated Moorish influence into their culture and vice versa. The Spanish brought African slaves to do the physical labor of settling the New World. This influence is still felt in various areas of the Americas and continues to migrate across the U.S.–Mexican border into the culture of the United States.

In the United States there are numerous temples and lodges of freemasonry that feature obelisks and statues of great men such as Imhotep. The Washington Monument, for example, is an obelisk, as is Cleopatra's Needle. Some of these cultural contributions, as well as those of other cultures, have been physically appropriated by U.S. citizens. The ancient obelisk built by Thutmosis III presently decorates New York's Central Park. This brings to attention the controversy of archaeologists, anthropologists, and other scientists conducting research in foreign countries. They often go there and claim their findings as their own and have them carted off to their own countries. At question is the violation of cultural and human rights: Do indigenous people have the right to keep their ancestor's cultural productions in their own land and with the people that created them? I say yes. The colonization of culture, especially for profit or decoration, is not ethically or morally acceptable. It is stealing. Many countries, like Africa, China, and Mexico, now have strong laws to prevent such thievery.

While conducting an Internet search on women of Africa, I discovered a page entitled "The Status of Women in Ancient Egyptian Society" by Peter A. Piccione (2001). He states that unlike the position of women in most other ancient civilizations, Egyptian woman seemed to have enjoyed the same legal and economic rights as the Egyptian man, at least in theory. This is reflected in Egyptian art and historical inscriptions. It is uncertain why these rights existed for woman in Egypt but nowhere else in the ancient world.

It may well be that men and women might not have been conceptualized in their familiar relationships as we know them. This is not to say that Egypt was an egalitarian society. It was not. Legal distinctions in Egypt were apparently based much more upon differences in social class than differences in gender. Rights and privileges were not uniform from one class to another, but within the given classes. It appears that equal economic and legal rights were, for the most part, accorded to both men and women.

According to Piccione's Web site, most of the textual and archaeological evidence for the role of women in ancient Africa survives from the elite classes. We know that women could manage and dispose of private property, including land, portable goods, servants, slaves, livestock, and money (when it existed). A woman could administer all her property according to her free will. She could conclude any kind of legal settlement, and could appear as a contracting partner in a marriage contract or a divorce contract. She could execute testaments, free slaves, and make adoptions. She was also entitled to sue, using the law to settle disputes.

It is highly significant that a woman in Egypt could do all of these things without the need of a male representative. Avangelin Veyna (1986) demonstrates that some of this was true for Spanish women, especially in New Mexico, until the U.S. war to acquire Mexico, when white male dominance was established. This amount of freedom was at variance with that of white American women of the same period. African influence is also felt in the *tapalos*, the head covering of Spanish and then Mexican women in the United States until the early 1950s.

There were several ways for an Egyptian woman to acquire possessions and real property. Most frequently she received them as gifts or as an inheritance from her family or spouse (Piccione 2001). She could also engage in purchases with goods that she earned through employment or she borrowed.

Under Egyptian property law, a woman had claim to one-third of all the community property in her marriage (i.e., the property that accrued to her husband and her after they were married). When a woman brought her own private property to a marriage (e.g., as a dowry), this apparently remained hers, although the husband often had the free use of it. In the event of divorce, her property had to be returned to her. She was also entitled to any divorce settlement that might be stipulated in the original marriage contract. A wife was entitled to inherit one-third of that community property on the death of her husband, while the other two-thirds was divided among the children, followed by the brothers and sisters of a deceased spouse. A woman was free to bequeath property from her husband to her children or even to her own brothers and sisters (unless there was some stipulation against such in her husband's will). She could also disinherit children and/or could selectively bequeath that property to certain children and not to others.

Slavery was no stranger to Africa. Under self-enslavement, women often received a salary for their labor. Two reasons forced women into such arrangements: as payment to a creditor to satisfy bad debts or to be assured of one's provisions and financial security. However, this fee would equal what the slave that the provider had to pay for her labor; thus, no "money" would be exchanged. Since this service was a legal institution, a contract was drawn up stipulating the conditions and the responsibilities of the involved parties. In executing such an arrangement, a woman could also include her children and grandchildren, alive or unborn. If such women married male "slaves," the status of their children depended on the provisions of their contracts with their owners.

However, based upon the Hermopolis Law Code of the third century B.C., the freedom of women to share easily with their male relatives in the inheritance of landed property was restricted (Piccione 2001). According to the provisions of the Hermopolis Law Code, where an executor existed, the estate of the deceased was divided up into a number of parcels equal to the number of children of the deceased, both alive and dead. Thereafter, each male child (or that child's heirs), in order of birth, took his pick of the parcels. Only when the males were finished choosing were the female children permitted to choose their parcels (in chronological birth order). The male executor was permitted to claim for himself parcels of any children and heirs who predeceased the father without issue. Female executors were designated when there were no sons to function as such. However, the code is specific that, unlike male executors, they could not claim the parcels of any dead children.

It is uncertain how literate Egyptian women were in any period. Piccione's Internet site suggests very low figures for the percentage of literate in the Egyptian population. According to Piccione, other Egyptologists would dispute these estimates. In any event, it is certain that the rate of literacy of Egyptian women was well behind that of men from the Old Kingdom through the Late Period. Lower-class women certainly were more illiterate. Middle-class women and the wives of professional men perhaps were less illiterate, and the upper class probably had a higher rate of literate women. This tendency is true all over the world even today.

If African American women have this as part of their history, what happened? First of all, the status of women in Egypt does translate into that of women in other parts of Africa, and thousands of African women were transported in the United State as slaves. If they survived, they and their offspring were isolated from their mother culture. Women from different areas were thrown together and their mother cultures had to go underground. They became secret cultural practices, some of which have survived to this very day. These ordinary and extraordinary roles are not the only ones in which we see African women cast in ancient Egypt. Although they do not appear frequently in the historical record, women appear as the victims of crime (including rape), as the perpetrators of crime, as adulteresses, and even as convicts. However, the percentage of women as criminals was very small compared to that of men (U.S. Federal Bureau of Investigation 2001b), and this is a worldwide tendency that also remains today.

## AFRICAN WOMEN IN AMERICA

Since slavery, the life of black women has improved. We even see a few of them speak with great authority; and the number of African American women is growing in the media. They have derived limited benefit from the fact that the American male population grew faster than the female population. The fact that there are about 6 million more women than men makes it harder for African American women to find partners. This is true for women in general, but because African American females have a much higher educational attainment than African American males and the attached earning power, adult women frequently find themselves without male partners.

This is also true for older women, who tend to have less education. The male-to-female ratio declines with age. For persons age eighty-five and over, it was roughly 49 males for every 100 females. Further, the nation's baby boom population, fifty-plus years of age with about a 51-percent female population, is expected to grow by 50 percent during this decade (U.S. Bureau of the Census 2000a).

According to government statistics, the nuclear family has revived a bit (U.S. Bureau of the Census 2001b), but three in ten households were maintained by women. African American female single-parent households have held steady. What is increasing is revenues for women-owned businesses (U.S. Bureau of the Census 2001), and next to Asians, African American women fare very well in this category.

The remarkable attainment of African American women is astonishing, especially when one focuses upon slavery and its legacy upon these women. The story of African slave women in the United States has been told many times by scholars better equipped than I. Because of the efforts of African American scholars, we have learned some very important facts about women during this dark time of U.S. history. In the Americas, slavery and the repercussions of it are historical; they have been, are, and will be felt until we adequately deal with the fact that it happened. What is more wretched is that the practice of human bondage may change over time, but the effects remain the same. The same can be said about sexism.

For example, the Spanish brought the idea of slavery and slaves to the New World, which we have already established was a very old world (New Mexico Spanish Genealogy Society 2001). It appears that the first slaves were males brought by Spanish men. With slavery also came white male dominance over African women. White colonists in the South brought over even more slaves. Until 1840, black men greatly outnumbered black women. Women were more frequently sold and purchased at auction than contracted for. Once captured and on U.S. soil, the African female social order broke down. Tribes were separated and individuals were shipped to different plantations. Slaves underwent a process of forced resocialization, cultural genocide, and the replacement of their languages and cultures with a new one.

Some of these women worked in the most intimate settings of white female and male homes, but most of them labored intensely outside of the homes of their white owners. In these relationships was a nasty secret. White men had easy sexual access to African women, who gave birth to numerous mixed-blood babies. These women were generally raped. Very few, like Sally Henning, who gave birth to the children of Thomas Jefferson, came to reap any benefit from relationships with white men.

In May 1999 I was reading my online newspaper (www.afroam.org; Phinney 1999) when I ran across an article about the descendants of Sally Heming, a black slave, who were invited to the Thomas Jefferson reunion. The Charlottesville, Virginia, meeting marked the first time descendants of former U.S. President Thomas Jefferson's alleged mistress were invited to a Jefferson family reunion. "Every family has an in-group and an out-group, and a reconciliation that has to take place," said Mary Jefferson, a descendant of Sally Hemings, one of President Jefferson's slaves and his reputed lover. The African American descendents were the out-group, and the white group at the May weekend declined, during a family business meeting, to allow relatives of Hemings to officially join the family's eighty-six-year-old Monticello Association. They also blocked a vote to offer Hemings's descendants, about three dozen, honorary membership, which includes burial in the family cemetery, until a paternity claim was researched. The association appointed a committee to conduct more research into the paternity issue and allowed Hemings's descendants inside the hotel ballroom for the membership debate. While in office, Jefferson, the nation's third president, was publicly accused of being the father of several of Hemings's children. Members of Hemings's family have passed down the paternity claim through the generations. In November

1998 a DNA study concluded that Jefferson was likely the father of Eston Hemings, Hemings's youngest son (Phinney 1999). Descendants of both families felt the reunion was mostly productive, although there was some tension. Some of the Hemings family feels the nation is looking to the family for leadership in healing some of the wounds of slavery and segregation. But a Monticello Association member made a motion to ask the Hemings guests to leave the room during a discussion of "family business." A 30 to 23 vote to let the Hemings group stay generated applause from about 250 persons in attendance. After the meeting, Lucian Truscott of Los Angeles, the Jefferson descendant who first invited the Hemings, told news reporters that there had been "an element of racism" in the arguments to deny immediate membership.

A slave woman had little choice in the selection of mates. To her master she was nothing more than a laborer and a breeder, but intimate relationships of her choice with slave men frequently took place. Just as black men were chained and branded, so were women after being herded off the ship that they had arrived on nude. Some women gave birth to children in the stench of the ship and later in the scorching hot sun of the fields they were forced to work in. For the white slave owner, slave women giving birth was an economic interest (James and Davis 1998). The more babies a black woman had, the better; they were free laborers. After her child was born, the slave woman was allowed to nurse and fondle the infant only at the slave master's discretion. Black women anguished over being separated from their children when they were placed on the auction block. When they resisted openly, they were flogged. In some cases slave women killed their children rather than subject them to the oppression of slavery.

At the expense of their own children, black women were in charge of caring for the slave master's children, and they are often presented as being important and necessary figures in white households. Black women existed to do the nasty household work still performed by women with little or no pay. She not only had to fight off the sexual advances of the white slave owner, but also those of his white male hired hands. Black men were relatively powerless to do anything about the sexual advances of white men. If the woman refused she was likely to get whipped. While the "master" whipped her, black men were forced to hold the women to the ground.

In some cases, black women admired the white skin of their masters or felt that copulation with white men would enhance their slave status (African American Women's Archives 1999). In their minds there was also the increased possibility that a mulatto offspring would achieve emancipation. The admiration of white skin was not very different from the slave mentality that caused some blacks to identify with their masters and act ruthlessly toward other slaves. In some cases, black woman submitted sexually to play a role in saving the life of a black man. If she did, she could prevent her husband from being whipped or otherwise punished.

Women like Harriet Tubman were instrumental in the liberation of the slaves. They gave the first critical accounts of actual conditions, but some Anglo-Americans unwittingly rendered some of the first insights into slavery via their personal papers and letters. Duke University in Durham, North Carolina, has collected Anglo-American perspectives created by white women and men that contain textual references to African-Americans. They shed light on the lives and experiences of African-American women (see African American Women's Archives 1999).

## BLACK WOMEN ENSLAVED

Most of the records are not gender detailed, but contain references to activities and communities plus valuable commentary on the religiosity, work, family life, and political activity of black women and men. They do so with varying degrees of bitterness, paternalism, racism, sexism, and honesty about the current attitudes of white people. It is important that a researcher relying on this information be aware of the complex assumptions from which information stems. Most Anglo-American perspectives on African-American women consist of observations made from considerable social distance. When focusing upon shared experiences between blacks and whites, it is imperative to recognize the existence of separate realities resulting from an intricate system of social constructs and power relations, which created great differences between the two groups and their world views.

Although Anglo-American perspectives have been used as the primary sources of documentation on black slave life in the United States, they should not be perceived as the primary perspective, nor as a singular point of view. Other work exists by African Americans and other scholars, diarists, travelers, teachers, and merchants with direct contact with ex-slaves after emancipation. Most interesting are the attitudes that are documented, especially those of white women. Attitudes transfer into actions, and together they force official and unofficial policy.

The Duke University collection (African American Women's Archives 1999) frequently renders white female attitudes about black women. For example, a Mississippi slave owner's daughter writes in anger that her father's slaves are deserting the plantation. She repeatedly notes that slaves are being "persuaded off" the plantation by older slaves. One interpretation of her use of the term "persuaded" is that without encouragement slaves would not otherwise be motivated to leave the plantation. Although this form of thinking might seem ludicrous to us, one must question and observe from which sources the daughter derives this perspective.

Female slaves were "hired out" as punishment (African American Women's Archives 1999). The Archibald Boyd letters include letters from slave trader Samuel R. Browning reporting on the health of the slaves, the conditions of the market, and the effect of a cholera scare on his sales. One letter describes a woman who gave birth while being marched about by the trader.

Some female slave history and talent was stolen and sold for profit. The Rankin–Parker collection (African American Women's Archives 1999) contains the autobiography of the Reverend John Rankin and the biography of John Parker, an ex-slave who Rankin worked with for the underground railroad. John Parker was born into slavery and bought his freedom in 1845. This collection includes the story of Eliza's (a female slave) escape across the Ohio River, and was later supposedly used by Harriet Beecher Stowe when writing *Uncle Tom's Cabin.*

The underground railroad helped secure slave freedom. Some Indian people also assisted runaway slaves. Freedom seekers stayed with the tribes, learned their ways, married, and had children (Katz 1986). Some interesting women's stories in need of more research and a feminist perspective are those of Diana Fletcher, who lived with the Kiowa, and Wildfire, who later changed her name to Edmonia Lewis but lived with the Chippewa for two years. In addition, there are many photographs of Indian women with children of mixed blood (*The Indians of California* 1994), but their identity is not known and little insight is offered into their experiences.

Southwestern Indian women became familiar with African American U.S. military men. They knew them as buffalo soldiers, and feared them just as much as they feared members of the white U.S. military. Most tribes were curious about their skin color, but this was not the basis for fear. Fear was rooted in what the U.S. army meant to Indian people.

The Duke University collection includes a volume entitled "Letters on Slavery." There one learns about the institution of U.S. slavery. The subjects discussed include conditions and treatment of house servants, field hands, and women gang leaders, and the role of female slaves as healers. African American healers, like those in the American Indian and Latino cultures, have long been revered in their communities. Some of these practices continue until this very day.

Although the majority of white women took advantage of their white privilege, it is worthy to note that some white women were sympathetic to the slaves. Jane M. Cronley's short stories and memoirs (Cronley 2001) are devoted in large part to documenting her family's relationship with their slaves both before and after Emancipation. Also included in the Duke University collection are two small volumes dealing with the 1898 Wilmington race riot. These appear to have been written by Jane Cronley and are highly critical of the white residents of Wilmington, North Carolina, whom she condemns as persecutors and murderers of innocent blacks.

Rosalyn Therborg-Penn (1998) relates more information on African American women's involvement in both electoral and nonelectoral politics after reformation. She reveals a comprehensive portrait of the African American women who fought for the right to vote in her book entitled *African American Women in the Struggle for the Vote, 1850–1920.* The women's stories of why they joined and how they participated in the U.S. women's suffrage movement are analyzed by Therborg-Penn, who informs us that not all African American women suffragists were from elite circles. Some of them were from the working class, and some were professional women from across the nation. Some employed radical, others conservative means to gain the right to vote, but contrary to the movement being presented as a white women's movement, black women were unified in working toward gaining the ballot to improve both their own status and the lives of black people in general. This was not the experience of Mexican American and American Indian women, however; they do not appear to have been active in this movement. They either lived too far from the center of such activity or the white-female-controlled movement did not target them.

One should not conclude that slaves and ex-slaves left no records. They left them in the form of songs, music, prayers, and oral histories taken by others. They even left written material revealing the difficulty of seeing the sale of closely related slaves and the efforts of free black men to recover their wives from white owners who refused to set them free. African Americans also documented various disputes, including those over wages and the relations between white teachers and African American students. These two issues, unfortunately, are still with us to this day.

In *The Story of the Lord's Dealings with Mrs. Amanda Smith, The Colored Evangelist,* Amanda Smith (1893), born into slavery in Maryland in the 1830s, tells how her father purchased her freedom and moved her to Pennsylvania, where she grew up and assisted runaway slaves. In the tradition of her father, she purchased a freeborn sister who had been sold into slavery and went on to be a missionary in Africa. Her autobiography contains an account of her life, work, faith, and travels in America, England, Ireland, Scotland, India, and Africa as an independent missionary.

From 1936 to 1938 over 2,300 former slaves from across the South were interviewed by writers and journalists with the support of the Works Progress Administration (WPA). Most of these former slaves were born in the last years of slavery or during the Civil War. They provided firsthand accounts of their experiences on plantations, in cities, and on small farms. The women of this era were transition women, much like the buffalo women among the Native Americans. Their narratives remain a resource for understanding the lives of America's 4 million slaves. These narratives can be found on-line, transcribed verbatim from the interview transcripts collected by writers of the WPA from 1936 to 1940.

Due to the wonderful Web site produced by the Corcoran Department of History at the University of Virginia in Charlottesville (American Hypertext Workshop 1996), we learn of Emma Crockett, who spoke about whippings: "All I knowed, 'twas bad times and folks got whupped, but I kain't say who was to blame; some was good and some was bad." There are a number of reasons for her inability or unwillingness to name names and be more specific about brutalities. Perhaps her memory was failing her. This is not unreasonable for someone eighty years old. The threat of retribution could have made her hold her tongue; or perhaps in her old age she had come to view her life as a slave with equanimity and forgiveness. She also told her interviewer that under slavery she lived on the "plantation right over yander," and it is likely that the children or grandchildren of her former masters or her former overseers still lived nearby. While the racial language might be offensive to modern readers, it is important to remember that these narratives were conducted sixty years ago in the Jim Crow South. Just as these former slaves survived into the twentieth century, so had the ideology of white supremacy that underpinned the slave society of the American South.

## RECONSTRUCTION AND REDEFINITION

Juneteenth is the oldest known celebration of the ending of slavery and the African American struggle for freedom (Juneteen.com 2002). It dates back to 1865, when on June 19 Union soldiers led by Major General Gordon Granger landed at Galveston, Texas, with news that the war had ended and that all slaves were now free. This was two and a half years after President Lincoln's Emancipation Proclamation, which had become official on January 1, 1863. Texas was a long way from the central seat of government, but whites had adequate communication for that period of American history. Why did it take so long? Perhaps whites did not want blacks to receive the information.

The period following the Civil War and the emancipation of slaves is known as Reconstruction. For African American women, this was a time of defining themselves and their people. The word also refers to the process by which the Union restored relations with the Confederate states after their defeat. Reconstruction lasted from 1865 to 1877 and was one of the most controversial periods in the nation's history.

The loose ties established between black men and women during slavery were in many cases dissolved after emancipation. Some black women remained with their men, but some black men began beating black women (American Hypertext Workshop 1996). This had been a practice reserved only for white men. A major concern during Reconstruction was the condition of the approximately 4 million freedmen (freed slaves; the term includes women). Most of them had no homes, were desperately poor, and could not read and write. During this period the federal government attempted to tend to the problems of helping the newly freed slaves find jobs, housing, and a means of acquiring an education. But white resistance was intense and the programs were undermined, and former slaves, especially the women, received little support.

Insight into this period can be gained from Harriet Jacobs, who wrote her story under the pen name of Linda Brent (American Hypertext Workshop 1996). Jacobs wrote because she wanted to inform and promote action among Northern women over the condition of slave women in the South. There is some controversy about whether or not she actually wrote the book, but in it she writes about slavery as "deep, and dark, and foul." Jacobs tells of being sexually exploited in her *Incidents in the Life of a Slave Girl*. To free herself from her sexual persecution, she first went into hiding and then escaped to the North. Her mother died when Jacobs was six years old, but she reports she had a kind mistress. Jacobs was fifteen when the mistress died, and the husband pursued her sexually. To escape this, she encouraged a relationship with a white unmarried lawyer and bore two children. Her son was born when Jacobs was sixteen, and her daughter when she was eighteen. Because her situation was intolerable, Jacobs left her children and ran away. The lawyer and his daughter tried to locate her and return her to slavery. At the age of forty, Jacobs was purchased and then emancipated by "Mrs. Bruce," an abolitionist. One Web site (htttp://xroads.virginaia.edu/~HYPER/hypertex.html) poses some questions leading to a critical discussion about the authenticity of Jacobs as the author of *Incidents*. For example, why did the book not receive the literary and historical attention it deserved until the 1900s? It is possible that it did not because Jacobs was a woman, and a black women at that. This manifests the sexism and racism in the literary and publication worlds. The book was published in 1861, edited by L. Maria Child Boston. Perhaps it was not as important for abolitionists as earlier works. Jacobs's life also brings into question the concept of motherhood, the abandonment of children, the need to survive, her reacquaintance with her children, and the consequences of being a literate slave.

As African Americans struggled with a new lifestyle, the forces of racism and sexism worked against a better way of life. Their civil rights were restricted by laws that prevented them from voting. They could not move freely in society or own property. Lynching and killing occurred regularly, and the federal government became ineffective at providing opportunities and protection. Thus, African Americans began to establish their own institutions. Some of them developed outstanding reputations, such as Atlanta University (now Clark Atlanta University), Fisk University, Hampton Institute, and Howard University, but it was at Stelman College, a women's college, that many women honed leadership qualities.

The Freedmen's Bureau did not solve the serious economic problems of African Americans. Many males traveled west, where there were fewer people, to be cowboys. Black women were in the West also. There they lessened their suffering of racist threats and violence, but there were still laws restricting their civil rights and the rights of Mexicans and Indians. Legal restrictions on black civil rights arose in 1865 and 1866, when many Southern state governments passed laws that became known as the black codes. These laws were like the earlier slave codes. Some black codes prohibited blacks from owning land. Others established a nightly curfew for blacks. Some permitted states to jail blacks for being jobless. The black codes shocked a powerful group of Northern congressmen called Radical Republicans. These senators and representatives won congressional approval of the Civil Rights Act of 1866, which gave African Americans the rights and privileges of full citizenship. In June 1866 Congress proposed the Fourteenth Amendment to the Constitution, which gave citizenship to blacks. It also guaranteed that all federal and state laws would apply equally to blacks and whites. In addition, the amendment barred former federal and state officeholders who had supported the Confederacy from holding high political office again.

None of the defeated Southern states had yet been readmitted into the Union, and Congress declared that none could rejoin until they ratified the Fourteenth Amendment. U.S. President Andrew Johnson urged the states to reject the amendment, and all the former Confederate states except Tennessee did so. Tennessee then became the first of the eleven defeated Southern states to be readmitted into the Union. The Fourteenth Amendment was finally ratified by the required number of states in 1868, and in 1870 the Fifteenth Amendment guaranteed citizens the right to vote, though this right did not apply to women.

Most of the chief legislative and executive positions were held by Northern white Republicans who had moved to the South and by their white Southern allies. Angry white Southerners called the Northerners carpetbaggers. This suggested they could carry everything they owned when they came South in a carpetbag or suitcase. Some African Americans males were elected to important posts during Reconstruction. Most of them had college educations, an option not available to women.

By the early 1870s Northern whites had lost interest in the Reconstruction policies of the Radical Republicans. They grew tired of hearing about the continual conflict between Southern blacks and whites. Most Northern whites wanted to put Reconstruction behind them and turn to other things. Federal troops sent to the South to protect blacks were gradually withdrawn. Southern whites who had stayed away from elections to protest black participation started voting again. White Democrats then began to regain control of the state governments from the blacks and their white Republican associates. In 1877 the last federal troops were withdrawn. By the end of that year the Democrats held power in all the Southern state governments.

After the Civil War most whites simply could not accept the idea of former slaves voting and holding office, and a system of deterrence that endures in a different configuration today was set in motion. As a result, attempts by Southern blacks to take advantage of their civil rights were met by increasing violence from whites in the South. In 1865 and 1866 about 5,000 Southern blacks were murdered (Freedman's Bureau 2002). The racists targeted black men, but black women were also victimized. Many women and girls witnessed false charges filed against their men and castrations. They witnessed and endured beatings, strangulations, and rape. Black women and men in the south lived in terror. There was no protection from the law; it was designed and controlled by whites. One of the largest hate groups was the Ku Klux Klan (KKK).

During the late 1800s, blacks, Mexicans, and Indians increasingly endured and resisted inhuman treatment at the hands of whites. Their social conditions reflected beliefs held by whites that whites were born superior to people of color. They were more intelligent and had more God-given talent, a better work ethic, and higher moral standards. Throughout the United States laws were passed and social practices were firmly in place that required that the races be separated on trains and in churches, schools, hotels, restaurants, theaters, and other public places.

Throughout this country discrimination took on latent and manifest functions. It was hidden but put into social practice, and it was written as public policy. Laws simply worked against people of color. In 1883 the Civil Rights Act of 1875, guaranteeing blacks the right to be admitted to any public place, was declared to be unconstitutional. In addition, the Civil Rights Act of 1866 and the Fourteenth Amendment to the Constitution, ratified in 1868, had forbidden the states to deny equal rights to any person. But in 1896 the Supreme Court ruled in *Plessy versus Ferguson* that a Louisiana law requiring the separation of black and white railroad passengers was constitutional. The court argued that segregation in itself did not represent inequality and that separate public facilities could be provided for the races as long as the facilities were equal. In practice, however, this was not accurate. When they existed, nearly all the separate schools, places of recreation, and other public facilities provided for people of color were far inferior to those provided for whites, but the "separate but equal doctrine" became the basis of race relations and was extended throughout the United States until the 1950s.

## THE CIVIL RIGHTS MOVEMENT

Following the emancipation of slaves, many black women, children, and men went north, but some stayed in the South, where they maintained African American traditions to this very day. Many women migrated to work as house and hotel maids and in factories. They contributed heavily to the general economy and to their own households. In the North, other women found an outlet for their talents and used their creativity as a way of providing for themselves and for others. Female creativity was at its height during the Harlem Renaissance of the 1920s. This important period in African American history produced some of the most outstanding American intellectual, literary, and musical classics. It was a time of poetry, dance, and economic power. It is this period that gave Josephine Baker a platform for her dancing talent, but then and now it was and is more difficult for black men to get jobs. Women can more easily transfer their domestic skills to gain employment as housemaids, bar maids, cooks, and waitresses.

Today, many black women work outside their homes. The most recent U.S. Bureau of the Census (2001b) information indicates that about 12 percent (7 million) of employed women are black. This means that about 51 percent of black women are employed for pay. According to the Bureau of the Census, black women participate in the labor force almost at the same rate as white women. However, this was not true during World War II, when men were sent to various places in Europe, the Pacific, and Africa to fight. A few black men flew airplanes, but most were ground soldiers. The women stayed home, contributing to the war effort by sacrificing what little they had. Unlike white women, African American and Mexican American women were not as frequently employed in the war industry, especially at higher paying jobs, but they were present. At the end of the war men had the GI Bill available to them. The men who took advantage of it went to college. A few went to acting schools, some became barbers, some bought homes, and others entered into the professions, primarily via black colleges and universities.

Because women had never been counted as part of the war effort, they received no GI benefits unless they served in the active military during the war. Again, many more white women than women of color qualified for the GI Bill, and African American women did serve in the military (Sheldon 1996). The GI Bill created a chasm, an educational and socioeconomic gap between men and women that exists to this very day. It is more or less pronounced from culture to culture. Native Americans, for example, did not take as much advantage of the GI Bill as did African Americans, and therefore lag behind other women in all social and economic categories.

One social and economic category in which women have made dramatic changes is their high school and college graduation rates. They are increasingly delaying marriage and childbirth to attend college and establish careers. The National Center for Education Statistics (2000) relates that more than twice as many women as men teach in both public elementary and secondary schools. Almost all hold a bachelor's degree and 64 percent have at least ten years of full-time experience. There are about 3 million public and private school teachers in the United States, and there is a shortage of teachers of color.

As a result of the combined efforts of the civil rights and black feminist movements, African American women have become teachers who frequently stress black history. White women still earn only seventy-seven cents to every one dollar earned by males. The median earning rate of black women ($25,117) compared to those of white males ($38,869) and white females $28,080) demonstrates a need to close the gap. Like Latinas, African American women earn less than white women do, and Native American women barely participate in the economy of the United States (U.S. Bureau of the Census 2000a). Even today, African American, Asian, and Latina women are highly employed as private household and daycare workers in the homes of white women. The racial and ethnic groups are most highly concentrated in these positions where they are most highly concentrated as a population. In the Southwest, for example, most of the domestic help in white households is Latino. On the West Coast, it is Latino, Asian, and African American. My conversations with domestic workers in Los Angeles with women of color have shown that they are forced to leave their children without adequate supervision in order to earn money by cleaning homes that are superior to theirs, cooking food that is generally healthier than theirs, and taking care of children who are whiter than theirs. There is something fundamentally wrong with this and with how African Americans have experienced some of their social history. These women, however, brought these issues to the attention of the civil rights movement of the 1960s, and keep them foremost in our mind as we move toward the feminization of racism.

Three major factors encouraged the beginning of the contemporary civil rights movement for people of color. Men of color had served with honor in World War II. In fact, Mexican American men were the most highly decorated in that war (Trujillo 1990). Black, Native American, Asian, and Chicano leaders pointed to the service records and the military treatment of these veterans to exhibit the injustice of racial discrimination against them. African Americans in the urban North made economic gains, increased their education, and registered to vote. There soon followed numerous civil rights organizations and African American women were immediately involved. Many of them took their lead from women like Mary Church Terrell, who helped found the National Association of Colored Women as early as 1896. She also advised government leaders on racial problems. In the 1950s and 1960s, major court battles were won, there was a period of peaceful protests, and civic unrest led to the enactment of historic new civil rights laws. Contrary to the male-dominant depiction, women were at the forefront.

However, women in all the movements had to justify having their issues addressed by men in the movement. Female university and college students were highly active, and many became scholars. In the early part of the 1960s social scientists became interested in the African American family because it was interested in poverty. Most social scientists saw poverty as a "social problem," and blamed the poverty of people of color upon the family patterns among these people. White social scientists interpreted families of color as "deviating" from the white "norm." The black family was targeted as having more female heads of households than the white norm, and was therefore deviant and abnormal. People of color not only had higher unemployment rates; they had higher criminal justice rates, less political power, less education, and poor health. White social scientists claimed that the way to solve these problems was to build a more stable family modeled after the white patriarchal pattern.

In 1965 the U.S. government published a booklet entitled "The Negro Family: The Case for National Action." In it the U.S. Department of Labor stated the Negro community had been forced into a matriarchal structure because the institution of slavery led to a breakdown in the family and created a matriarchy, a culture in which women were dominant. This matriarchal family structure was held responsible for contributing to "emasculation," the taking away of manhood. In other words, the disempowerment of black people was partly caused by black women. No attention was given to the fact that black women were just as powerless as black men, and even more. This myth of black matriarchy has had widespread influence, and is even widely believed today. In 1970, Maxine Williams and Pamela Newman wrote *Black Women's Liberation*. They gave voice to many black feminists when they wrote that the idea of a black matriarchy was something African Americans had to become informed about, resist, and expose.

During the height of the civil rights movement, Williams and Newman brought attention to the fact that due to a shortage of black men most black women were forced to accept gender relationships on male terms. They also revealed that black women, like Chicanas and Latinas, were struggling to fulfill the beauty "standards" of a white western society. Twenty years ago it was common to see women of color wearing blond wigs, rouge, and lipstick. Today the objective for some is still to get as close to the white beauty standard as possible. In spite of the fact that bleaching creams and hair straighteners were and are used, women of color cannot change their black or brown skin. Asian women have a similar situation; even if they enlarge and round out their eyes with surgery, they are still Asian.

Even today's "minority" models tend to have white features. Some women of African descent have reclaimed African names. African American women have followed the advice of bell hooks (1989), who maintains that for many exploited and persecuted people the struggle to create an identity, to name one's reality, is an act of resistance. The process of domination devalues identity by devaluing language, culture, and appearance. Maintaining a sense of self, therefore, is a form of resistance. Resisting assimilation means holding on to culture. Another perceived attack on black culture is the "touchy" subject of black men with white women.

In the late 1960s and early 1970s, the "black is beautiful" campaign and black feminism encouraged black women to develop self-esteem and play a more prominent role in the movement. Foremost among them was scholar, author, and activist Angela Davis (James and Davis 1998), but black men in the movement still felt women should not take the lead. Authors like Williams and Newman (1970) give us some fine examples. For example, Stokely Carmichael declared that the position of women in the movement was "prone," and some years later, Eldridge Cleaver stated women had "pussy power." Eventually, the Black Panther Party altered its view, saying "women are our other half," and Alice Walker (1983) gave us the term "womanist" to refer to black feminism. Later, some women of color from other cultures adopted the term.

When writing their political statement, the Republic of New Africa (Williams and Newman 1970) stated they wanted the right of all black men to have as many wives as they could afford, because this is the way things were in Africa. This is an example of what black women faced in some aspects of the civil rights movement (Williams and Newman 1970). However, in the 1960s and throughout his life, Dr. Martin Luther King, Jr. urged African Americans to use peaceful means to achieve their social goals. Cesar Chavez urged Mexicans and Asians to do the same. University and college students organized and some joined in coalitions to resist the war in Vietnam. Women began to exchange details of their experiences in the movement. However, they did not give up on the men. With them, they staged sit-ins, boycotts, marches, and "freedom rides" (bus rides to test the enforcement of desegregation in interstate transportation). The hippie movement and the women's movement during the early 1960s combined with efforts of the civil rights groups to end discrimination in many public places, including restaurants, hotels, theaters, cemeteries, colleges, and universities. In some cases these coalitions were controversial. Generally they were short lived, and some of this history is violent, but activists remained committed to advancing the cause of civil rights and human rights in the United States.

Several women of color rose to the forefront during the civil rights movement of the latter part of this century. Among them was a seamstress and civil rights activist in Montgomery, Alabama, who became a symbol of women who dared to take bold action to attain their civil rights. In 1955, Rosa Parks was arrested for disobeying a city law that required blacks to give up their seats when white people desired to sit in their seats or in the same row. Montgomery's African American population protested Parks's arrest by refusing to ride the buses. Their protest lasted 382 days, and ending only when the city abolished the bus law. The boycott became the first organized mass protest by blacks in Southern history.

Numerous cities and towns remained unaffected by the civil rights movement. African American leaders, therefore, felt the United States needed a clear, strong federal policy that would erase all remaining discrimination in public places. To attract national attention to that need, African Americans were joined by other groups of color and some white people to organized a march on Washington, D.C., in August 1963. More than 200,000 took part in what was called the March on Washington. A high point of the March on Washington was a stirring speech by Martin Luther King Jr., who told the crowd that he had a dream that one day all Americans would enjoy equality and justice. Cesar Chavez and members of the American Indian movement joined King in the effort. Soon afterward, President John F. Kennedy proposed powerful laws to protect the civil rights of all U.S. citizens, but many white people opposed the legislation.

This led to civic unrest. In some places riots broke out, and assassinations of civil rights leaders and protesters took place. Issues of police brutality made the headlines, as did economic deprivation and social injustices suffered by Asians, Chicanos, and Native Americans on reservations and in cities, and by farm workers of all color. Violence and riots were witnessed in the African American and Chicano Watts section of Los Angeles in 1965, in the predominately Chicano east side of Los Angeles, in Detroit and Newark in 1967, and in Cleveland in 1968. Persons were killed at Wounded Knee, where American Indians were trying to reclaim lands unlawfully taken by the U.S. government.

After the Detroit riots, President Lyndon B. Johnson established the National Advisory Commission on Civil Disorders, also known as the Kerner Commission, to study the causes of urban rioting. The commission put much of the blame on the racial prejudice and discrimination of whites against blacks, but all people of color suffered. One must ask why African Americans have received so much credit for the civil rights movement when so many other cultures were involved. I feel it has to do with the fact that white citizens think in dichotomies and categories. Black is the opposite of white and is easiest for them to recognize, but African Americans have also lived with white people longer and in closer proximity. Early in U.S. history they learned white language and culture better than the other ethnic groups. Because African Americans openly resisted oppression in centers of white settlement where there were more people, newspapers, and centralized government, they get most of the attention. In addition, African Americans have had their own means of training scholars, writers, attorneys, and so on and the other populations have not. In addition, they controlled their own churches. This gave them a weekly platform by which to discuss civil rights issues. The opportunity to meet regularly and to hear various perspectives, think about them, and decide on a course of action are all skills and resources required to resist public policy that is discriminatory, and women were, like they are now, the majority in black churches.

In 1968 President Johnson recommended better housing and increased economic opportunities for poor people and established the National Commission on the Causes and Prevention of Violence. It attempted to reduce the dissatisfaction that contributed to riots and other violence. Since then the issue of housing has become public and has been of grave concern to women of color, especially black women involved in welfare rights efforts. Today, women head over 60 percent of the two-or-more-person households. These households are maintained by women under forty-five years of age (U.S. Bureau of the Census 2001b). Of the 14 million women living alone, over half of them are sixty-five or older. About 55 percent of American households contain married couples, but most of these couples do not have children living at home.

## SENIOR CITIZENS

According to Census 2000, older women outnumbered older men by a ratio of 141 women for every 100 men. The sex ratio increased with age, ranging from 118 for the sixty-five to sixty-nine group to a high of 237 for persons eighty-five and over. Thus, the older population is not only getting older, but growing as a population. A child born in 1998 could expect to live 76.7 years, about twenty-nine years longer than a child born in 1900.

The major part of this increase occurred because of reduced death rates for children and young adults, and future growth is expected. This growth of older

Americans slowed somewhat during the 1990s because of the relatively small number of babies born during the Great Depression of the 1930s. As has been mentioned, the older population will burgeon between the years 2010 and 2030 when the "baby boom" generation reaches age sixty-five. By 2030 there will be about 70 million older persons, more than twice their number in 1999, and they will make up 20 percent of the total U.S. population. Minority populations are projected to represent well over one-fourth of the elderly population in 2030. Between 1999 and 2030 the white Anglo population sixty-five-plus years old is projected to increase by 81 percent, compared with 219 percent for older minorities. This includes Hispanic growth rates of about 328 percent, 131 percent for African Americans, and 147 percent for American Indians, Eskimos, and Aleuts combined. Asians and Pacific Islanders are estimated at 285 percent (U.S. Bureau of the Census 2000d).

The most recent statistics suggest that older men are much more likely to be married than older women, and that almost half of all older women are widows. Divorced and separated older persons are relatively rare. However, their numbers (2.2 million) have increased significantly since the end of the decade, when approximately 1.5 million of the older population were divorced or separated (U.S. Bureau of the Census 1999b).

While a small number of older Americans lived in nursing homes three years ago, the percentage increases dramatically with age. The number of African American women living in nursing homes is only slightly increasing. There are two things keeping African American and other older women of color from utilizing nursing homes: cost and the tremendous fear of ill treatment. The National Center for Health Statistics (2000b), in "An Overview of Nursing Home Facilities," estimates that households containing families headed by persons sixty-five-plus years old reported a median income of $33,148. This renders a median income of $33,795 for whites, $25,992 for African Americans, and $23,634 for Hispanics.

The Social Security Administration (Aragon 2001; Casares 2002) maintains that the major source of income, about 90 percent, for older persons was their federally sponsored Social Security checks. Almost 4 million elderly persons were below the poverty level. About one of every twelve (8.3%) elderly whites was poor in 2000, compared to 22.7 percent of elderly African Americans and 20.4 percent of elderly Hispanics. These higher than average poverty rates for older persons correlated with living in central cities, but rural poverty is just as damaging. There was an 11.7 percent rate of national rural poverty. It was highest in the South, where older female African Americans were concentrated.

Sometimes these older women live alone. Older persons living alone or with nonrelatives were much more likely to be poor than older persons living with families. The highest poverty rates, almost 60 percent, were experienced by older Hispanic women who lived alone (U.S. Bureau of the Census 2000c).

More often than not, older African American women have a low home-ownership rate. Of the more than 20 million households headed by older persons, about 80 percent were owners and 21 percent were renters. Females of color were disproportionately underrepresented as homeowners and overrepresented as renters. President George Bush, in his state of the union address on January 30, 2000, encouraged an effort to increase "minority" home ownership, but did not mention women, whose educational attainment varies considerably by race and ethnic origin. Roughly 73 percent of whites, 68 percent of Asians and Pacific Islanders, 45 percent of African Americans, and 32 percent of Hispanics had concluded high school at the end of the last decade (U.S. Bureau of the Census 1999a).

Health and health care are related to education and income. About 30 percent of all older persons surveyed for the 2000 census assessed their heath as fair or poor, compared to 9.2 percent for all persons combined. There was little difference between the sexes on this measure, but older African Americans (41.6%) and older Hispanics (35.1%) were much more likely to rate their health as fair or poor than older whites (26%). With poor health comes limitations on activities because of chronic conditions increase with age. Today more than half of the older population reports having at least one disability (U.S. Bureau of the Census 2001a), and most older persons have at least one chronic condition. The most frequently occurring conditions per 100 elderly at the beginning of this century were, in descending order, arthritis, hypertension, hearing impairments, heart disease, cataracts, orthopedic impairments, sinusitis, and diabetes. Older people accounted for well over one-third of all hospital stays and about 50 percent of all days of care in hospitals. Older consumers averaged $3,000 in out-of-pocket health care expenditures (cost not covered by insurance). Older African American women cannot afford such costs (U.S. Department of Health and Human Services 2000).

In 2000 there were about 36 million families with children under eighteen living with them. Of these, single parents headed about 30 percent. African American families with children under eighteen are almost three times as likely to be maintained by a single female parent, as are white families. Households maintained by black women with children have difficulty purchasing and maintaining a home. Shelter and having a home is a fundamental need of humans. When President Bush encouraged home ownership for "minorities," he maintained that establishing respect for women needs to be a "priority" in the U.S. war with Afghanistan (Bush 2000). He did not say it would be a priority in our own country, where African American women find themselves homeless seniors and single women with children.

Only about 2.2 million American households contained three generations within them. Populations of color ranked the highest among such households, but this tendency is being threatened by the economy and the drive toward individuality motivated by the dominant white value systems being taught to black and other children of color. Thus, black women and other women of color are at high risk of poor or no housing, bad health, little or no insurance, high medical costs, and loss of family support that was once there for them. This is a social embarrassment to America that draws international attention.

## HISTORICAL TRAUMA

Also drawing international attention is the violent historical trauma experienced by people of color in the United States. Trauma, like war, is always violent, and violence can be an undeclared war. Unfortunately, the women of Afghanistan have become political footballs in a male-dominated game. A war upon U.S. female poverty among women of color would take the women of color and the United States a long way toward respect. It would assist how the county is perceived internationally. In spite of the fact that several countries stepped forward to support the United States, the September 11 incidents made it clear that the United States is not well respected or even admired throughout the entire world. Until it is eradicated in the United States, other countries will hold this contradiction to the American dream, to equality, freedom, and justice for all, up to international scrutiny.

Violence can manifest in incarceration, and being trapped in a female role is for some women something like being in prison. Over a million and a half people are forced to live in jails in America. Approximately 120,000 of those people are women (U.S. Department of Justice 2000). There has been growth in the rate of incarceration of females. The common profile of the imprisoned female is that of a young, single mother with few marketable skills, a high school dropout who lives below the poverty level. The majority of the women are between the ages of twenty-five and thirty-four, and an estimated 90 percent have alcohol- or drug-related histories.

Eighty percent of convictions among women are for nonviolent drug or property crimes. These crimes are often family related, due to poverty. Many women are charged as accessories to crimes committed by male relatives or companions, often without the knowledge of the women (Morales 2002). The sharp rise in female incarceration rates can be attributed to the advent of mandatory minimum sentences for drug law violations. Convictions on offenses for which defendants once received probation can now result in very long imprisonment or even life without the possibility of parole. Although a greater number of white women than women of color are arrested, black women are eight times more likely than white women to be sent to prison. Black women are disproportionately represented in the following areas of legal abuse: overarrested, overindicted, underdefended, and excessively sentenced (Morales 2002; also see www.infosh.org/gulas/women).

Mothers constitute more than 80 percent of the women in prison. When mothers are imprisoned, their children are also. An estimated half-million children are separated from their imprisoned mothers. The decades-long sentences that are now common can either entirely wipe out the reproductive lives of young female prisoners or prevent them from playing any role in the lives of their children as they grow from infancy to adulthood. Children of incarcerated mothers are more prone to becoming entrapped in the vicious cycle of foster care, juvenile detention, and prison.

Conditions for women in prison are physically and psychologically brutal in ways particular to their female gender. Male guards are typically assigned to prisons for females. These women have great difficulty in defending themselves physically and legally from sexual coercion and assault, which is common and routinely results in pregnancy (U.S. Department of Justice 2000). The United States has become the world leader in its rate of incarceration. It has surpassed South Africa and the former Soviet Union, and the black male rates of incarceration in the United States far exceed that of black males in South Africa. And it is racist and sexist. This does violence not only to African American men, but to society in general and specifically to the national character and how it is perceived around the world. The term violence has come to imply certain assumptions. It is associated with pain and harm.

The injustice to African Americans and other populations of color is physical in the form of poor health, poor housing, exclusionary education, and a lack of political representation. But it is also psychological in the form of the need to combat low self-worth and community worth based upon such a frivolous factor as color. The violence is also spiritual. The forced conversion of Africans to Christianity magnified any physical or psychological trauma. If one does not believe in God, the spirit, or the soul, then one can then discount or dehumanize those who do. Nonbelief not only discredits the population; it does not recognize God and the godlike qualities believers maintain are germane to the human experience. At the international and local levels, if one discounts the spirit or the soul of those who do not share the views of U.S. Christianity, then it is easier to wage war: kill, mutilate, rape, disfigure, and heave painful atrocities upon those who differ. This is violent, and this has been thrust upon most of those in the United States who are poor, homosexual, people of color, or women.

There is something fundamentally wrong when things are violent. The hate and anger necessary to escalate, to be outraged to the point of rioting, social organizing, and even war, robs humans of humanity, and crimes against humanity are the worst kind because they threaten not only human life, but also the life of the planet. They desecrate and are another form of violence against that which allows life: the Earth that renders a place to walk, eat, and sleep. Violence destroys animals necessary to the ecological cycle of which we humans are a part, and pollutes the very air and water so vital to all existence.

## TOWARD TRUTH AND TRUST

Defining crimes against humanity has been limited to men. Until very recently, defining crimes against women has not been a priority for national leaders, but it has been one of the top concerns for feminists around the world.

I know that for over thirty years U.S. women of color have struggled to make racism a feminist issue and have received minimal feminist support. The plight of Afghan women, unfortunately, has been politically manipulated to demonstrate the monstrosity of the enemy. This is another factor that makes it easier to kill them during war. To some degree the manipulation of the issue has opened the eyes of Americans to sexism, but it has rendered a limited view, one that isolates Afghan women to a place far away, out of reach, and out of the sight of the United States.

It is only logica, therefore, to contend that sexism is a problem rooted in the Taliban, not in global male patriarchy, which thrives in the United States and is exported in its unique form throughout the world. This is one reason why "they" hate us. We, the citizens of the United States, have not dealt with either racism or sexism. We have exported it to other cultures, just as it was imposed upon American Indians and Chicanos. Like the AIDS virus, it has attached itself to immigrants, penetrated their culture, and when it is has invaded, it turns on its host to destroy it.

The Bureau of Justice Statistics tracks the incidence and level of crimes committed in America. The National Crime Victimization Survey (NCVS) is the single most comprehensive source of information on the experience and consequences of violent crimes against women. The following summarizes some of the NCVS findings based upon a nationally representative sample survey of females age twelve and over. It entailed about 400,000 individuals conducting the interviews.

The results are that female victims of violent crime were most often between the ages of twenty and twenty-four. Women who were young, black, Hispanic, never married, with lower family income and lower education levels, and in central cities were the most vulnerable to becoming the victims of violent crime. Nearly two in three female victims of violence were related to or knew their attackers. White and black women experienced equivalent rates of violence committed by intimates and other relatives. However, black women were significantly more likely than white women to experience incidents of violence by acquaintances or strangers. Except for rape, females were significantly less likely than males to experience all forms of violent crime between 1987 and 1991. This trend continues into the year 2002.

Female victims of violence experienced injury in 34 percent of the incidents. When the offender was an intimate, they experienced injury in 59 percent of the incidents. Thus, the better the offender knew his female victim, the more he hurt her. About three out of four female victims of violence resisted the actions of the offender, either physically or verbally. This resistance was helpful in 61 percent of the incidents. In 55 percent of rape incidents, the attacker was not a stranger; 43 percent of rapes occurred at or near the victim's home. About one in four attacks on females involved the use of a weapon by the offender. One in three of these involved a firearm. Nearly half the victims of rape perceived the offender to have been under the influence of drugs and/or alcohol at the time of the offense.

About half the women victimized by violence reported the crime to the police, and among those who didn't, about six in ten said that they considered the matter a private or personal one or they felt the offense was minor. Women do not report because they generally know the attacker and fear retaliation against themselves or their families. They also know the history of men of color with the police. It is a violent one, one that has impacted women by removing their men. The violence that women of color have endured is not only physical. It is cultural, psychological, and spiritual.

Some forms of violence are not readily seen or easily measured. One of these is the psychological and spiritual violence of racism and sexism combined. There are no models by which to teach people how to heal from what often is a traumatic experience. We do know, however, that there are contributing social factors producing a complexity that involves both social circumstances and personal choices. For example, absentee fathers contribute to the disorder of the African American value for family by not contributing to the formation of living arrangements and children supported by women in their absence. It also renders a stereotype that African American families are matriarchal because the women chase off the men.

The idea of black matriarchy does psychological and spiritual harm to American society by rendering negative sexist stereotypes of men. Those who contend that black women are too strong and men cannot live with them not only stereotype black men as weak and abandoning their families, they produce a rationale by which to accept that men of color make children without the responsibility of practicing birth control and providing maintenance. The emasculation of men makes it easy for men to leave and not bond with their children. They damage not only their own spirit, but the spirit and psychological make-up of their children. The mother, then, has to work harder to produce a well-adjusted child. Because she has so many variables impacting her life, her spiritual and emotional make-up suffers.

Contrary to the stereotype, there is a middle class in African American society. Unless it is that of a celebrity, little notice has gone to the actual lifestyles and social contributions of middle-income black families. Celebrity window dressing disguises the fact that there is a rise of middle-income black families, but it is deceiving, because the majority of the population is poor and lower working class.

A higher income lessens life's economic stress, but does it lessen racist and sexist stresses upon individuals and families? It renders time and energy to develop a family plan that includes the ability to purchase education, housing, transportation, insurance, and recreation. Racism, however, transcends class; higher income does not erase sexism. Thus, middle-income groups of color, for the most part, still have to deal with racist stereotypes and treatments, and women still endure sexism in their own homes, their culture, and the general society. Thus, middle-income families of color are not always the same as the white middle class in values and racial consciousness. Most middle-income persons have their own value systems and cultural manifestations. When the *New York Times* notes that black middle-class families exhibit a striking trend toward smaller families (Holmes 1998), I suspect they are talking about a middle class rooted in African American society who can now can afford some the things white middle-class families can afford. This make them middle income, but does it make them middle class in the way we consider middle class in mainstream America? No, as there is still the racial barrier.

The author of the *New York Times* article, Steven Holmes, notes that married black women gave birth to 357,262 babies in 1970. By 1996 that figure dropped to 179,568, a decline of nearly 50 percent, twice the drop in birth rate among married white women, but it is anticipated that married middle-income African American women will continue with this trend. The reduction of child birth rates for married middle-class black women has dropped because higher-income families, regardless of race, generally delay giving birth. They tend to have more education, and they tend to move away from neighborhoods, parents, and relatives who can provided a support system that includes childcare.

Those who have studied the phenomenon feel the decline in birth rate among two-parent African American families is caused by forces not found in the larger white population. Black couples often want to maximize the benefits they offer their children in order to ensure they will have a better chance to compete in a racist society. The drop in birth rate has had a significant effect upon the appearance of illegitimacy, where the percentage of births to unmarried women is approaching 70 percent. The number of single women has increased in the African American community. Holmes notes that statisticians and demographers note that the starlling high percentage of unwed mothers is not the result of more single African American women giving birth. In fact, that percentage has been declining for the last twenty years. It reached a forty-year low in 1996. Instead, the high proportion of black babies being born out of wedlock is mainly a function of a statistical comparison to the steep drop in the number of children being born to married black women.

Some feminists urge young women not to bring children into this world without a firm commitment from a sexual partner. This often means that he is going to raise or provide financial support for his children. African American men are urging men to do the same, but many men have problems fulfilling their responsibilities and in doing this they feed the race war that is much like the Cold War the United States once had with the Soviet Union: A war can be an undeclared war; a hot one like U.S. troops in Vietnam, or one like the cold hostilities toward the Soviet Union that lasted from World War II in the 1940s until the 1990s.

## RESTORING RESPECT

Children of women in prison usually live with their grandmothers or other custodial parents and they tend to be poor. Over 30 percent (more than 4.2

million) live on incomes below the poverty level (U.S. Department of Justice 2000). White custodial mothers are more likely to receive child-support awards than are custodial fathers. Most custodial parents with awards have a legal agreement entered through a court, government agency, or other legal body insuring child support. When men and women receive child support they receive about the same amount (about $3,767 in 1995). In 1997 (U.S. Bureau of the Census) the number of mothers receiving child support was much lower than fathers receiving child support. The fact remains today and it is estimated that the total unpaid child support is about $1 million. Visitation and joint custody are associated with higher child-support payments, and many child-support awards include health care insurance. This startling low rate of U.S. men paying child support renders serious questions about payment and how men feel about children. The immediate problem for women of color, of course, is collecting the child support.

The likelihood of receiving some or all the child support due women varies according to socioeconomic group, age, and marital status (U.S. Bureau of the Census 2001b). Nonpoor women collect child support more often than poor women do. The percentage of white women who receive child support payments is about 73 percent, compared with 59 percent for African American and 58 percent of Hispanic women. Women age thirty and over (71%) are more likely to receive child-support payments owed them than women under age thirty (65%). Women who are never married collect less child support (56%) than women who were once married (73%). Women with at least a bachelor's degree are more likely to receive child support due them (79%) (U.S. Bureau of the Census 1995).

Withholding child support is often a weapon wielded by men to harass women. I wonder how long it will take U.S. courts to charge men who do not pay child support with harassment. It was a highly educated black woman, Anita Hill, who put the discussion of gender discrimination and sexual harassment into American living rooms for several months. With the televised confirmation hearings of Supreme Court Judge Clarence Thomas, Anita Hill united American feminists in making public the issue of sexual harassment.

Today, more black women are resisting gender-role typecasting. They are reclaiming their heritage, going to Africa, and decorating in an African décor. In fact, people have recognized the shared domination of nonwhite people and women as a result of white male supremacy. What remains now is educating the next generation in healing what they have inherited. If nothing else, September 11 moved the world into specific camps, and many chose that of world unity. Today one hears more often that there is but one race on the earth, the human race. Does this really mean we are beginning to heal from discrimination? Only time will tell.

The history of African American women and other women of color in the civil rights movement has shown that humans can bring about change. Our challenge to heal from the damage done to our own citizens by deep-rooted divisions is hard to embrace. Primary among African Americans is the hope that we can, but also primary is their history in a white-dominated society characterized by the profit motive, individualism, upward mobility, and competition.

Perhaps bell hooks (1996) lends some encouragement when she notes that "this nation can be transformed. . . . We can resist racism and in the act of resistance recover ourselves and be renewed." hooks is enraged by racism. In her latest collection of the essays, *Killing Rage: Ending Racism*, hooks contends that racism in the United States is as violent as it has ever been and that there is a systematic effort to deny it. Most Americans want to believe that there is equality in our economic and cultural lives, but even after September 11 there is not.

White people do not carry all the blame. People of color go along with the status quo because they are reaping the benefits of color blindness. Most are content that they are no longer being physically hanged and raped without the alternative of limited access to the judicial system. The O. J. Simpson trial demonstrated the power of money and connection to the judicial system, but even then most people deny and do not want to hear about the continued existence of sexism and racism. As hooks tells us, it serves to keep the lid on a situation that some fear requires violence to heal. But there are nonviolent means.

Primary among them is education, and recognizing the structure, the function, the goal, and the social impact of sexism and racism. Discrimination makes society dysfunctional. As hooks sees it, the answer is rage. Rage releases the pain and destructiveness of racism, and it must be acknowledged. But rage can be energy harnessed for the redefinition of education. It can be channeled to constructive ends by taking the form of art, poetry, and music aimed in a healing direction. Anger should not be feared, for it can be put into action that is positive.

Female anger needs to be recognized when it manifests in depression. Anger can make poor women work to escape poverty, but only if they can get jobs and education by which to qualify for jobs. They can become leaders. Anger can change the hierarchically structured society we live in into a less gender-structured world, for the betterment of all.

Healing from the simultaneous effects of racism and sexism requires reparation, and most Americans do not want to discuss reparation because they think it will cost what they value the most: money and land. I find contradictions when the subject of reparation is approached. To most Americans of color, it appears that the U.S. government is more willing to make reparation to healthy middle- and upper-income people with insurance who lost relatives in the attacks on September 11 than they are to the mutilated descendants of the slaves, of massacred American Indians, and of displaced, disempowered Chicanos. Yes, there are contradictions. They are in the form of inconsistencies between payments to the Japanese for incarceration during World War II and denial of it to Chicanos and American Indians for stealing their resources. No reparation has been made for taking and destroying the land, stealing the gold and silver, killing thousands of people, and subjecting those who survived and their descendants to the debilitating elements of prejudice and discrimination.

The sooner we admit that sexism and racism exist to render unfair opportunity to white men and to limit competition for control of money and its resulting power, the quicker we will recuperate and gain the respect of our current enemies. This means displacing the system that maintains racism and sexism. This is why America was attacked. This is one of the first steps in retribution: equal access.

Reparation does not have to be in the form of large sums of money, but it can. There is no need to fear. There is money enough to go around. The problem is that it is concentrated in the hands of a few who exclude the majority. What is important is how we spend it. Let us invest it in the healing of our country. We do not want to do this because the United States is addicted to power. The truth is that world power is diffused already. This was demonstrated in how the entire world did not rush to come together to fight what America called global terrorism as easily as the United States had hoped.

The truth is that we have moved into a world economy where credit cards have been accepted in North, Central, and South America as well as in Europe, Israel, Japan, and China. Women of color want ownership of what America symbolizes and justice. They want the United States to own up to its past and its mistakes, to apologize, and to take part in reflecting the face of their country's global future. Another truth is that many women and people of color want men to liberate them, and this is not realistic. One cannot expect the oppressor to be the liberator. African American history teaches us this. Yes, there a few white people who will fight for the liberation of the oppressed when they view themselves as not being the persecutors. But when they are struggling to get a job, buy a home, and feed and clothe their children, they probably will not.

The truth is that there is little trust of whites. It is not in white people's interest to relinquish white privilege, and most white people do not want to admit they thrive on white advantages and walk on colonized land. The white-controlled feminist movement has not dealt effectively with the white privilege of colonization ensured them by their white forefathers and to some degree their foremothers. The issues surrounding color and territorialism was one of the strongest factors contributing to the cold race war. If white feminists want to address all women's issues, they must address their own liberation from sexist and racist privilege, and this means addressing retribution. We need to live in the land of the free. We need justice for all. We need to mend broken treaties and repressive immigration policy. This must be done if what we want is a relatively peaceful global existence. Many want women of color to forget their past and "go on with it." The truth is, it is never too late for justice, and we have gone for too long without it.

# REFERENCES

Administration on Aging. 2000. "A Profile of Older Americans." Department of Health and Human Services. Washington, D.C.: U.S. Government Printing Office.

African American Women's Archives. 1999. "American Perspectives on African American Women." Manuscript sources at the Special Collections Library, Duke University. Also available at: <http://www.scriptorium.lib.duke.edu.collections>.

AFRO-America. 1999. "UPS Donates Nearly One Million to Support Groups for African Americans in Atlanta." Afro-American Newspaper Company of Baltimore. Web site. Available at: <http://www.afroam.org>. Last visited November 17, 2002.

American Hypertext Workshop. 1996. Corcoran Department of History, University of Virginia, Charlottesville. Available at: <http://www.virginia.edu.history.html>.

American Online News. 1999. "Jefferson's Slave Kin Shunned." Associated Press, May 17. Available at: <http://www.womenshistory.about.com/library>.

Aragon, Roy. 2001. "You and Social Security." Statement made at a National Hispanic Council on Aging Conference, San Diego, California, October 24.

"Black and White Women: What Still Divides Us." 1988. *Ladies Home Journal*. March, pp. 4–6.

Bush, George W. 2001. "State of the Union." Public address by the President of the United States. Televised nationwide, February.

———. 2000. "State of the Union." Public address by the President of the United States. Televised nationwide, January 30.

Casares, Augustine. 2002. Statements made at a New Mexico Hispanic Council on Aging monthly meeting. Albuquerque, May 27.

Cronley, Jane M. 2001. "Letters on Slavery." Duke University Special Collections. Available at: <http://www.scriptorium.lib.du/collections/african-american-women>.

Edwards, Audrey. 1998. "Black and White Women: What Still Divides Us." *Ladies Home Journal*, March, p. 14.

Freedman's Bureau. 2002. Available at: <http://www.freedmansbureau.com/search/KKK>. Last visited November 16, 2002.

Frink Brown, Janice. 1999. "Girl, 12, Pleads with Mayor, Police Chief to Reopen Case of Slain Brother." Baltimore: *AFRO-America*, 1. Available at: <http://www.afroam.org>. Last visited November 16, 2002.

Holmes, Steven A. 1998. "Black Couples Are Favoring Small Families." *New York Times*, April 5, pp 1A, 5A.

hooks, bell. 1996. *Killing Rage: Ending Racism*. New Haven, Conn.: Owlet.

———. 1989. *Talking Back: Thinking Feminist, Thinking Black*. Boston: South End Press.

———. 1981. *Ain't I a Woman: Black Women and Feminism*. Boston: South End Press.

*The Indians of California*. 1994. Alexandria, Va.: Time Warner (Time Life Books).

Jacobs, Harriet. 2001. "Incidents in the Life of a Slave Girl Written by Herself." Available at: <http://www.xroads.virginia.edu>. Last visited November 17, 2001.

James, Joy, and Angela Davis. 1998. *The Angela Y. Davis Reader*. Oxford: Blackwell.

Juneteenth.com. 2002. "History of Juneteenth." Available at: <http://www.juneteen.com/2002>. Last visited November 16, 2002

Katz, William Loren. 1986. *Black Indians: A Hidden Heritage*. New York: Atheneum.

Morales, Carmen. 2002. Interview at Old Town Sheraton Hotel, Albuquerque, New Mexico.

National Center for Education Statistics. 2000. Telephone interview with Janet Davis. See also *We Measure America: Women and Education*. Washington, D.C.: U.S. Bureau of the Census.

National Center for Health Statistics. 2000a. "Consumer Income" (P60-209). Available at: <http://www.infosho.org/gulas/women> (updated February 22).

———. 2000b. "An Overview of Nursing Home Facilities: Data from the 1997 National Nursing Home Survey." Hyattsville, Md.: Advance Data no. 311.

New Mexico Spanish Genealogy Society. 2001. "400 Years of New Mexico History, 1585–1998." Available at: <http://www.nmgenealogy.org>. Last visited May 23, 2002.

Phinney, David. 1999. "Family to Recognize Slave Descendants?" Available at: <http://www. NISCNEWS.com> and <http://www.womenshistory.com>. Last visited November 16, 2002.

Piccione, Peter A. 2001. "The Status of Women in Ancient Egyptian Society." Available at <http://www.library.nwu.edu/class/history/B94/B94women.html>.

Robinson, Joynty, Maya Angelou, and Tritobia H. Benjamin. 1996. *Bearing Witness: Contemporary Works by African American Women Artists*. London: Rizolli International.

Sheldon, Kathryn. 1996. "Brief History of Black Women in the Military." Women in Military Service for America Memorial Foundation. Available at: <http://www.womensmemorial.org.BB41998.html>.

Smith, Amanda. 1893. *The Story of the Lord's Dealings with Mrs. Amanda Smith the Colored Evangelist*. Chicago: Meyer and Brother. (Special Collections Library, Duke University.)

Smitherman, Geneva, ed. 1995. *African American Women Speak Out on Anita Hill–Clarence Thomas*. African American Life Series. Detroit: Wayne State University Press.

Therborg-Penn, Rosalyn. 1998. *African American Women in the Struggle for the Vote, 1850–1920*. Blacks in the Diaspora Series. Bloomington: Indiana University Press.

Trujillo, Charlie. 1990. *Soldados: Chicanos in Vietnam*. San Jose: Chusma House.

U.S. Bureau of the Census. 2001a. "Americans with Disabilities." Public Information Office. Washington, D.C.: U.S. Government Printing Office.

———. 2001b. "Profile of Nations Women." Public Information Office. Report by Renee E. Spraggins. Washington, D.C.

———. 2001c. Telephone interview with Patricia Gallegos, Public Information Office.

———. 2001d. *Update on Country's African American Population*. Public Information Office. Washington, D.C.: U.S. Government Printing Office, March 21.

———. 2000a. "Black Population in the U.S.: March 2000." PPL-142, Current Population Survey. Washington, D.C.: U.S. Government Printing Office.

———. 2000b. "Census Facts for Women's History Month." Current Population Survey.

———. 2000c. "Population Projections of the United States by Age, Sex, Race and Hispanic Origin: 1995–2050," P25-1130). Available at: <http://www.census.gov/population/www/hispanic/\.html>.

———. 2000d. "Race and Hispanic Origin with Special Age Categories: Middle Series, 1999 to 2000." Current Population Survey. Washington, D.C.: U.S. Government Printing Office.

————. 2000e. "Projections of the Total Resident Population by 5 Year Age Groups." Washington, D.C.: U.S. Government Printing Office.

————. 2000f. "Women-Owned Firms Compared to All U.S. Firms by State: 2000." Washington, D.C.: U.S. Government Printing Office.

————. 1999a. "Educational Attainment in the United States." Washington, D.C.: U.S. Government Printing Office.

————. 1999b. "The Older Population in the United States: March 1999." Current Population Reports. Washington, D.C.: U.S. Government Printing Office.

————. 1997. "Three in Ten Households Were Maintained by Women in 1996." Washington, D.C.: U.S. Government Printing Office.

————. 1995. "Child Support for Custodial Mothers and Fathers: 1995." Washington, D.C.: U.S. Governing Printing Office.

————. 1993. *We Measure America: Women and Work*. Washington, D.C.: Department of Labor Women's Bureau.

————. 1990. *We Measure America: Women and Their Racial and Ethnic Backgrounds*. Washington, D.C.: Population and the Current Population Survey.

U.S. Department of Health and Human Services. 2000. "A Profile of Older Americans." Administration on Aging. Washington, D.C.: U.S. Government Printing Office.

U.S. Department of Justice. 2000. Bureau of Justice Statistics, National Crime Victimization Survey. Available at: <http://www.infosho.org/galus/women>.

U.S. Department of Labor. 1965. "The Negro Family: The Case for National Action." Office of Policy Planning and Research. Washington, D.C.: U.S. Government Printing Office.

U.S. Federal Bureau of Investigation (FBI). 2001a. ""United States Crime Index: Rates per 100,000 Inhabitants." Public Information Office. Washington, D.C.: U.S. Government Printing Office.

————. 2001b. *U.S. Crime Statistics on Women*. Washington, D.C.: U.S. Government Printing Office.

Veyna, Avangelin. 1986. "Women in Early New Mexico: A Preliminary View." In *Chicana Voices: Intersections of Class, Race and Gender*, edited by T. Cordova. Austin: University of Texas Press.

Walker, Alice. 1983. *In Search of Our Mother's Garden*. New York: Harcourt Brace Jovanovich.

Williams, Maxine, and Pamela Newman. 1970. *Black Women's Liberation*. New York: Pathfinder Press.

# CHAPTER 5

# Asian and Pacific Islander Women

In a sometimes inhumane and complex world where technology, trade, and politics are international and technical and cultural literacy is important for a better quality of life, some people get lost and severely distorted. This became very clear when I began the research for this chapter on Asian and Pacific Island women. I first purchased a new computer and hooked up to the Internet. In my naïvete I searched the topic "Asian women." Much to my resentment, the results rendered a variety of sex Web sites from various countries. The same happened to me when I typed in "Latinas" and "black women," but to a lesser extent. I learned that one has to be more specific and type in "U.S. Asian American women, social issues," and that there was a consequence to being technically and social illiterate because I came to understand that once I visited those sex sites they continued to send me e-mail. To this very day I receive two or three e-mails every day selling sex. These sites market women to men in a huge trade that is international. In the United States many feel the sting of this international trade among immigrant women who are stereotyped as stupid, poverty bitten, and hungry to be in America.

## IMMIGRATION

Most U.S. citizens cannot see that Asian and other women can improve society and contribute to world peace. Few have taken advantage of this free cultural education to learn diverse languages, or to obtain multicultural contact and behavior. After the September 11 incident and the war declared upon the Taliban, it became more evident that the world needs peace. After September 11 we need to know more about the diverse citizens of the world, not only because it is the moral or profitable thing to do, but because our lives depend on it.

More than one of every three foreign-born persons in the United States is a naturalized citizen, and Asians number very high among them (U.S. Bureau of the Census 2001). They, like other foreign born, live in family households that are larger than those of (native born) in the United States. Of the family households with five or more people in them, Asians ranked relatively low, with 22.2 percent. Latin and Central Americans had the highest number of households with five or more people (35.1 percent and 42.1 percent, respectively).

More foreign born in the United States are in the thirty-year-old category. Females and males born in the United States are about equal. The highest percentages of foreign born are between the ages of four and nineteen, and between thirty-five and forty-four, however the younger the population is the larger it is, except for the twenty to thirty age category. Educational attainment among foreign born varies by region of birth. The highest percentages of high school graduates were found among those born in Asian countries (U.S. Bureau of the Census 2000a) (see Table 5.1).

Foreign-born residents earn less than those who are native born. Unemployment rates were similar between foreign-born men and women at 4.4 percent, but unemployment rates differed between foreign-born men and women

**Table 5.1**
**Percentage of Population Twenty-Five Years and Over with at Least a High School Education by Nativity and World Region of Birth**

*Source*: U.S. Bureau of the Census 2000. "U.S. Foreign Born by Country of Origin." Washington, D.C.: U.S. Government Printing Office.

by 5.5 percent and among native women at 4.3 percent. However, the unemployment rates were not statistically different between native women and native or foreign-born men, or between foreign-born women and foreign-born men (U.S. Bureau of the Census 2000b).

Immigration is but one variable affecting Asian women's lives, but even native-born Asians are stereotyped as immigrants. The women are considered to have immigrated to the United States for sexually linked reasons, and are suspected of prostitution. On the contrary, they are much more than this. An overview of their origins and social conditions reveals a group of diverse women who contribute to the richness of U.S. society by providing alternative approaches to problem solving, artm and healing (see Table 5.2).

Pacific Island and Asian populations are considered together for U.S. census collection and analysis purposes. This group, along with American Indians, is probably the least understood of America's residents. This misunderstanding challenges other Americans' conception of what constitutes the United States. Asian and Pacific Islander populations have a highly diverse history and social, religious, and political consciousness; and U.S. citizens are often confused by the differences. If the United States could overcome the hate instilled in its population by the political characteristics of war, it could confront and embrace the complexities and thus grow to be contributing global citizens.

In fact, with some concentration on eliminating social barriers, the United States could be highly equipped to enter into global citizenship. If we only concentrate on statistical data on Asian and Pacific Island people, we get a quick global perspective. Generally, the label "Asian and Pacific Islanders"

**Table 5.2**
**Asian Subgroup Populations in the**
**United States, 1990–2000**

*Source*: Asian American Federation Census Information Center, Based on U.S. Bureau of the Census, Census 2000.

refers to Chinese, Filipinos, Japanese, Asian Indians, Koreans, Vietnamese, Hawaiians, Samoans, and Guamanians. Census 2000 Current Population Survey reports that over half of the 7.2 million Asian and Pacific Islanders were females who live in the West. Asian females had a median age of thirty-one, compared with twenty-nine for Asian males (see Table 5.3).

Not only were the women older, but they had lower high school graduation rates than the men (74% versus 82%). Pacific Islander women and men, however, had very similar rates of high school graduation (75% and 77%, respectively), but the female rate was still lower. Less than 6 percent of Tongans, Cambodians, Laotians, and Hmongs have completed college; the high school graduation rate for Hmongs is only 31 percent (AsiaPacific.com 2000). Statistics for women in this group were not available in January 2002.

Sixty percent of Asian women and 63 percent of Pacific Islander women were in the labor force and worked outside the home (U.S. Bureau of the Census 2001). Of all U.S. women, only 57 percent participated in the labor force. Asian women maintained 12 percent of Asian households with no husband present. This was lower than the 19 percent of Pacific Islander single-parent households. When compared to white women, over three-fourths of white women have a high school degree and 18 percent have a bachelor's degree or higher. Fifty-six percent of white women participate in the labor force, and about 14 percent of white households are headed by women.

Asian and Pacific Island female median age is higher than that for white women. Asian women have higher labor market participation rates, while they maintain the least number of households with no male present. Clearly there are social factors that account for the differences. Among these are the commitment to work and to family.

**Table 5.3**
**Total U.S. Asian and Pacific Islander**
**Resident Population Estimate by**
**Percentage and Gender**

*Source*: Population Estimates Program, Population Division, U.S. Bureau of the Census, Washington, D.C. (Internet release date January 2, 2001).

*Note*: Projection to November 1, 2000. Numbers in thousands.

It has been my experience that very often the feminist movement is linked to higher family disruption and there is the myth that there is no such movement in the Asian and Pacific Island communities. I believe that some of the factors accounting for this myth includes the Asian female's need to address racial discrimination against her people and the fact that women have always been held in low esteem in Asian culture. The same low value for women is not traditional among Pacific Island women, but it has become more so as Islanders have interacted with Americans (Trask 1993). Added to this is the fact that the majority of women of color did not participate in the white women's movement of the 1960s, but chose instead to address women's concerns within the confines of their racial and ethnic groups. Contrary to the popular belief that Pacific Islander and Asian women are "old fashioned" and will not "speak up for rights," these women have participated in addressing the bilingual needs of their children by demanding bilingual education in the United States for at least the past thirty years.

I have established that the United States was not originally a nation of immigrants. Rates of immigration have varied substantially over periods of our history, as have the countries and cultures from which these immigrants originate. Until September 11 the United States experienced a period of high immigration. Immigrant children are of particular interest. The Public Information Office of the U.S. Bureau of the Census notes that the percentage of America's children and youth who are foreign born has been increasing steadily over the last several decades (2001).

Immigrant children may have special needs that can be addressed through the educational system. The percentage of children who are foreign born varies substantially by racial and ethnic background (U.S. Bureau of the Census 2001). In 1980 less than 2 percent of whites, blacks, and Native Americans were foreign born, compared to 40 percent of Asians and 14 percent of Hispanics. By 1990 the percentage of foreign-born Asian children had declined from 40 to 33.2 percent, while the percentage of foreign-born Hispanic children increased to almost 16 percent (U.S. Bureau of the Census 2000d).

Asian women have also been highly vocal on voting rights, immigration policy, and in addressing the injustices of the racism involved in American Japanese incarceration during World War II. Pacific Islander and Asian women have fervently defended themselves against sexism and demanded cultural sovereignty for indigenous people, and there is nothing old fashioned about it. What is old fashioned is the stereotype of Asian females as mail-order brides and prostitutes, and the wartime resentment toward them as "war brides."

## GLOBAL SEX TRADE

Although American wars fought by men in other countries have produced stories of sex for sale, let us not deceive ourselves into believing that Asian women are the only women subject to the sex trade. Nor should we believe they have much control over what happens to them. They do not. They and thousands of other women all over the world are involved in the male-dominated sex trade, and American men participate in it all the time. From my interviews with women and men who participate in it and live in the United States, I have learned that it works well for both males and females, at least on the surface.

According to my preliminary findings the more gentle process is that a woman writes to an American man and tells a friend that she has a friend who would like to know a man who is interested in marriage. Eventually the man writes to her and she writes back. They exchange pictures and ask one another several questions. Almost immediately the male will ask the female what kind of sex she is willing to engage in. I have only interviewed seven women, but they have revealed that some of the letters are graphic, and some are down-right nasty. The female chooses to continue the correspondence or not. If she continues, he generally tells her he wants to meet her. Eventually he goes to her country, they meet, arrange a marriage contract with the head of the household, and he brings her home to the United States as his wife. The Filipino women I have interviewed tell me they must first be married before they can leave their country.

I have also interviewed men who have obtained Filipino wives. Another way for females and males to meet is that certain men have "books" with pictures and a few details about the women and they market their information to men in this country. If a woman is "lucky" she gets a husband who does not beat her. Most of them work hard. They have babies, work outside the home, inside their own homes, and in the homes of the male's elder parents. She generally provides the unpaid services of a housekeeper and earns money that her socially incompetent husband often cannot. Usually her income is necessary to increase his status, which unfortunately is measured in the United States by how much one earns.

All of my subjects are white men who have written to and met more than one female. Two out of the four men for this interview have been married more than once to Filipino women. I understand that most of them are many years older than the imported female. Most of the men have married at least once, often to white women or other women of color. When I ask them why they chose to acquire a wife the way they did they answer that "white women want too much." When this is explored further they tend to not want to talk about it. Those who have talked to me say that women from other countries "turn them on" or that they wanted a wife who did not complain so much. I have heard Chicano men tease their American-born Chicano wives with the threat of replacing them with a good, quiet Mexican woman who can cook and grovel at his feet.

This kinder, more gentle form of the sex trade plays on human shortcomings and social injustices; namely, sexism, racism, and money. When it is less kind, women are stereotyped as loyal like dogs, even under conditions of stark poverty. There are advertisments on the Internet and other publications that target unhappy, lonely, and usually unattractive men who do not like their women too smart.

I have found that it is not that women involved in the sex trade are stupid. Often they are poor and come from violent situations and are sold, kidnapped, or tricked by male members of their families. Women are purchased and traded like chattel. They are trafficked within nations and across international borders to be cast into forced marriage and prostitution; girls are compelled into child pornography. The consequences to the women and girls are terrifying, often causing lifetime physical and psychological trauma. No documented opinions exist about the spiritual damage they incur, but it is not difficult to imagine.

Discussions at the Fourth World Women's Conference in Beijing, China, in 1995 revealed that because conditions in underdeveloped countries render so many women destitute, these women often sacrifice themselves for the family and or for their own betterment. In some cases females have paid a fee to participate. Sometimes entire families invest and expect a return on their commercial venture. Once she is married, she has made a commitment to do whatever it takes to get out of any potentially bad situations to empower her family by at least providing one less mouth to feed. Rarely is there everlasting love. These women simply adjust to what they get, often sending money home to support the family.

Feminists worldwide note that little attention is paid to the fact that many women have plans for their lives and that they sometimes do not include marriage. Some of them want education or better jobs. They are promised schooling and job training, but rarely do they receive it. Some of these women are forced to become addicted to drugs and are marketed as prostitutes.

As for other immigrant women the adjustment to the United States is difficult. Foremost among their complaints is that they are lonely. If they are lucky, they get to see their families every six years, or other female members of the family are brought to the United States.

The males I have encountered appear more contented. They sometimes complain that the "book" lied. There are claims that the "ladies" offering themselves to the golden prison of mixed marriages are from well-educated, outstanding, loving families. It is true that the family in the country of origin treats the white man well; they have to, he is going to support them. If, indeed, the white male bonds with the family from which he has isolated his wife, it is because he is a socially disconnected male who has to disguise his shortcomings by fulfilling his promises. The truth is that most women come from poor families and lie about education and social economic status in order to catch a man who will take them away from poverty.

Men complain because they get a private thrill out of fulfilling their fantasy of having women who are ready to engage in any form of sex, thinks they are wonderful, and work like beasts to meet any other need that arises. They do not consider themselves macho dogs that do not control their sexual energies and engage in relationships with sophisticated women who are their equal. They do not see themselves as emotionally and physically abusive and expanding the racist–sexist stereotype of foreign women. Contrary to popular belief, most of these women do not cherish the idea of leaving their country, and they aware that poverty and patriarchy forces them to sell out to the highest bidder. They spend days, months, even years crying for family and friends in the sexist–racist foreign culture of the United States.

Specifics of the sex trade were addressed in 2002 (Tessier 2002) as Pakistan and India grappled with war and terrorism. The nations joined five of their South Asian neighbors in signing a groundbreaking U.N. agreement meant to combat commercial sexual exploitation of women and children, mostly girls. "No civilized society can afford to ignore the welfare of its women and children," said Pervez Musharraf, Pakistan's military ruler and president (Tessier 2002). The pact defines trafficking in women and children as a violation of human rights. The countries involved in the agreement are called upon to pass criminal penalties against abusers, to take steps that promote children's well being, and to protect them from abuse, including educating them about their sexual vulnerability and strategies for self-protection.

Women and children are sold along the same trade routes traveled by drugs and weapons, especially in Southeastern Europe, and involve the same underground criminal mechanisms. In Asia the sex trade is one aspect of an enormous informal labor market that often includes debt bondage. In India, Pakistan, Myanmar, Nepal, and Thailand, for example, girls often are obligated to work as prostitutes to pay off money loaned to their parents or guardians. The girls are paid little money and most of their earnings must be used to pay their bosses for their food, housing, and transportation.

Precise statistics on the number of children captured by sex traders are difficult to obtain because sex trafficking is illegal and illicit; plus, what punishment exists is not harsh or even implemented. Where data exists, UNICEF (2002) informs that definitions vary. Some estimates include street children who may sell sex if someone makes an offer; others include children working virtually as slaves in brothels or massage parlors.

Selling sex does not discriminate by country. The Senate Foreign Relations Committee recently heard that up to 2 million women worldwide were sold or lured into becoming sex slaves, with 50,000 of them arriving in the United States annually. Officials told the committee that many of the women came from the Ukraine, Albania, the Philippines, Thailand, Mexico, and Nigeria. The sex trade draws girls and women to richer countries from poorer countries, such as Bangladesh, a nation that loses thousands of its children each year to sex traffickers. However, according to the Central Intelligence Agency, more than 40,000 children are smuggled yearly into the United States to work in the sex industry (Tessier 2002).

University of Pennsylvania researchers (Estes 2001) estimated 325,000 U.S. children age seventeen or younger are prostitutes, performers in pornographic videos, or have otherwise fallen victim to commercial sexual exploitation. Their three-year, $400,000 study was based on research in seventeen cities and included interviews with 200 child victims, most already in the legal system, and more than 800 state, federal, and local officials. University experts on juvenile law say it is the deepest investigation yet into the extent of the problem.

There are 72 million children age seventeen or younger in the United States. Richard Estes, a professor of social work at the University of Pennsylvania and one of the researchers for the Penn study, maintains the largest group of children involved in the American sex trade, about 122,000, is made up of children who have run away from home and turned to prostitution or pornography to get money for food or drugs. The second-largest group, about 73,000, is made up of children who live at home and are used by family or friends in exchange for money, food, drugs, or other enticements. The third-largest group, about 52,000, is made up of "throwaway" children who have been abandoned by parents or guardians and turned to the sex trade to survive. About 90 percent of the children are born in the United States.

Because the payoff for profiteers is enormous, the sex trade thrives in both urban and rural settings. Within the borders of poor countries, the sex trade provides a huge transfer of wealth to the poorest villages. In Thailand, for example, UNICEF (2002) estimates women working in the sex trade in cities send close to $300 million each year to rural areas.

The underlying causes of commercial sexual exploitation of children include poverty, gender discrimination, war, organized crime, globalization, greed, traditions and beliefs, family dysfunction, and the drug trade. UNICEF and human rights groups have documented the special threats of sexual exploitation spawned by war and armed conflict. Desperation often compels women and children to offer sex in exchange for food, shelter, vital documents, or safe passage through war zones. Refugees are especially vulnerable to demands for sex by camp officials, border guards, police officers, and military personnel.

According to UNICEF (2002), about 80 percent of the world's 35 million internally displaced people are women and children. In war, women are abducted, traded, raped, and forced to do household chores. Many foster relationships with men in order to escape terrorism. Generally, they come to the United States and encounter ridicule and intolerance (UNICEF 2002).

## MODEL MINORITIES

Very few women rise to the highest rung of the social economic ladder, especially Pacific Islander women. Pacific Islanders have much Asian influence and are indigenous to the islands. Most other Asian presence in the United States began as an immigrant experience, but now thousands are U.S. born. It is true that some chose to come to this country because of political and economic hardship in their own. However, some did not immigrate as freely as others did. Some are refugees, and especially Pacific Islanders consider themselves colonized and imposed upon by U.S. politics. Thus, some of them are not as happy with their U.S. historical experience. This displeasure is rooted in racism and sexism experienced in the United States, but many also miss their countries of origin and their cultural contexts. In addition, even though some have prospered in the United States, many are poor.

Advocates frequently complain that Asians are stereotyped as the "model minority." They have broken the boundaries of the immigrant experience and have experienced drastic upward mobility. This myth perpetuates the general impression that all Asian Americans are quiet manipulators, clever, prosperous, and well educated. It also negates the high rate of poverty, illness, incarceration, and lack of political power (South Asian Women for Action 2002). The myth has fostered distrust of Asians, and has limited their cultural integration into the dominant society. It has also hampered social intervention programs targeting disadvantaged women of this population. The model-minority myth masks the existence of enduring barriers and other problems that women encounter as they live in their own varied cultures within the dominant society.

Of primary concern for Pacific Islander and Asian women advocates is the intimate issue of birth control and women's fertility. Asian women, and perhaps men, appear to have more birth control than other women of color do. At the end of the last decade, whites had an average of 1.8 births per woman, compared with 1.9 births among Asian Americans, 2.0 births among Native Americans, 2.2 births among blacks, and 3.0 births among Hispanics.

As of February 1, 1998, the U.S. Bureau of the Census estimated there were 10.2 million Asians and Pacific Islanders, and most live in Hawaii and California. The population is young, more than six years younger than the median age for the non-Hispanic white population. Census 2000 indicated that Pacific Islander and Asian populations are characterized by rapid growth. The Asian and Pacific Islander population in the United States was estimated at 8.8 million, up from 7.3 million in 1990. Since the last census in 1990, the Asian and Pacific Islander population has grown at a rate of about 4.5 percent per year. Immigration to the United States accounted for much of the growth (about 86 percent). The rest was due to natural increase (births minus deaths). At the beginning of this century the combined population surpassed 34 million and represent about 10 percent of the total U.S. population (U.S. Bureau of the Census 2001). This, combined with the similar statistics for Latinos, changes the color of the nation. In fact, by the year 2025 one in four U.S. women will be Hispanic, American Indian, Asian, or Pacific Islander (Associated Press 2001).

When comparing data for the Asian and Pacific Islander population for previous years, it should be noted that they have traditionally been undercounted. Under- and overcounting people of color and different interpretations of the data affect not only their true number, but also the provision of social programs and the development and implementation of public policy. As with Native Americans, there is controversy about being counted and not being counted by the U.S. census. There are Pacific Islanders who feel the population should cooperate with government officials, and cite social programs as a benefit. Those who advocate not being counted feel that less government intervention in their lives is better (South Asian Women for Action 2002).

Patricia Barela, community partnership specialist for Census 2000 (part of the Decennial 2000) informed me that Native Americans were the most severely undercounted population in the United States. An intense campaign to get this population to respond was underway in 2000; response was slow and interpreted as resistance to increased government intervention and the perceived security of fixed amounts of money already disbursed to indigenous people.

Asians and Pacific Islanders vary on these topics because they are not a heterogeneous group. They differ in indigenous languages, cultures, and length of immigration. Not only were Pacific Islanders born on the islands, but several Asian groups, such as Chinese and Japanese, have been in the United States for generations and are counted among the native born.

Asians and Pacific Islanders are more likely than non-Hispanic whites to reside in metropolitan areas (U.S. Bureau of the Census 2001). Similar proportions of both populations reside in the suburbs of metropolitan areas. The proportion of Asians and Pacific Islanders living in central cities was almost twice that of non-Hispanic whites. They have toiled to rent and then own homes. More than 70 percent of non-Hispanic white households were homeowners. Asians and Pacific Islanders residing in central cities were less likely to be homeowners (41%) than renters (57%). In contrast, Asians and Pacific Islanders living outside central cities had a higher proportion of homeowners (61%) than renters (38%). This leads one to infer that a move into the city results in lower resources. Non-Hispanic white householders tend to be more owners than renters, regardless of whether they lived inside or outside central cities.

During the last census count, one-third of the doctorates were awarded to Asians in engineering and one-quarter were conferred in the physical sciences: astronomy, physics, chemistry, and mathematics (U.S. Bureau of the Census 2001). These data often promote jealousy among different ethnic and racial groups in the United States. It feeds the stereotypes and lumps Asians into one large pile with little attention to its diversity.

Just prior to Census 2000 the nation's total foreign-born population numbered 25.8 million, of which 24 percent were Asians and Pacific Islanders. Immigration rates varied, from 31 percent for Hmongs to 88 percent for Japanese. Hmongs are among the most recent Asian immigrant groups. Among Asians are counted Tongans, Cambodians, Laotians, and Hmongs, all relatively small populations. These smaller numbers may have to do with the circumstances under which Vietnamese were introduced to the United States.

Most of them came as a consequence of war. April 2000 marked the twenty-fifth anniversary of the end of the U.S. war in Vietnam. Not many communities observed that on April 5, 1975, 2,000 orphans were airlifted and flown from their native country. Of these children, 409 were babies and 300 were under the age of one year (Martin 2002). Some families, mostly men, assisted the United States during the war with Vietnam and were airlifted on April 29, 1975, in the largest evacuation of a population during wartime. According to data compiled by the United Nations, approximately 1 million Vietnamese people fled Vietnam and capture by the North Vietnamese and made it to refugee camps between 1975 and 1982 (CNN 1998). Many Amerasian children were left behind to suffer the abandonment and discrimination of being born during wartime from an American father and a Vietnamese woman. Some of these babies were airlifted to the United States as the result of work done by American women stationed in Vietnam (Martin 2002). Let us not forget that American women served in Vietnam during the war, and that they served during the Gulf War and the war with Afghanistan. As we move toward the feminization of racism and global harmony, we must ask what good is war, and what role do women have in it?

The U.S. Bureau of the Census (2000a) estimates 2 million Vietnamese people live in America. The largest number, between 200,000 and 300,000, live in Santa Ana, California. In contrast, roughly 20,000 Vietnamese people live in San Antonio and Austin combined. Most immigrants were brought to the United States as highly impoverished refugees.

The U.S. Bureau of the Census Public Information Office (1999b) profiled the nation's racial and ethnic minority population. Data collected in the March 2000 Current Population Survey (CPS) should not be confused with Census 2000 results (U.S. Bureau of the Census 2000a). The twenty-one tables, entitled "Asian and Pacific Islander Population in the United States: March 2000 (Update)," provide data on age, marital status, family type and size, education, labor-force participation and employment status, occupation, income and earnings, poverty, and tenure (owner or renter).

In March 2000, the CPS estimated that 80 percent of Asian and Pacific Islander family households were maintained by married couples, and 42 percent of these households had incomes of $75,000 or more. In addition, 44 percent of Asian and Pacific Islanders age twenty-five and over had a bachelor's degree or higher, and 86 percent had at least a high school diploma in 2000. In 1999 Asians and Pacific Islanders had a record-low poverty rate of 10.7 percent. There were 2.5 million Asian and Pacific Islander families; 13 percent were maintained by women with no spouse present and 7 percent by men with no spouse present.

Asian and Pacific Islander families tend to be relatively large. For example, 23 percent of Asian and Pacific Islander married-couple families had five or more members. Fifty-three percent of Asian and Pacific Islander households owned their homes. The highest proportions of Asian and Pacific Islander women worked predominantly in executive (about 18%), professional (20%), and administrative support (including clerical) jobs (23%).

Toward the end of the 1990s, census data indicate the proportions of Asian and Pacific Islander men and women in most occupations was similar, except in administrative support, farming, precision production, and transportation. There were more (22.5%) Asian and Pacific Islander females in administrative support than there were men (8.5%). Asian and Pacific Islander women also have slightly higher rates than men in executive administrative and managerial work (17.5% compared to 16.3%), and in the service category (11%), except in private household employment. College-educated Asian and Pacific Islander men were twice as likely as comparable non-Hispanic white men to work in technical (7% and 3%, respectively) and administrative-support occupations (10% and 4%, respectively). Pacific Islander and Asian women had a rate of 4.5 percent of working women in the technical and related support fields.

Similar proportions of college-educated Asian and Pacific Islander and non-Hispanic white women twenty-five years old and over were employed in executive, technical, and sales occupations. A higher percentage of college-educated non-Hispanic white women (49%) worked in professional occupations. The proportion of college-educated Asian and Pacific Islander women who worked in administrative jobs (20%) was about twice that of comparable non-Hispanic white women (11%), and the proportion who worked in service occupations was three times higher (6% and 2%, respectively). It appears that Asian and Pacific Islander women do well in administrative positions, but they are still more highly concentrated in the lowest paying positions.

The latest U.S. Bureau of the Census (2001) data on Asian Americans and Pacific Islanders reveals that 10.4 million Asian Americans and Pacific Islanders live in the United States and associated Pacific Island jurisdictions (colonies). These areas comprise approximately 4 percent of the total U.S. population. Asian and Pacific Islanders are the fastest growing racial or ethnic group in the United States. They are expected to reach 10 percent of the population by the year 2050.

A total of 40 percent of the combined Asian and Pacific Islander population do not speak English fluently, and there are more than thirty ethnic Asian groups (Asian Women in Business 2002). Even though the poverty rate of these families (14%) is higher than that of non-Hispanic white families (8%), the myth that Asian Americans and Pacific Islanders are the model minority persists. This implies that they have few health or social problems. However, emerging data on the population demonstrates significant disparities and barriers to health care and social service access; for example, the group lacks health insurance at a higher rate than the total U.S. population. Korean Americans are the most likely racial or ethnic group to be uninsured. An estimated 2 million Pacific Islanders and Asians are uninsured.

The citizenry suffer disproportionately high rates of hepatitis B, diabetes, cancer, and tuberculosis. Infant mortality rates in the U.S.–associated Pacific Island jurisdictions exceed the U.S. rate, in some cases by more than twice as much (2000). In fact, 40 percent of all infant mortality rates are among people of color (National Center for Health Statistics 2002).

## WOMEN AND THE CONSEQUENCE OF WAR

Asians remain a mystery to some U.S. citizens. Many feel they know them for their determination to work to get ahead, sometimes twenty hours a day. The Koreans are often victimized for attempts at building, refurbishing first a single building, then a whole block, and ultimately, as in the case of Los Angeles's Koreatown, an entire neighborhood. In my travels to lecture around the country, I have found that their presence is felt not only in Los Angeles, but also in New York, Chicago, El Paso, Philadelphia, and to varying degrees in other cities across the United States. Their physical presence is in the form of grocery and other shop owners and operators. In New York they are well known for their green groceries, which helps fill the consumer demand for healthy and natural food. Korean American industriousness irks some citizens, who perceive the newcomers as parasites who return nothing to the community. This resentment hardens into racism and Korean Americans are victimized by hostile citizens.

Koreans have benefited from the cultural and scientific advances made by China and Japan, but have also suffered repeated military attacks from both (MacDonald and Clark 1996). From them they have inherited influences on their language, religion, architecture, costume, and music, especially from the Chinese. Koreans adopted the Chinese language in government documents and in the sacred texts of Buddhism, a religion that came to Korea in the sixth century.

Western involvement in Korea is rooted in the European nations' efforts to parcel out bits of China to themselves. Korea had long been isolated from contact with any country but China, and she shied away from dealing with Westerners. It closed its doors to non-Chinese foreigners in 1866 and guarded itself from the United States after having watched it pressure Japan into a trade agreement in 1854. After much military maneuvering and violence, the Koreans reluctantly entered into trade with the United States. Although Korean rulers disdained foreign influences, some subjects were attracted to some aspects of Western culture, especially its freedom of religion. Christian missionaries, especially Catholic missionaries, converted thousands to Christianity (MacDonald and Clark 1996). Christians introduced the concept of democracy, as well as Methodism and Presbyterianism via mission schools. Japanese troops invaded and occupied the peninsula after an 1895 victory in their war with China. Students hated the foreign domination. The occupying forces despised the American missionaries, but carefully refrained from harassing citizens. Korean interest in U.S. democracy grew, and Japanese persecution grew against the Koreans. When the Japanese sided with the Nazi Germans during World War II, Koreans were ordered to toil in munitions plants and airplane factories. Many Koreans were shipped to Japanese coal mines, and decided that their hope of liberation lay with the allied forces that won World War II, which resulted in a divided, North and South, Korea.

Koreans have experienced anti-Asian behavior, gang violence, and discriminatory legislation. For example, in 1906, Korean American children were subjected, with those of Japanese and Chinese heritage, to a San Francisco ruling that Asian students could not attend public schools in white districts. Koreans remained in the United States because returning to their country of origin would have meant worse hardship. Japanese cruelty toward the native population in Korea equaled that of any occupying force. Japanese men stole Korea's vital rice crop, forced its people into heavy labor, and insisted that they adopt Japanese surnames.

Korea endured many conflicts because of the perception of other countries of it as a prize whose possession meant supremacy in the Pacific. Japanese rule ended with the close of World War II. Then, the "Land of Morning Calm" became the victim of yet another aggressor power struggle between the United States and the Soviet Union, who divided the country at the 38th parallel into North and South occupations. The northern half of the country was controlled by the Soviet Union and called the Democratic People's Republic of Korea. Beneath the 38th parallel lies the Republic of Korea. Koreans have immigrated to the land of freedom, liberty, and security to escape persecution. Today the offspring of original immigrants outnumber new arrivals (Women's Enews Inc. 2002).

This history, however, has not stopped some Korean and other Asian women from advancing in U.S. society. Asian women are active in their homes, in business, in the humanities, and in the social and physical sciences, and have made great contributions to the United States. The following are some examples: Mary Kawena Pukui was a Hawaiian author, translator, and editor who lived between 1895 and 1986; Yoshiko Uchida was a Japanese children's book author; and Anna May Wong was a Chinese actress who died in 1961. More contemporary women include Chinese Chien Shiung Wu, a nuclear physicist, and authors Bette Bao Lord, Maxine Hong Kingston, and Jade Snow Wong. Jade Snow Wong is also known for her work as a ceramist. Perhaps the best know Chinese female is Connie Chung, a television news anchor and reporter. Patsy Takemto Mink is a Hawaiian politician, and Wendy Lee Gramm is an economist. Dorothy Cordova is an archivist and community leader in the Filipino community and June Kuramoto is a musician of Japanese ancestry (Sinnott 1993).

There are many more gifted women. Each story is fascinating and an inspiration for research and business students, musicians, writers, artists, labor leaders, poets, and painters. Some of these women are young. For example, award-winning novelist Amy Tan, author of *The Kitchen God's Wife* (1991), based on her mother's response to Amy asking her to tell her about living in Shanghai, China, during World War II, was born in 1952. In addition, Japanese violinist Midori was born in 1971. The youthful genius has sold out concerts in New York's Carnegie Hall. Perhaps the most important contribution of all to this writer is that of Maya Ying Lin (Chinese), who taught the world about war. At the age of twenty-one the university senior entered a national contest to design a monument to be erected in Washington, D.C., honoring the veterans of the Vietnam War. She designed a highly polished black granite, v-shaped wall that not only won the contest, but which allows people to mourn, to deal with the anger and pain associated with the war, and to begin to heal. Many U.S. citizens resented that an Asian female's design was selected.

As a university professor I have taught and counseled hundreds of Asian students. The Vietnamese are often thought of with suspicion: They are misunderstood as rude, bad smelling, thin people with peculiar names who come from strange places with equally unusual names and practice peculiar relations. The Vietnamese students are called "gooks," a racist term used during a war that was never declared a war. They are stereotyped as impoverished, but with intense motivation to produce high economic and educational achievers at the cost of U.S. tax dollars. This contention is even held by a generation that was not born in the 1980s, when over a million people fled from Vietnam after the United States could not win the war being fought there. Many Vietnamese who helped the United States during that war were brought to this country because it was feared what would happen to them under Communist rule (McGuire 1991). They became refugees or they disappeared completely. Some were airlifted to the United States. Some came in boats and were called "boat people." Many were shipwrecked, drowned, or rescued by passing boats. If discovered by the Communist government, they were sent back to Vietnam. The most unfortunate refugees were pirated, robbed, beaten, kidnapped, sold as slaves, or even tossed overboard.

According to my Vietnamese students in the early 1980s, Vietnamese integration into the United States was not easy. They could not get food like that found in Vietnam, and they were forced to change their diets. Americans complained of the odor created by rice and fish sauce, a staple in their diet. Many complained that the immigrants were given welfare to assist them in escaping their lack of income. But slowly the large families went to work and school and tried to abandon their tonal language to learn English. Since the Vietnamese alphabet has no f, j, w, or z, the immigrants mispronounced many words and were ridiculed.

When Vietnamese women first came to the United States they wore garments open at the sides below the waist. These were worn over loose trousers, whose style was the same for men. Chopsticks were used at home, and they had to get accustomed to silverware and learn American democracy, a system unlike Communism, in which the public theoretically controls the production and distribution of all goods and services. With them they brought a tradition of poetry, calligraphy, and a calendar consisting of the lunar month, the time between one full moon and the next full moon, which is approximately twenty-nine and one-half days. Most of these women were traumatized. Nancy Webster (2001), a thirty-year-old career female, remembers having flashbacks of bombs exploding as a newly relocated child in the United States. She experienced this from the age of four to thirteen.

The Americanization experience of female refugees from Vietnam is slowly being documented. In Vietnam the parents arranged most marriages when their children were very young. In the United States women want to choose their husbands. In Vietnam families lived in close proximity to one another, but in the United States many women are choosing to live far from their families, and to visit infrequently (Sinnott 1993). Some choose to go to college. Others marry white men, an act generally disliked by most families. These women give birth to "mixed" children, who sometimes do not fit comfortably in white society and are uncomfortable in Vietnamese communities. Even these women have triumphed. Not only have they survived war and relocation; some have healed from the ravages of war and they, themselves, are viable contributions to the country. Unfortunately, many are still trying to heal.

The Vietnamese are from Southeast Asia, an area consisting of Vietnam, Kampuchea (Cambodia), Myanmar (Burma), Indonesia, Malaysia, the Philippines, Singapore, Thailand, and Laos. Although the Vietnamese were forced to flee their country under fear of death, the Chinese and Japanese immigrated a bit more freely, primarily opting for a higher standard of living. Many Asian women immigrated into the United States as wives of military men.

It appears that people who enter the United States of their own free will achieve more than those who were introduced as a consequence of war, as slaves, or as refugees. One sees this more clearly when one analyzes the situation of indigenous people compared to their conquerors. Pacific Islanders are poorer, and Asians have more resources than African Americans, Native Americans, and Chicanos. This is important because it answers various questions about why some immigrants experience more upward mobility than others. Europeans have assimilated into the general population far better than Native Americans, Mexican Americans, and African Americans. The answer is linked to the fact that immigrants know they will have to change and give up some cultural aspects of themselves in order to achieve their reason for coming to this country. Those colonized and brought against their will resist incorporation into the new society for extended periods of time. In addition, with white skin comes more privilege.

Southeast Asia is a tropical region of more than half the size of the U.S. mainland. Its population is nearly 442 million (McGuire 1991). It is made up of two long peninsulas that jut to the south from China and India, plus many islands further south and east. The Malay Peninsula contains parts of Burma (now Myanmar), Thailand (formerly called Siam), Malaysia, and the city-state of Singapore. The island countries include Indonesia, another part of Malaysia, Brunei, and the Philippines. The Indochina Peninsula contains Vietnam, Laos, Cambodia, and part of Thailand. Only Thailand has kept its independence through the years. All other countries were conquered by foreign countries: Burma and Malaysia by the British; Indonesia by the Dutch; the Philippines by the Spanish and the Americans; and Vietnam, Laos, and Cambodia by the French.

When I taught at Metropolitan State College in Denver, Colorado, many students and local residents imagined Vietnamese women preparing and eating fish, frogs, dogs, bloody chicken, and rice. I witnessed this. I also saw and heard it in Lowell, Massachusetts, Los Angeles, California, and San Antonio, Texas. I heard many say that in their minds these women had a past of driving motor scooters, working in the fields, taking their shoes off before entering the house, using outdoor toilets, smoking, and prostitution. When the women arrived in the United States they suffered from diarrhea. The food and water were strange. Many needed medical attention, and there were language problems. The women could not speak English. They spoke their own dialects and French. This was insulting to the Americans. When the women came to this country they left behind a life of keeping house, tending animals, sweeping streets, Buddhist pagodas, and a tradition of prayer and meditation, forgiving, and canceling debts. Their traditions included going out at night to socialize where there was much activity.

In 1965 American bombs began to fall upon the population in Vietnam. The French had colonized the country prior to this. It is at this time that Americans became introduced to the small thin people who were not to be trusted. They fought and lived in tunnels with very small entrances. Some hid and lived under the American encampments. Some set booby traps, caused the death of very young American men, and became the mothers of bastard Amerasian children. The war was confusing to Americans. They did not understand that there were North and South Vietnamese with a variety of loyalties. Thus, it was hard for them to tell the difference between the allies and the enemies.

Like women from Vietnam, Native American, Latina, and Asian and Pacific Islander women know the terrors of war. It is in their recent cultural memory. In a way, African American women also know war. They and other people of color are the survivors of a race war, and they often do not trust whites and members of other groups. Although some indigenous tribes accepted runaway slaves into their tribes, others had war experiences with the buffalo soldiers, the African American calvary men who protected white interests in the West.

Two of my colleagues and another acquaintance have traveled to Vietnam during the past five years. They report there are now museums on the war in Vietnam. Every weapon that was used during the war could be fired by both men and women. Today the war contributes to the tourist economy. Young men hock war memorabilia in the street. Some of it is fake, but the war was not. In Vietnam there are now thousands of young people fathered by U.S. soldiers. These children have not fit easily into Vietnamese society. Many have grown up in orphanages.

Until the mid-1940s, emperors and empresses ruled Vietnam. It was not until World War II that the temples, tombs, shrines to ancestors, and palaces where the monarchy lived could be visited. U.S. bombing nearly destroyed these places. Since stabilizing the society was imperative, restoring monuments was not a priority until more recently.

Women who came to the United States missed Vietnam, its flora and fauna, their traditional foods, relating to their families, attending cultural festivals, home parties, and the communal nature of washing clothes at the river. Until recently, they could not visit their homeland. In Lao Chi, near the Chinese border, there are border disputes. Until 1992 the border areas were closed to tourists. This made a journey across Asia impossible, but Vietnam is now open to tourism. In the north one can experience the shyness of women, who giggle when you ask them a question. Highland and hill tribes live their linguistically and culturally diverse lives in an area that reminds me of Machu Picchu in Peru, high and breathtaking in beauty. There are fifty ethnic groups. The Hmong number about 700,000 and some of them still wear large plaid wool scarves of bright colors. Some have never heard of Americans. Little girls in bright clothing wear earrings and necklaces and blouses with decorated collars. Both women and girls sew by hand and they are learning what tourists like. This is affecting their cultural production, much like the railroad and the tourists it brought to the southwestern part of the United States affected Pueblo Indian production. Indians stopped producing cultural items that they then sold to tourists. Instead, they produced for the tourist market, changing shapes, designs, and colors to meet tourists' tastes.

Even though some Vietnamese women feel isolated, not all women are isolated for too long a period. Some have organized and it is not uncommon to see a few of them as delegates for Asian and Pacific Islander women at women's conferences. This was especially true at the U.N. Fourth World Women's Conference in Beijing, China, in 1995. Asian countries were represented in varying proportions. The most important thing I learned there was that women have basic gender issues in common. The rest is racial and economic politics.

## ASIAN WOMEN'S HEALTH

The "model minority" myth has limited integration of Asians and Pacific Islanders into mainstream society. The lack of integration is most apparent in the low health levels experienced by the populations. There are public health intervention programs targeting Asians, but the myth of the model minority masks the barriers and problems that Asian American women encounter in accessing health care. Most Asian women do not perceive themselves to be at risk for health problems because most feel they are healthier than men are. Because women are hard working in spite of being ill, because of the high cost of medical care, and because women always place others before them, they are not encouraged to seek health care by others.

Poor or bad health robs individuals of the pursuit of happiness and harmony. However, today's women face serious health concerns, such as heart disease and cancer. Many diseases take unique forms and are specific to women. In 2002, heart disease was the leading cause of death for both women and men in the United States, but women were twice as likely to survive it. Men were two to three times more likely to die from lung cancer. The U.S. Department of Health and Human Services maintains that compared with rates for whites, coronary heart disease mortality was 40 percent lower for Asian Americans. Although cancer is the second leading cause of death among American women, for Asian and Pacific Islanders it is first. The National Center for Health estimates the average life expectancy for American women is seventy-nine years. In 1999, the Center for Disease Control and Prevention and the National Center for Health Statistics (NCHS) indicated that disparities in the health status of Americans remain widespread. These disparities are evidenced in mortality, morbidity, and the utilization of health service statistics. Women of color are not immune from the ailments that ravage the health-delivery system in the United States.

During the 1990s, death rates for Asian American women were lower than for white women in every age group. Homicide was the leading cause of death for young black females fifteen to twenty-four years old. During the same period, death rates for American Indians under forty-five substantially exceeded those for white Americans. High blood pressure, lupus, and HIV/AIDS disproportionately affect women of color. At the end of the last century, for females thirteen and over, the AIDS rate for black, non-Hispanic females was 2.4 times that for Hispanic females and 14 times that for white, non-Hispanic females. In 2002 the Hispanic female rate rivals the black female rate.

In a University of California study the prevalence of obesity is substantially higher for non-Hispanic black women (50%) and Mexican American women (48%) than for non-Hispanic white females (MEDTEP 2000). In the preventive and prenatal care category, only 60 percent of American Indian and black mothers receive early prenatal care. Among Hispanic mothers in the United States, only 59 to 65 percent of Mexican American, Central and South American, and Puerto Rican mothers receive prenatal care. Reasons for this are generally associated with poverty, but some of these women are more relaxed about childbirth. Asian ethnicity and national origin impact infants' birthweight. Researchers at the MEDTEP Research Center on Minority Populations at the University of California, San Francisco, analyzed the relationship between Asian ethnicity–national origin and the likelihood of low-birthweight infants among 50,044 Asian and 221,866 white women. They found that low birthweight rates among Chinese and Korean women ranged from 3.5 percent to 4.7 percent, well within the national goal of no more than 5 percent low-birthweight infants. On the other hand, low-birthweight rates among Cambodian, Filipino, Indian, Japanese, Laotian, and Thai women ranged from 5.3 percent to 8 percent, well above the goal. The low-birthweight rate for white women was about 4 percent. The relative risk of very low birthweight was significantly elevated among Filipino women relative to white women, although the absolute difference in incidence was only 0.3 percent. Asian Indian women were almost twice as likely to have moderately low-birthweight infants as white women.

Like other women, Asian and Pacific Islander women act as the primary caregivers for their families and communities. This has limited their time and energies to make their own individual well-being a priority. There is also the pervasive myth that Asian women are not at risk for breast cancer because they are small breasted. This untruth has been exacerbated by the fact that many demographers treat all Asian ethnic groups as if they were one group, thus hiding any variances between different groups. For example, according to the latest U.S. Census data (Asian Women in Business 2002), approximately 14 percent of U.S. Asian Americans lived in poverty, but when broken down by ethnic group, the rates ranged from 65 percent of Hmong living in poverty to less than 10 percent for Japanese Americans.

Women's health varies by ethnicity. In 1999 Asian women had the lowest rates of vaginal infections. Ethnic breakdowns for breast and cervical cancer incidence rates have become widely published only in the last few years. The range of breast and cervical cancer incidence shows varying high rates for women of color with regard to breast, cervical, uterine, ovary, lung, colon–rectum, and stomach cancer. According to the Asian American Cancer Society, the breast cancer incidence per 100,000 for some women of color in 1999 was as follows: African American 95.4, Chinese 55.0, Filipino 73.1, Hawaiian 105.6, Japanese 82.3, Korean 28.5, Vietnamese 37.5, Alaskan native 78.9, American Indian 111.8, Hispanic 16.2, and white 69.8. American Indian women have the highest incidence of breast cancer, but Vietnamese women have the highest incidence rate of cervical cancer (43 per 100,000). This is seven times the rate for Japanese women (5.8 per 100,000), and more than twice the rate for Hispanic women, which is the second highest for all racial and ethnic groups (16.2 per 100,000).

Even though breast cancer incidence and mortality rates are lower for Asian American women, the disease burden in this population is not inconsequential. The assumption that Asian American women are not at risk for these diseases contributes to diagnosis at stages with poorer prognosis. Not only are women more ill when they do receive medical attention, there are very few culturally sensitive service providers available. There are other barriers to providing care for Asian and other women of color. These barriers include accessing cancer screening services, financial burdens, lack of childcare, fear of breast cancer as a fatal disease, lack of familiarity with the screening process, and language differences.

Although breast cancer is rare among men, it is more deadly. The biggest risk factors for breast cancer are being female and getting older (Asian American Breast Cancer Society 1999). More than 75 percent of women who are diagnosed with breast cancer are age fifty and older. Most women (about 80%) who get breast cancer do not have a family history of the disease. Only 5 to 10 percent of all breast cancers are inherited.

AIDS is still a national problem. In 1991 the number of black, non-Hispanic females with AIDS was fourteen times the number of white, non-Hispanic females and 2.4 times the number of Hispanic females. Also, a national concern is hypertension, the most prevalent circulatory condition for women of all ages and races. Hay fever and chronic sinusitis were the most prevalent respiratory conditions for women in 1991. A smaller percentage of Hispanic women have high cholesterol than do black women or white women.

In the area of preventive care, cesarean delivery was the most common operative procedure for women in the United States. The number of cesarean deliveries rose from 4.5 percent in 1965 to 24.1 percent in 1986, and remained at about this level through the early 1990s. The Asian American Breast Cancer Society notes that fewer than 50 percent of women conduct breast self-examination twelve or more times a year. Only 50 percent of women have a pap smear and 53 percent report having had a breast examination by a health professional. In 2000, younger women were much more likely to have had a pap smear within the year than older women.

With regard to the use of health resources, women visit doctors more often than men. The greatest gender difference in utilization occur during the child-bearing years. For females and males, utilization steadily increases with age, and the gender difference declines with age. Most Asian American women do not visit the doctor regularly and are at a high risk for developing osteoporosis, especially during and after menopause (Minority Health Resource Center 2002). The disease is characterized by low bone mass, which makes bones susceptible to fracture. If not prevented or if left untreated, osteoporosis can progress painlessly until a bone breaks, typically in the hip, spine, or wrist. A hip fracture can limit mobility and lead to a loss of independence, while a vertebral fracture can result in loss of height and stooped posture. It is a disease that is preventable and treatable. Studies indicate that Asian Americans share many of the risk factors that apply to other women. It important to understand what osteoporosis is and what steps can be taken to prevent or treat it.

There are several factors that increase chances of developing osteoporosis. These include a thin, small-boned frame, previous fracture or family history of osteoporotic fracture, and estrogen deficiency resulting from early menopause (before age forty-five), either naturally or from surgical removal of the ovaries or as a result of prolonged amenorrhea (abnormal absence of menstruation) in younger women (National Institute of Health 2001a). Its onset may occur with advanced age, a diet low in calcium, cigarette smoking, excessive use of alcohol, and prolonged use of certain medications. African American women, Chicanas, and other Latinas are at a lower level of risk than Asian women are, but they are still at significant risk.

A number of facts highlight the risks that Asian American women face with regard to developing osteoporosis: Asian and white women have osteoporosis more often than black women due largely to differences in bone mass and density. The average calcium intake among Asian women has been observed to be about half that of other population groups. Calcium is essential for building and maintaining a healthy skeleton. Asian women generally have lower hip-fracture rates than white women, but the prevalence of vertebral fractures among Asians seems to be as high (herSource 2002). In recent decades there has been a sharp increase in hip-fracture incidence in some parts of the Far East. In fact, it is estimated that about half of the expected 6.3 million hip fractures worldwide in 2050 will occur in Asia.

Slender women have less bone mass than heavy or obese women and are therefore at greater risk for osteoporotic bone fractures (National Association of Women's Health Organizations 2002). Building strong bones before the age of thirty-five can prevent osteoporosis. A healthy lifestyle can be of critical importance for keeping bones strong. To help prevent osteoporosis, eat a balanced diet rich in calcium, exercise regularly (especially by engaging in weight-bearing activities), do not smoke, and limit alcohol intake. I recommend finding a doctor with a feminist orientation and talking to that doctor if a family history of osteoporosis exists or if women no longer have the protective benefit of estrogen due to natural or surgically induced menopause. Doctors may suggest that bone density be measured at menopause through a safe and painless test. Keep in mind that each culture also has ways of addressing the same health concerns. Asians often lead the way in homeopathic medicine.

Although there is no cure for osteoporosis, there are treatments available to help stop further bone loss and reduce the risk of fractures. Studies have shown that estrogen can prevent the loss of bone mass in postmenopausal women, but many women of color are fearful of taking estrogen. The current generation is the first to experience a higher incidence of estrogen therapy. For additional information and resources, I suggest contacting the Minority Health Resource Center (P.O. Box 37337, Washington, D.C. 20013–7337; call (800) 444–MHRC or fax 301–589–0884). In addition, the National Association of Women's Health Organizations (NAWHO) has an Asian Women's Reproductive and Sexual Health Empowerment Project. Their mission is to improve the overall health status of Asian American women and families. NAWHO is committed to addressing gaps in research, information, and knowledge about women's reproductive and sexual health care needs. The Asian women's project intends to educate women and lead them to increased access to reproductive and sexual health care, including family planning services with expanded reproductive and sexual health options. One key strategy for addressing and challenging these inequities is gathering baseline data on Asian American women and sharing and discussing these efforts with health care providers, policy makers, the Asian American community, and the general population at large.

The Asian Women's Reproductive and Sexual Health Project has a number of studies showing that Asian women are the least likely to utilize clinical preventive health services, especially pap tests and breast cancer screening, unless they are in severe pain or have symptoms that interfere with daily functioning. Reproductive and sexual health issues directly affect the quality of women's lives and are influenced by one's cultural background, socioeconomic conditions, familial relations, and social environment.

The project also notes that one of the major factors influencing the use and knowledge of reproductive and sexual health services among Asian American women is that Asian women tend to view gynecological ailments as important and legitimate only when they directly concern pregnancy or prenatal care. Many Asian American women have a limited understanding of the range of reproductive health technologies available and feel uncomfortable discussing contraception with their partner(s). In addition, Asian American women generally do not receive much information on their reproductive and sexual health concerns, are reluctant to discuss their reproductive health concerns with family or community members, and often have no other sources of information for their health needs.

In 1995 the National Asian Women's Health Organization examined the use of reproductive health technologies by Asian American women in California via a survey of six California counties with significant populations of Asian Americans. One-half of the 674 Asian women surveyed had not visited a health care professional for reproductive health needs in the past year. Of those surveyed, 25 percent had never visited such a professional, and two-thirds of the women did not always use contraceptives or protection, even though the majority of them were sexually active. This survey received coverage in fifty articles in both ethnic and mainstream newspapers, two television interviews with network affiliates in Los Angeles, and radio coverage on over fifteen stations in the Bay area and in Los Angeles.

Of course, there are those who do not want to expand women's reproductive health and choice options. This subject is thought of as personal and can be an issue of control for some men and for some religious organizations, and is a topic of many debates. Organizations on both sides of the issues exist. The following are but a few. Catholics for a Free Choice (CFFC) is an independent nonprofit organization engaged in policy analysis and advocacy on issues of gender equality and reproductive health. They are based in Washington, D.C., and work in the Catholic social justice tradition. CFFC is affiliated in the United States with Catholic Organizations for Renewal and Women Church Convergence. It works internationally and has four partner organizations in Latin America and a network of volunteer activists in several South American countries.

Since 1969, the National Abortion and Reproductive Rights Action League (NARAL) has promoted reproductive freedom and dignity for women and their families. With a grassroots network of thirty-five state affiliates and 500,000 members nationwide, NARAL educates Americans, works to help elect pro-choice candidates, and advocates for pro-choice legislation to secure women's freedom to choose. Along with defending reproductive choice from assaults by the radical right, NARAL is leading the way to promote policies that will make abortion less necessary.

Reproductive health and freedom issues are cross-cultural. The National Black Women's Health Project is a Washington, D.C., membership organization focused on self-help and health advocacy. The project administers and develops programs to bring about more equitable distribution of health care resources and to empower all African American women to take greater control over their personal and community health and social well-being. In addition, the Pro-Choice Public Education Project (PEP) is a new and pioneering national collaborative of nearly fifty pro-choice organizations working together to reach, educate, and energize the nation's pro-choice majority. Each year, Planned Parenthood health centers nationwide provide high-quality, affordable reproductive health care and sexual health information to more than 5 million women, men, and teens. Planned Parenthood prides itself on welcoming everyone, regardless of race, age, sexuality, disability, or income. They note most Asian and Pacific Islander women have never sought services.

## FOREVER ALIENS

One of the reasons Asians and Pacific Islanders hesitate to seek service has to do with how they are ridiculed and debased by the general society. Not only is their language and accent made fun of, they are seen as foreign. In spite of the fact that there are several generations of American-born Asians and Pacific Islanders, they forever remain aliens in the minds of most Americans. To be Asian or Pacific Islander is to very frequently be asked, "Where do you come from?" The constant flow of immigrants does not help to break the mindset that all Asian women are immigrants, with limited English and in need of mentoring to learn American ways.

Having a history of generations living in America and being fluent in English and in the American culture plus fluent in an Asian or Pacific Island language is a skill that is generally not compensated, especially in the health field, where health varies according to immigrant status. Dr. Martha Sotomyor (2002) noted at a recent meeting on elder abuse that if Asian women are in the country illegally, they fear securing health services because they live frightened of scrutiny and deportation. Few "Americans" can distinguish among Pacific Islanders and other Asians. Language and custom differences make it difficult for most white Americans to provide adequate services for them. The original Asian immigrants were Chinese, and the introduction of the Chinese to the United States and the hostility they encountered in the United States has impacted other Asian and Pacific Islander populations. New immigrants inherited the neglect and animosity of relations between whites and Asians. This is why some whites cannot distinguish among Pacific Islanders and Asians. Their need to dehumanize and simplify people of color extends this lack of differentiation to Hispanics, Indians, and blacks.

The first arrival of the Chinese, 155 years ago (Leadership Education for Asian Pacifics 2002), is part of an intricate political and economic relationship (generally push–pull) between Asia and the United States. From her birth, the United States sought to establish herself as a new power among old nations. Citizens saw their "manifest destiny" as westward expansion across the continent to the Pacific and beyond to Asia. The Chinese were recruited as laborers in the economic development of the new Western territories (Zinn 2001). Most of the first immigrants were men, who were caught between the white laboring class struggling for better working conditions and the capitalist exploitation of labor. The Chinese became scapegoats for the growing pains of the U.S. labor movement in the West and were subjected to much oppression.

Debates centering on white superiority over yellow (Chinese) inferiority became nationally known as the "Chinese Question." In the 1960s women's issues were often referred to as the "Women's Question." The answer to increasing Chinese presence in the United States was the passage of the Exclusion Act of 1882, which almost eliminated Chinese immigration. Furthermore, Chinese who were already in America were declared ineligible for citizenship. Yet even under these unstable conditions, Chinese communities thrived.

In the nineteenth century, Western nations and Japan sought to carve up China in their own interest. Following the defeat of China in the Opium War of 1839–1849, Chinese seaports were forced open to foreign trade. The Chinese signed contracts to work in Southeast Asia and the Americas and fell victim to the "coolie" trade, a cruel working relationship between laborers, suppliers, and owners. Many went to Hawaii to work in the sugar cane industry. A series of "unequal treaties" gave Western nations, and later Japan, commercial privileges and extraterritorial concessions. The United States claimed a share under the Treaty of Wang-Hsia, and sought to insure her privileges through the enunciation of the "Open Door Policy" in 1899. In addition, the corrupt and incompetent ruling class of China failed to provide effective leadership in the face of foreign aggression. Unregulated opium traffic and peasant rebellions signaled the demise of the traditional imperial order, and under the flag of trade marched merchants, missionaries, and Marines.

Leadership Education for Asian Pacifics (LEAP; 2002) notes that the Chinese were not the first Asians in the Americas. The first recorded settlement was Filipino in 1763 in New Orleans. Nineteenth-century immigration, however, was predominately from Kwantung, China, to California. Some Californians hoped to harness the newly arrived cheap pool for the development of the frontier. Some even hoped to enslave them, but opposition to slavery ran high for fear of rejection of admission into the Union, and the Chinese fought back. Sometimes there was cooperation between the populations. The participation of Chinese merchants in celebrations of George Washington's Birthday, Independence Day, and California's admission into the Union not only added color to the civic festivities; it encouraged some people. The majority did not share this optimistic view. The manners and habits of the Chinese were repugnant to many in California.

In 1852 the Chinese population increased sharply. Male presence was keenly felt in the gold mining fields of California in the 1850s. They also contributed much to building the transcontinental railroad connecting the East and West coasts of the United States (LEAP 2002) in the 1860s. While the display of Chinese festivities in the city delighted the white population, their presence as competitors in the mines and as laborers was not welcomed even though they worked abandoned claims. There was an especially intense conflict with the Irish, many of whom also disliked blacks, because the Chinese came to the United States to escape crop failures in Ireland.

In spite of the hostility and harassment facing the Chinese, they remained competitors and established settlements and businesses throughout the western frontier. In 1854 there were laws forbidding Chinese from testifying against whites (LEAP 2002). Even though they were seen as exotic, as barbaric, and as watchdogs of gambling or opium dens, they managed to own shops and laundries. Some supported the continuation of Chinese opera, and proceeded with their distinctive writing traditions, which most whites considered scribbling. Poverty and patriarchy endured, and women with "lily bound" feet were brought to the United States to be brides. Meanwhile, the men worked on the railroad, and some discovered and unearthed the skeleton of a great mastodon. In addition, there were many gardeners who fed the shop owners who sold a variety of goods, including brooms, cloth, feed, tools, and the brightly decorated dragons so often associated with the Chinese.

In the late nineteenth and early twentieth centuries Japanese, Filipinos, Koreans, and Asian Indians immigrated. Unlike European immigrants, who were allowed to become citizens and encouraged to take part in all aspects of life in the United States, Asians were denied citizenship and kept out of the mainstream (Zinn 2001). Most western states made it illegal for alien women and men who were not citizens to own land. In 1882 Congress passed the Chinese Exclusion Act, preventing the importation of Chinese laborers. U.S. courts refused citizenship to Asians because they are neither white nor black. In 1907 the same restrictions were applied to Japanese laborers, and in 1917 the Immigration Act enforced a literacy test and banned immigration from all countries in the Asia–Pacific Triangle except the Philippines, which was a U.S. territory (Sinnott 1993). In 1906 California law barred marriage between whites and "mongolian" Asians. It was not until after World War II that the exclusion laws were revised. In 1944 the War Bride Act removed racial restrictions for Asian brides and permitted them entry into the United States. In 1945 the War Brides Act made it possible for the wives and children of U.S. servicemen to enter the country and become citizens. The military discouraged U.S. soldiers from such unions, and when the women and children arrived on the mainland they were subjected to much scrutiny and discrimination.

The Immigration Reform and Control Act of 1986 made family relationships and work skills the basis for allowing immigrants into the United States.

After years of exclusion from the mainstream and having limited roles in their own culture, some women emerged to address their concerns within the Civil Rights Movement of the 1960s. This aroused a new generation of Chinese to a broader consciousness. The lessons of the past and the search for identity and voice were intertwined with the hope of the future. Chinese women now number among those advocating for their people.

But there is still sexism and racism, and some women support this. In my April 30, 1999, e-mail was the following "joke," forwarded to me by a woman. Only an edited version is rendered here:

### Learn Korean In Five Minutes!

| English Phrase | Chinese Interpretation |
| --- | --- |
| Are you harboring a fugitive? | Hu Yu Hai Ding? |
| Stupid Man | Dum Gai |
| Your price is too high! | No Bai Dam Ding!! |
| I think you need a facelift | Chin Tu Fat |
| It's very dark in here | Wai So Dim? |
| Has your flight been delayed? | Hao Long Wei Ting? |
| That was an unauthorized execution | Lin Ching |
| I thought you were on a diet | Wai Yu Mun Ching? |
| You are not very bright | Yu So Dum |
| I got this for free | Ai No Pei |
| Your body odor is offensive | Yu stin ki pu |
| Pew! Does this bathroom stink! | Hu Flung Dung? |

I was unappreciative of the "joke," and was told I was overreacting. The woman did not recognize that the "joke" was insulting. Also insulting is the continuing stereotype that Asian women are passive and good housekeepers: The underlying assumption is that even women feek they have license to ridicule, stereotype, and insult Asians. They not only quietly keep their own houses clean, they make excellent servants. The license to ridicule and stereotype is tied to ignorance, but also to the belief that immigrants in the United States are illegitimate and not real Americans.

From 1903 to 1905 Koreans immigrated to Hawaii as strike breakers against Japanese sugar cane and pineapple field workers (LEAP 2002). Americans are most familiar with Koreans who immigrated in the mid-1960s into the United States from South Korea. They came to escape the devastating effects of the Korean War (1950–1953). They clustered in and near two major cities on each of the U.S. coastlines: New York and Los Angeles. They have inherited the beliefs about Chinese and have also been subjected to anti-Asian immigration legislation. For roughly forty years Koreans were barred from entering the United States. They then were allowed to enter the United States under a strict quota limiting the number of Koreans to 100 per year. This quota was finally abolished in 1965. By the late 1960s a population of several thousand South Koreans grew to be hundreds of thousands.

Many cultures believe one can die of a broken heart. Today the separation between body and mind is lessening. Many are recognizing that bodies cannot heal without attention to the spirit, the soul. This belief is most common among populations of color in the United States, and is considered unscientific by established medicine. This has placed limits on male-dominant white medicine, and there is now a movement toward a more holistic medical tradition. The people of Asia have known about holistic health for centuries, and one of the highlights of my life was visiting female doctors in China. Asia has brought the United States acupuncture, tai chi, anesthesia using less than half the amount of drugs that would be used in the United States, different massage methods, and healing herbs. They also give us a different geography of the body and its chi (energy).

The chi functions differently in women, some of whom are masters at mixing herbs and prescribing and combining them with Western medicine. In the United States, women can be seen working as doctors and in herbal pharmacies, where scorpion, lizard, and ginseng root are recommended to increase the chi, the vital life force. Other prescriptions include shavings of deer antler and remedies to increase heat or undo the stagnation of energy. It is not unlike the Latino *curanderismo*. Herbs are boiled, mixed, and drunk as teas. Some taste bad, as do many pills prescribed by U.S. mainstream doctors, some of whom will admit that the power of the mind helps medicine work.

The chi is made up of circuits or channels of energy. The difference between men and women is with regard to the nerve paths. Asian doctors have sensitivity to the chi when it rises or pulls back, and they have viable practices. Contrary to popular belief, massage is much more than making the muscles feel good. It is about opening up channels to allow blood to flow and rid the body of toxins. It assists in realigning and opening up the chi. This, combined with herbs specifically prescribed for the patient, can be highly effective.

There are people's parks in Shanghai and all over China. Every morning citizens exercise by engaging in tai chi, a series of gentle movements based upon Daoist philosophy and the martial arts. The idea is that the body has to move. The person has to figure out his or her center and focus the mind. One cannot have health unless the body is maintained. Here, health is a philosophy of life, not just the absence of illness. How one lives—one's philosophy, thoughts, and emotions—shapes healing and illness as much as how one behaves affects physical well-being. Being peaceful circulates the chi. It lessens obstruction of energy flow. The goal is to get it to move more freely, and it moves more freely when it is balanced. Ying and yang are a part of the Daoist beliefs about the balance of the body and the mind. Figuring out where the imbalance is is necessary in order to fix it with needles, massage, or herbs. The goal is to teach the patient how to heal, to teach the patient how to concentrate, to use his or her mind to change his or her health. This is one of the goals of meditation.

Human beings, including human thought, emit energy. The will is a kind of energy that goes out of a master's body and can be absorbed by others. In the United States we often refer to this as "vibes." This is a sense, not an understanding, and in my opinion sexism and racism are often sensed by the people. They can pick up this energy and it burdens them, but the sexist and racist is also burdened, and this transmits into the society and blocks it from progressing. Perhaps the mixing of Chinese and Western medicine can be a model for healing social ills.

## PACIFIC ISLANDER WOMEN
## AND CULTURAL LIBERATION

There are over 30,000 islands in the Pacific Ocean, which takes up more room on Earth than all the land put together. The Pacific Islands include Polynesia, Melanesia, and Micronesia. The Polynesian Islands are scattered across a triangle covering the east-central region of the Pacific Ocean. The Hawaiian Islands in the north, New Zealand in the west, and Easter Island in the east bound the triangle.

On many of these islands there are still thatched-roof huts, coconuts, beaches, sugar cane, coral reefs, and exotic fish, and parts of them offer some of the best diving environments in the world. But this area is being threatened. Some of the stereotypes have been hurtful to the people, the hills, and the mountains, which are being bombarded by pollution. In some places growing sugar cane is becoming a thing of the past, and there is now a need to protect the coral reefs. Women can no longer travel alone, and many things have changed, but we still stereotype island people of color as being lazy and having a disregard for time. To many, Pacific Islanders are dark-skinned people who dress in loose-fitting, brightly colored clothing and appear to wear no underclothes. Stereotypes include images of topless women in a paradise where everyone eats a lot of fish and pork. The women make great servants, they are pretty and pleasing when they are young, and their mothers are fat. This population has a history of headhunting, cannibalism, ancestor worship, and many secrets. Drinking is the main hobby of men. Women were once sacrificed to erupting volcano spirits, and people once believed that there was nothing beyond their land. Therefore, they were and continue to be ignorant.

To the missionaries, indigenous island people were savages. Both men and women had long hair and bathed in the ocean. Flies were everywhere. Therefore, the natives were unclean. They were unscientific and superstitious. Their superstition led them to believe that waterfalls, rocks, and jungles had spirits within them, and sex was indiscriminate. Many of the stereotypes are tied to Christian missionaries, who interpreted the indigenous world view as non-Christian and the work of the devil. It was the role of the missionaries to Christianize and civilize them. One priority was to dress the women in Western-style clothing.

From the very beginning there were efforts to denounce the Christians and their cultural ways. Later there was a movement to denounce foreigners and their attempts to colonize the indigenous. In the 1940s during World War II, some of the islands, especially Solomon Island, experienced intensive fighting between Americans and the Japanese. This left unexploded mine fields, rusting guns, tanks, and other scars of war upon a peaceful people.

There are 107 dialects in the Pacific Islands. Most code switch. They speak both English and many still speak their own language. Code switching is considered speaking pigeon. In the nineteenth century, Europeans kidnapped thousands of Malaitan men and took them to work on sugar-cane plantations in Australia. On this island, in the twentieth century, the women were frequently photographed with umbrellas and carrying babies wrapped in a cloth around their necks.

As in Malaita, many Pacific Islander women breast feed their babies and many still give the appearance of being shy. Their history includes stories about a time when families built villages and when shell money was used in the purchase of land, pigs, and brides (Grant 1994). Visitors lament the changes. According to Pacific Island feminists they prefer the days when, other than a healthy smile and pretty white teeth, Pacific Islander young women appeared to have no personality. But contemporary young women have the struggles of all colonized and formerly enslaved people: balancing their indigenous culture against that of the colonizers. This means they are subject to the stresses of combined sexual and racial discrimination.

On July 28, 1999, I caught the end of a program entitled *The Human Experience* on the Learning Channel. The focus was upon the interaction of humans. Upon conclusion, the narrator said that there is a build-up of pressure for people of color that is based upon having to deal with bigotry and injustice. This pressure leads to health risks that include depression, stroke, and heart attack. People of color have known this for some time. When I worked as a mental health worker in a southern Colorado state hospital, I had an alcoholic African American patient. This patient was hospitalized, treated, and released several times. I came to the conclusion that his primary problem was that he was attempting to gain employment, which he linked to validation of his manhood. We released him to a racist society that offered little or no employment to black men. In part, he would drink to numb the pain of this and was returned to the hospital by his family.

Although it is sometimes easier for women to transfer domestic skills to the labor market, their employment is generally at a lower level. This is primarily due to the cumulative effects of sexism and racism, and causes much stress. The task before mental health workers is how to treat women of color, whose presenting problem when they seek or are mandated to procure mental health treatment is depression. Generally, depression is internalized anger. I say liberate the women; change their status in society. Redefine their worth and role. If the Communist government of China can launch a huge campaign to increase the value of girl babies to keep them from being smothered to death because boys are preferred, the United States can also launch a campaign to better the image of women. In 2002 there is no data on the results of the campaign, but liberation from exploitation, from discrimination, from injustice, and from sexual harassment is imperative for people of color, who combined are now the majority population in the United States (U.S. Bureau of the Census 2001).

It is my belief that few Americans want to hear about the liberation of people of color from their oppression. In fact, most doubt that there is persecution of people of color. They do not see it and they do not feel it. Even some people of color maintain this. They believe that all one has to do is work hard to get ahead, but liberation is not about having more money. It is about being comfortable everywhere one goes. It is about learning and teaching one's culture in school as a matter of fact by having it integrated into how material is taught and how the schools and the districts are structured. It is about being taught an indigenous language as the first language.

What few persons know is that there is a very strong sovereignty movement among Pacific Islanders. Many of those active in the movement resent tourists. They see it as taking advantage of the heritage of the colonization of the islands. The current sovereignty movement emanates from the growing frustration and frequent protests that have taken place over the last two decades, as well as the organization that has gone on in preparation for claiming sovereign-nation statue. Trask (1993) and Dudley and Agard (1990) give a good account of where the sovereignty movement is today in Hawaii and present a number of clearly explained models for nationhood that have been proposed by various island sovereignty groups. Some of the issues include the desire to

Have colonized land returned to the indigenous

Speak the indigenous language in both private and public places

Relate with the natural world publicly and unashamedly

Think their own thoughts and to pursue their own aspirations

Restore the status of women

Develop indigenous arts

Worship indigenous gods

Follow an indigenous moral system

See indigenous people whenever they look around

Be Hawaiian again by making contributions to the world as Hawaiians

Have a Hawaiian presence in the world community

Exist as a Hawaiian nation

This movement is felt strongly in Hawaii and, like American Indians did for the quincentennial, Hawaiians emerged with a good deal of literature for the Centennial Commemoration (1893–1993), which marked the one-hundredth anniversary of relationships with the United States. Authors like Haunani Kay Trask (1993) and Michael Kioni Dudley and Keoni Kealoha Agard (1990) write about the relationship as colonial, and outline how life was fairly routine prior to the coming of the white man and women.

Prior to the coming of the white man, life was rich in poetry, symbols, myths, and art. Hawaiians created sculpture, feathered capes, helmets, leis, and other objects of adornment. They had an entire civilization that included a successful relationship with nature, the land, forests, animals, and the ocean. Their world view included a philosophy that humans participated in a con-sciously interrelating cosmic community in which all beings protect and care for others (British Broadcasting Corporation 1987). There were 6,000 species of plants, animals, and insects. No other place in the world had this number of native species. Hawaii's extreme isolation, 225,000 miles from the nearest continental land mass, made it a home to plants and animals that evolved in their own special way without outside influences until humans arrived. Those humans were the Polynesians.

Peli, the first goddess, resided beneath Killawaa with its lake of lava and volcanic crust. She was and still is a fearsome and untamable spirit controlling the living and the dead. When she exploded, trees and stumps were what re-mained of once thriving forests, or what remained of people who had angered Peli. But vegetation grows quickly. This does not tame the primeval destruc-tion of a volcano as a constant threat creating a labyrinth of tubes and caverns that permeate the islands. Ancient people lived here. Records of the native population are engraved on the walls of the water-filled depressions and flooded lava tubes. Exclusive wildlife dominated by tiny fish, which appear copper in color, and other unusual flora and fauna attract birds, some of which are on the endangered species list. Many species are already extinct.

The islands are still being created. Like culture, the environment is not un-changing. On the islands the change process is represented in the origin of the animal world, which is linked to the human world and begins on a reef where coral once became worms, then became fish, and finally arose as humans. This notion is no more far-fetched than other creation stories and theories of evolution.

The edges of the island are steep and swept by waves. Some fish spend their entire lives in the waves of the reef, which also builds the island. Each fish has a duty, a function. They vary in color and markings. Some are in disguise; flat with bumps that looks like sand. There are huge eels, puffer fish, octopus, and jellyfish. Some are transparent. Some glow like blinking signs or alien space-ships. Here also reside sea horses and manta rays more than ten feet wide. Some creatures have strange-looking spindly legs. Some are day fish. Others are night fish. Some do not even swim; the ocean currents move them.

On some islands seals spend much of their time feeding in the ocean, sleep-ing on the beach, or fighting over females. Male birds can be seen trying to mount female birds. The power of femaleness is well respected in an environ-ment where living with lava is a way of life. It crumbles into pebbles, and into sand to form black beaches, new land. Kauai is the largest island, home to the rarest and most unusual birds. Its moisture-laden trade winds make it the wettest land on the planet (British Broadcasting Corporation 1987). Here there are waterfalls and showers that wear away the island.

The Hawaiian Islands number seven in total, but Oaho, with the city of Honolulu, is the most popular. Five million tourists spend $2 billion a year. Tourism is the main industry of most of the islands. From all over the world people are attracted to surfing, sailboating, and spending hours in the sun watching the half-naked bodies of others. There is much money to be made renting outrigger canoes, selling treatments for sunburn, sunscreen, sandals, aloha clothes, and hotel accommodations. One can catch a bus or a paddy cab, rent a motor scooter or a car, and go on sightseeing tours in a helicopter.

There are museums and archives, college and university campuses, aquariums, and cultural centers. One can purchase jewelry, macadamia nuts, and even visit the USS *Arizona* memorial, a U.S. sunken ship that met its demise on December 7, 1941, when it was bombed by the Japanese. This incident instilled hatred in the hearts of many U.S. citizens toward the Japanese. Such was the hatred that the Japanese were incarcerated in concentration camps during the war. They lost their homes, their businesses, and their possessions, and endured severe discrimination. In Hawaii the Japanese are often disliked by the indigenous as foreigners who came to colonize.

Hawaii is the home of huge corporations. One sees the huge pineapple fields and can learn about the people. Some tourists are serious students. Others are simply curious, and a couple of hour's visit to the Polynesian Cultural Center is enough for them. They can return home to tell their friends how they learned to dance the hula, saw the crafts of villagers, and experienced demonstrations about basket weaving, opened coconuts, and even saw a native climb a tree to get a coconut.

The sale of culture and the environment is big business. Swimmers give exhibitions of cliff diving. For a price, one can attend a roasted pig and fish feast that includes a variety of fruit drinks, and one can learn about the whaling industry, take a glass-bottom boat ride, and enjoy indigenous music with an "American" twist. With some interest, it is easy to learn something about King Kamayamaya and Queen Liliu'okalani and the Faulkin Islands, visit churches and missions and the summer homes of royalty, and go on nature walks, but for the most part indigenous people do not control this. Business, politics, and education are controlled by whites, those who came to the island much later (Trask 1993).

## PACIFIC ISLANDER SOVEREIGNTY MOVEMENT

As a result of the need to control their lives, a number of pro-nation groups meet regularly. Collectively they are known as the sovereignty movement. They plan and educate other Hawaiians about the need to take back the land

and live as free Hawaiians. There are 309 distinct nations existing by treaty within the territorial limits of the United States. Like Native Americans, the native Hawaiians want to enjoy some areas of complete sovereignty and some areas of limited sovereignty. They want their own territory, their own government structures, their own laws, to collect their own taxes, and they want to be protected by American federal law with regard to their culture and religion. Even though being a state offers all this, members of the sovereignty movement want American culture and ownership of land removed from the islands.

This movement is rooted in the way Hawaii was annexed to the United States and in the treatment of Queen Liliu'okalani (note the Anglicized spelling). There are numerous books, at various reading levels, and several Web sites with information on Queen Lydia Liliu'okalani, who was born in Honolulu on September 2, 1838, and died on November 11, 1917. She was the last sovereign Queen of Hawaii, who was deposed by the advocates of a Republic for Hawaii in 1893. Liliu'okalani was the third child of High Chief Kapaakea and the Chiefess Keohokalole. Her brother was King Kalakaua. Her family came from a long line of royalty (Liliu'okalani 1991).

She became fluent in English and was influenced by Congregational missionaries. As a young girl she rode horses and attended parties and teas. She traveled into the countryside, sang, and participated in songwriting contests. She became engaged briefly to Prince William Lunalilo, who later ruled Hawaii from 1873 to 1874, but she eventually married a *ha'ole*, a white man named John Owen Dominis, on September 16, 1862. Dominis would serve the monarchy as the Governor of O'ahu and Mau'i. Liliu'okalani and Dominis had no children, and according to her private papers and diaries the marriage was not fulfilling. Dominis died shortly after she assumed the throne. The queen never remarried.

Liliu'okalani ascended the throne of Hawaii after the death of her brother, King Kalakaua, who had become king upon the death of Lunalilo in 1874. Both Lunalilo and Kalakaua were without heirs, and Kalakaua named his sister, Liliu'okalani, heir apparent upon the death of their younger brother in 1877. King Kalakaua, who in the eyes of most indigenous Hawaiians had been a weak leader, died in San Francisco in January 1891.

When Liliu'okalani assumed the throne, she suggested that there should be a new constitution for Hawaii, because Kalakaua had been forced to submit to the "Bayonet Constitution" of 1887, which had limited the power of the monarch and weakened the political power of native Hawaiians. American interests felt threatened and began to talk of the annexation of Hawaii by the United States in order to reestablish an economically competitive position for the sugar interests. To do this, they formed the "Committee of Safety."

Native Hawaiians desired more detachment from American influences and supported self-empowerment through the queen's new constitution. In 1893 Queen Liliu'okalani sought to strengthen her position through a new constitution. It was Queen Liliu'okalani's right as a sovereign to issue a new constitution, but the group against her thought only of protecting their financial interests in sugar by overthrowing the institution of the monarchy. On January 16, 1893, the Committee of Safety fabricated a need for U.S. protection of the USS *Boston* in the port of Honolulu. The American minister in Hawaii, John L. Stevens, called the *Boston's* troops to take control of Iolani Palace and various other government buildings. The Committee of Safety, with the use of musket and canon, then deposed the queen, abrogated the monarchy, and established a provisional government that in 1894 became the Republic of Hawaii.

The colonists, composed largely of Americans, petitioned Washington in 1893 to be annexed by the United States, but they were first denied because this did not serve U.S. interests.

In March 1893 James H. Blount, the newly appointed American minister to Hawaii, arrived representing President Grover Cleveland. Blount listened to both sides, annexationists and restorationists, republicans and royalists, whites and natives, and concluded that the Hawaiian people were on the side of their queen. When Blount returned to Washington he and Cleveland agreed that the queen should be restored. Blount's final report implicated the American leaders in the illegal overthrow of Queen Liliu'okalani. President Cleveland took the position as American minister to Hawaii away from Blount and instructed him to speak directly to the queen and offer her the crown upon the condition that she pardon and grant general amnesty to those republican annexationists who had dethroned her.

Liliu'okalani initially refused to grant general amnesty, but by mid-December she changed her mind and offered clemency to her political enemies. Liliu'okalani's delay had compromised her political position and President Cleveland had released the entire issue of the Hawaiian revolution to Congress for debate. The big money interests (annexationists) went to Washington, D.C., and lobbied Congress against restoration of the monarchy. On July 4, 1894, the Republic of Hawaii with Sanford B. Dole as president was proclaimed, and was immediately recognized by the U.S. government.

In 1895 Liliu'okalani was arrested and forced to reside in Iolani Palace. After weapons were found in the gardens of her home, she was accused of knowing about resistance activities. She denied knowing about the weapons and stated she was unaware of the activities of the royalists. Her supporters kept her abreast of the news in Hawaii by sending her flowers wrapped in daily newspapers. In November 1896 she was released and was allowed to travel and speak openly and freely. She journeyed to Washington in December 1896 to speak to the president, but by this time Cleveland was on his way out of the presidency and no longer able to assist her or her desire for restoration.

Eventually the queen resigned herself to the fact that she and Hawaii had been colonized, but she always maintained that Hawaiian sovereignty was inherent and could not be taken away by force. Liliu'okalani evoked loyalty and sympathy from native Hawaiians until her death. Visitors from abroad and officials of the United States would call upon the queen as a gracious gesture of respect. She continued to live for nearly two decades at Washington Place while receiving an annual pension from the legislature, which by 1917 was $15,000 a year. She also received income from her various landed properties and was present at most state occasions. With dignity and political courage she refused the offer to attend the annexation of the islands ceremonies. She simply could not bear to see the Hawaiian flag lowered and the U.S. flag replace it. Her pain and loss were also the pain and loss of all other Hawaiians and they resonate until this day.

Today Liliu'okalani represents all that is virtuous in Hawaii's grand past. She sought to preserve Hawaiian sovereignty and traditions, and wrote her memoirs, *Hawaii's Story by Hawaii's Queen* (Liliu'okalani 1991). In 1866 she wrote the Hawaiian national anthem, "He Mele Lahui Hawaii." In 1876 her song "Aloha Oe" ("Farewell to Thee") became the first Hawaiian song to become popular outside the islands. Liliu'okalani died from a stroke in 1917 during World War I. A sculpture of her exists on the grounds of the state capitol in Honolulu. Marianne Pineda of Boston sculpted it and the dedication describes her as "a symbol of the character and spirit" of the Hawaiian people.

## WOMEN OF THE SOVEREIGNTY MOVEMENT

In the spirit of Queen Liliu'okalani, women are at the forefront of the sovereignty movement. The subject of Hawaiian women's leadership was controversial at first. The men were feeling unsupported and eclipsed by women's leadership. They felt personally injured when women took the lead. Hawaiian women seek a collective self-determination (Trask 1993). They want to achieve sovereignty through and with their people and their men. They do not want to be separate from them as individuals or as splintered groups. They see such individualism and separation as promoting confusion and alienation, the very maladies that afflict people with industrial history. Hawaiian feminist liberation does not mean upward class mobility and incorporation into mainstream culture. It means that gender struggles occur laterally, within the context of Hawaiian culture. They see their lives as having more in common with their men and other indigenous people than with white women, who have also been despotic to Hawaiians and are seen as interlopers.

My conversations with Hawaiian feminists reveal that they see the lack of control over their bodies as a result of colonialism. Poor health is traceable to the Americanization process and the loss of land, where they once lived as healthful people on native food. The high rate of breast cancer is related to forced assimilation, junk food, supermarkets, and the "American" diet. High infant mortality, oppressive working conditions, and low wages are all related to loss of self-government and the loss of control over their lives. Haunani Kay Trask (1993) interprets white feminists as unable to see the causal connection between indigenous life conditions and their status as colonized people. The failure of this vision is a result of their white privilege. They see domination of Hawaiian females but refuse to see the oppression of women as a product of colonialism. White feminist presence in the colonies is an indication of their privilege. Trask asks, what are white people doing in the middle of the Pacific Ocean? She answers, living off native land, culture, and people.

Many women of color, including Haunani Kay Trask (1993), have experienced white feminists as foreigners revealing that their first loyalty is to the white culture. This loyalty results in a rejection of the sovereignty of indigenous people and the acceptance of white imposition. Even on the mainland, they insist on residing in Indian country. One cannot expect the profiteers of tyranny to liberate and confront the role they play in oppressing others. Evidence of this is experienced when white feminists insist their definition of feminism is the right one. They use their white power, status, and privilege to ensure that their definition supersedes that of indigenous women.

Haunani Kay Trask (1993) and other island feminists seek nationhood in unity with other Hawaiians. They are primarily native people to whom the white man introduced money as a means of exchange. The white man (the early settlers were men, but women quickly followed and reaped the benefit of being attached to men) is also seen as having coerced the king into dividing up the islands. They compelled him to institute communal land with private land ownership, which resulted in much indigenous land lost to white people when the white man used the king to purchase private property. Later they kidnapped the queen and held her prisoner. Those in the movement also point out that the white man brought diseases and reduced their numbers from around 1 million in 1778 to less than 40,000 a century later. Captain Cook's men are targeted as having brought venereal disease and its accompanying suffering of insanity and death. Cook was only in the islands for a few days in 1778 before a storm forced him to leave. When he returned a year later, word of his arrival had spread throughout all the islands (Trask 1993).

Those Hawaiians who are most adamant about seeking restoration and sovereignty are those whose relatives, in the years after Hawaii's annexation as a territory of the United States, saw laws passed forbidding them to practice aspects of their culture, including religion and speaking their own language. It was not secret that the majority of indigenous people did not want to become "American."

Those seeking statehood over a hundred years ago profited greatly from it. Native Hawaiians have not. Many are without food, shelter, skills, education, and jobs. Many resent not being able to live in villages without intense poverty, and they lament the loss of the bartering system and a society that was based on generosity and communal concern (Trask 1993). Prior to the switch to capitalism, fishermen and farmers gave freely, and everyone flourished.

When Captain Cook arrived in the islands, some Hawaiians, whose gods were thought to appear in human form, mistook him for a god. This story is reminiscent of the arrival of Hernan Cortes in Mexico in 1521. Montezuma and his priest first thought Cortes was Quetzalcoatl, a god who they were expecting to return to the Earth about the same time as the Spanish arrival. Like some Mexican Indians, who could not conceive of a man dressed in armor a horse draped in armor, some Hawaiians thought the clothes Cook wore were different-colored layers of skin. The shiny buttons on his coat were thought to be flashing lights from within him. This is not an unusual story considering that indigenous people knew nothing about white men and their culture. Their world view simply did not include horses and guns. This phenomenon is similar to the white man's inability to conceive of spirits in the forest, the mountains, and the sea, and desire to see such beliefs as ignorance and the work of the devil. When the Western world came to Hawaii the Westerners had knowledge of life, culture, and the ways of various continents. In contrast, the island people did not have the same experience and Hawaiian chiefs made tragic mistakes in learning how to trade sandalwood. Within one generation Hawaii was almost completely stripped of its sandalwood forests and Hawaiians were in great debt. In the end, they lost their traditional lifestyles to the system of paid work.

## LESBIANS, GAYS, AND HAWAIIAN MARRIAGE LAWS

Then came the missionaries, who brought with them two convictions: that theirs was the one true religion and that white society was superior to that of the Hawaiians. The Hawaiians who attended missionary schools tried to assimilate while continuing to function from a Hawaiian perspective. This was especially difficult when missionaries could not get past the cultural dress, which they saw as public nudity, and the body adornment of the Hawaiians. In addition to direct physical and spiritual conflict, there were great misunderstandings between the two groups because of language differences. When white people were occasionally awarded land to live on, there was the unexpressed provision that they could live on the land until permission was rescinded. Westerners did not understand this. They accepted it as a gift, to be held in private ownership. When the natives wanted use of the land returned, fighting, name-calling, and stereotypes that lead to mistrust were common.

A current understanding of the indigenous struggle is made complex by the fact that only some indigenous people want sovereignty, and many are mixed blood. The sovereignty movement is occupied with concentrating on how to create unity and come to an agreement on how to be inclusive. Some suggestions on how to move toward sovereignty call for the need for groups to take up clearly defined models of nationhood, to live with them and work with them to flush out deficiencies through public presentations and debates. Some suggest that it is time for the Hawaiian community to begin viewing the various sovereignty groups as political parties and the nationhood models they propound as their platforms. Under this model, the parties can then vie for the public's vote through presenting their models and winning popular support. This guarantees community input.

Another difference that fragments unity and peace among Americans is that of sexual preference and/or sexual orientation. Lesbian, gay, bisexual, transsexual, and transgender issues frequent communities of color. These factors came into the national spotlight when Hawaii very publicly engaged in an eight-year battle to decide whether or not to recognize same-sex marriages. Although the decision is being appealed and American society is still locked in bitter debate, Hawaii decided it does not recognize same-sex marriages, and remains a place with more sensitivity and privilege to homosexuals.

Thus, some women of color face another form of discrimination, homophobia. There are people in the world who believe lesbian women and gay men are abnormal, and they exert an extraordinary amount of pressure upon them to make them heterosexual, or stop having sex with their same gender. The issue is more complex than gays and lesbians. The gay rights movement has expanded to include bisexuals, transgender, persons who change their sex, and persons who cross dress. At one end of the discrimination scale is name-calling and avoidance. At the extreme end is violence, which includes beating up and killing homosexuals. Hate crimes against people of color are also common, and they are similar to what happens to lesbian women and gay men. Hate crimes intensify if the victim is also a person of color.

An increase in knowledge and consciousness has manifested in the increase of reports of hate crimes against lesbian, gay, and bisexual Americans. Only in rare circumstances, however, are they adequately investigated and prosecuted. In most states laws are not adequate to allow this. In June 2002, C-SPAN broadcast a panel presentation by well-known lesbian and gay activists. It was noted that only twenty-two states and the District of Columbia include sexual orientation in their hate crimes statutes. Getting hate crimes statues established in most states has been an ordeal. Twenty-one states have hate crimes laws that do not include sexual orientation, and eight states have no hate crime statutes (C-SPAN 2002). The FBI's 1996 collection of hate crime statistics revealed that hate crimes against lesbians, gays, and bisexuals are a serious national problem (FBI 2001). In 1997 anti-gay hate crimes accounted for nearly 14 percent of all hate crimes. Currently, only two federal hate crime laws include "sexual orientation" as a protected group (C-SPAN 2002). The Hate Crimes Statistics Act, which originally became law in 1990, was reauthorized by the 104th Congress through the year 2002. After this year ends the U.S. Congress will revisit the act. This law calls for states and localities to voluntarily report all hate crimes to the FBI, which is mandated to compile these statistics into an annual report.

This law, however, does not punish anti-gay or racial hate crimes; it simply tabulates the reported crimes in jurisdictions that provide statistics to the FBI. The Hate Crimes Sentencing Enhancement Act, which was part of the Violent Crime Control and Law Enforcement Act of 1994, provides for sentencing when it is proven beyond a doubt that the crime committed was a hate crime. This is difficult to prove because it requires a proof of motivation and state of mind, difficult psychological areas of personal behavior. Because federal law enforcement agencies do not yet have jurisdiction over anti-gay hate crimes, this law can only be used against hate crimes based on sexual orientation when the offense occurs on federal property, such as a national park.

A person can feel hate or resentment in various ways. Another concern is the current immigration struggle that involves binational lesbian and gay couples. The outcome of this controversy is of serious consequence to lesbian and gays, and involves the right to be married. Currently the most controversial court case testing this assumption involves Hawaii, which is willing to recognize lesbian and gay marriages. Most state will not allow same-gender couple to marry. Most lesbian women feel the restriction of same-sex couples with regard to marriage is unconstitutional. Various lesbian and gay centers engage in organizing public education and outreach efforts to protect the lesbian and gay right to marry from legislative and judicial attack. They also continue to strive to achieve full equality for same-sex married couples with respect to immigration.

Lesbian and gay couples have a unique struggle when they face immigration. For many foreign national partners, immigration law has erected barriers that manifest as a lack of options to obtaining legal status. This means there is no way to find legal employment, no chance of ever leaving the United States and returning to live with the ever present fear of separation by deportation. In this context the Hawaii marriage case offered hope and binational couples have become increasingly aware of what it may finally mean for them. Many binational couples feel that if they could legally marry the immigration laws already established to ensure the unification of families would finally apply to all. Fundamental to this belief is that marriage is a basic human right. Making a life-long commitment to another person is something not denied to heterosexuals, and denying it to homosexuals is not only unconstitutional but immoral. To gay activist Andrew Sullivan insuring marriage rights is the most important issue (C-SPAN 2002).

Many lesbians of color are in committed, long-term relationships that often take on many of the responsibilities associated with civil marriage. Unlike legally married people, however, lesbian and gay men cannot share in the economic and legal benefits of civil marriage. Should a state allow same-sex couples to marry, the other states, according to many legal scholars, would have to recognize that union and provide all the legal and economic benefits currently given to married people. Thus, the issue has gone from a personal to a political and economic agreement.

Other social issues affecting lesbians include protecting their rights as they age, getting adequate health care, promoting viable research, and teaching aspects of lesbian life in schools. Primary among their critics are elements of the religious and military communities. One often hears that God loves the homosexual but does not love what the homosexual does. This is known as "hate the sin, love the sinner." In the military there exists a "don't ask, don't tell" policy that silences lesbians and gays. Lesbians and gays simply want what the rest of U.S. society wants: the right to earn a living, to be politically represented, fair treatment in the judicial system, to participate in their religion, to have good health, and to get a well-rounded education. Thus, the gay rights movement wants what women of color want: to end discrimination in various elements of their existence. The gay movement, however, differs in that it stresses different issues. I believe the issues differ because they experience discrimination in aspects of life different from women of color and that the difference is rooted in color, class, and gender. Persons in the lesbian and gay rights movements adhere to different value systems. For example, in the military and in other government entities they seek an end in discrimination to sodomy laws. People of color have not stressed this because, on the whole, behavior that warrants this attention is not perceived as affecting all of them; but there are women of color for whom lesbian and gay rights issues are important. Their identity is based on the color of their skin and their sexual orientation. Here is a fine opportunity for coalition. The women's and civil rights movements and the gay movement can address issues of gender, color, and sexuality on behalf of the gay and lesbians of color in their communities.

Like the women's movement, the gay movement has not made an end to racism a priority. I believe this has not been done because the movement is white male dominated with more focus on white male issues. For example, men of color seek access to upward mobility in the military. Because white men already hold the highest ranks, they can pay attention to changing marriage and sodomy laws. The same is true for white women in the military. They hold higher ranks than do women of color. However, concerns of access to upward mobility affect the lesbian woman of color because she is hindered by decisions made within the military based on preference for white heterosexual males and females and for heterosexual males regardless of color. In this hierarchical scheme, the lesbian of color is at the bottom.

In July 2002, C-SPAN televised a panel presentation by prominent personalities in the gay rights movement: Norah Vincent, Andrew Sullivan, Carmen Vazquez, and Richard Goldstein noted they want to be honored as they exist, not on how people want them to be. They simply want to be judged by the kind of human being they are (C-SPAN 2002). Vincent felt child custody was a primary issue. Aside from the custody issue, Goldstein agreed with Vincent, but notes that 66 percent of persons in the gay rights movement are white liberal males and some have profited from their white middle-class male privilege via the efforts of the whole. His feeling is that the gay rights movement must uplift the entire gay community. Some members of the movement feel that conservative gays and lesbians hurt the gay rights movement. Some people of color also feel that conservative persons of color, especially those in decision-making positions, harm the communities of color when they support conservative perspectives on public policy. They are charged with becoming "window dressings" placed on exhibit by those who control in an effort to placate charges of discrimination. Vazquez noted that change in gender expression should be social and legal, but the laws alone have not ended racial discrimination. According to her, "people had to fight like hell" for change.

The intensity of the divisions within the gay rights movement was witnessed on this C-SPAN program. It demonstrated how conservative and liberal approaches to problem solving fragments the movement and how race is ignored. However, all the panel members who appeared on the C-SPAN program agreed that gender conformity is what they all resisted.

After almost forty years in the civil rights and women's movements it is my opinion that Vazquez is correct and that it takes two approaches to promote social change by the human rights persons of the United States. Someone must be "inside" the structure negotiating and others must be "outside" placing boisterous social pressure using the national and international media to bring about social change. This is a heated battle, but conservatives and liberals must talk to one another in order to establish agreement on the final outcomes, set some boundaries, and move forward to address common issues with forgiveness about the style in which it is done.

I further agree with Vazquez that sex among gay, lesbian, transsexual, bisexual, and transgender persons is a private matter between the person and a receptive partner. Vazquez advised the audience to cease presenting the issues as white and privileged because there are many persons of color within and outside of it who share the same concern over gender restrictions. She challenged the national media to address life and death health issues in the lesbian and gay communities, and challenged lesbian and gay advocacy organizations to put their money into addressing such grassroots issues.

The panel mentioned maintained that the gay, lesbian, bisexual, and transgender movement is a decentralized movement. There are various leaders at various times, addressing various issues. For some the movement is the way to get a meaningful life. Being gay is not an attack on heterosexuality. I understand this to mean the lesbian and gay rights movements attack is on the fact that gender is socially constructed and that the movement seeks gender fluidity. Social change is a struggle against the constricted roles one is placed into because of biological traits. As Vazquez noted, "It is against a system of discrimination and system of privilege."

What does this mean for women of color? In order to be more inclusive in promoting the feminization of color, they and members of the lesbian and gay rights movements, the predominantly white women's movement, and the movement of people of color should agree to fight for an end to discrimination based on gender and race. In feminizing racism they then could address the concerns of women and men of color in their movements, and solidify their coalition efforts in a mass campaign.

I would like the reader to note that this calls into question a dichotomous, up–down, good–bad, black–white, and female–male world view. The world view of people of color tends to be more inclusive, holistic in its approach. Skin color and sex are biological characteristics. Because they manifest in cultural privilege for the white male, politics and culture are not separate entities. They are on a continuum where attitudes manifest in behavior. When women do not act like women and men do not act like men, they are judged as betraying their gender, as attacking the social norm that is seen as limited, but safe, for many. I, however, question that safety. Gender role constriction is much too narrow, too binding to produce peace. When one deviates from the straight and narrow path there are heavy consequences. They are at least demonized and at most killed. We have seen it in the racial and ethnic movements and we now see it in the lesbian movement. Although it was not made a national issue, in the smaller circles of lesbian conversation, the California woman who was killed by her neighbor's dog outside her apartment in 2001 was killed because she was a lesbian.

In order to heal and bring about a more cohesive, peaceful society, we must change the culture. The reasons why issues of equality are still with us is because what we have been doing has not worked. Those things that have worked should be acknowledged and/or revised to assist other social change movements. Social change can be accomplished by utilizing culture. It can be done via art, music, and poetry, much like how the Chicano and black civil rights movements utilized the mural tradition of Mexico. This discussion has given me insight into leadership. There does not need to be one leader. No one gives people permission to advocate for equality, and we cannot believe that the oppressor will liberate us from discrimination.

## HEALING SUGGESTIONS

From the study of Pacific Islander and Asian women we learn about perseverance, the ability to hold on to life, to a concept, we learn about an entrepreneurial spirit, an idea of fairness and liberation. We also learn to adapt, adjust to social stress, and change, which is a key element in the lives of women of color. These survival skills add to the reasons for feminizing racism. Women of color are role models for others to emulate. They teach us to highly value education and family, to be flexible citizens of the world because Asian women represent great numbers of the women in the world. They frequently are caught up in international politics and policy. For the Philippines this has meant violence. In the Philippines, as in the Hawaiian sovereignty movement, women have been in the leadership roles (Women's Enews Inc. 2002). Other women continue, sometimes trapped in gender roles, to contribute to a world economy, where they teach us about utilizing the world's resources carefully and about survival with respect for the Earth and the environment and the link to human rights and injustice.

Until this time the appeal for social justice has been rooted in the civil rights guaranteed under the U.S. constitution. An international perspective forces us to examine human rights, especially those extended by the United Nations. A missing element in the cry for human rights is anger and passion. Not enough women have excavated the anger buried deep inside of them. They are afraid to look at how their lives have been disturbed, controlled, and negotiated away because of their relationships with men, because they do not value themselves enough, and because the U.S. government has deceived them into false consciousness. Women of color teach humans to love and respect themselves and their fellow human beings enough to demand healing from sexism, to hold men and their power in balance, and to proceed to make social contributions.

This is not to say that men are mean, nasty, and ugly. Some are, and they will hurt women, but I believe most men simply want to protect their own interests. For me the truth of the matter is that most male's bottom-line interest is in keeping women subservient in order to continue their male privileged life. Somehow some have lost the ability to identify with women and to see that women and men are related. To unify the diverse population of the country we must form partnerships with other humans and protect not only our civil rights but also those of others. A change in perspective is necessary. The study of Asian women teaches us to take a longer view of history. We must perceive that an attack on one group is an attack on the country and on the fundamental principles of democracy. This is why legislation forbidding hate speech and other hate crimes is necessary. To begin the change, we must first look within the national character of the nation and change the characteristics of individuality, upward mobility, and profit as an orientation.

From Asian women we learn that people must engage in internal critique and examine how well U.S. culture is working. Based upon my review of women of color, I propose it is not working very well, and that a review of its leading characteristics reveals that at the heart of it is the negative consequences of competition, individualism, upward mobility, and marginalization. Competition and individualism marginalize all of us and do not take advantage of the full human order to provide equality in the quality of life for all. The opposite of competition, individualism, and upward mobility is cooperation, community, and unity. There is strength in diversity. It provides more than one way to solve problems. Up until now, the U.S. character has included repression and violence against the majority of its population.

To better achieve the goals of freedom and justice for all, we must correct the history that is currently being taught in schools and universities and reconceptualize the nature of a multiethnic and multiracial country. This means resocialization and giving new or added meaning to symbols and gestures. Strengthening the nation means having women of color in top decision-making positions and having current leaders declare that there is power and strength in ethnic diversity and that an attack on any ethnic or racial community will not be tolerated. This nation must become a place where we respect and recognize individual efforts, and where the man in the White House does not cheat on or demean his wife.

Certain things have to happen to empower women of color. First is increasing the level of health, for without health, a person cannot make many social contributions. One might think that correcting health status would lead to increased economic, educational, and political power. This chain-reaction form of thinking works in theory, but is not practical, for the roots of discrimination are so deeply ingrained that we must attack the symptoms of health, education, economic, and political power all at the same time. This takes commitment and money, money that some do not want to invest in creating a more powerful country because they define power as force.

To heal the nation from the injustices of sexism and racism, we must confront what is fragmenting feminist efforts in the United States: racial intolerance. To heal from racism we must accept that women of color are U.S. citizens, not foreigners. From them we can learn various cultures and languages. Learning these skills translates into cultural literacy, an ability necessary in global communication. Most women have been cut out of U.S. global interaction. White men have controlled it, and most white women have held on to the power associated with their men and their skin color. Thus, they adjust to secondary privilege. This is a cowardly way to live, and to change means redefining and giving up that secondary position and proceeding as self-defined females within a global context that puts an end to racism. The need for this global skill in the arena of feminism can no longer be denied.

## REFERENCES

Asian American Breast Cancer Society. 1999. "Asian Women and Breast Cancer." Available at: <http://www.breastcancer.inf.com/bhealth/asian>.

Asian Women in Business. 2002. "Census 2000." E-mail: < info@awib.org>.

AsiaPacific.com. 2000. "Census 2000." Available at: <http://www.AsianPacific Universe.com>. E-mail: <api@hrsa.gov>.

Associated Press. 2001. "Deaths during Pregnancy Hit Minority Women More." Available at: <http://www.USATODAY.com>.

British Broadcasting Corporation. 1987. *Hawaii: Islands of the Fire Goddess*. Nature Series, vol. 1, no. 3. Bristol: British Broadcasting Corporation.

CNN. 1998. "Cold War: Episode 11." Available at: <http://www.cnn.com/SPECIAL/coldwar>.

C-SPAN. 2002. Wilson Center for National Affairs. New York: The New School. Book TV, June 27.

Dudley, Michael Kioni, and Keoni Kealoha Agard. 1990. *A Call for Hawaiian Sovereignty*. Honolulu: Na Kane O Ka Malo Press.

Estes, Richard. 2001. Interview at University of Pennsylvania, Philadelphia.

Fuentes, A., A. Afflick, and B. Hessol. 1997. San Francisco: *MEDTEP Research Center on Minority Populations*, 145 (2): 148–155.

Grant, Glen. 1994. *Obake: Ghost Stories in Hawaii*. Honolulu: Mutuai Publishing.

herSource. 2002. "Osteoporosis and Asian Women." Available at: <http://www.hersource.com/osteo/cl/asian>.

Leadership Education for Asian Pacifics. 2002. Telephone interview with Marta Gomez, Denver Colorado, January 12.

Liliu'okalani. 1991. *Hawaii's Story by Hawaii's Queen*. Boston: Charles E. Tuttle.

MacDonald, Donald Stone, and Donald N. Clark, eds. 1996. *The Koreans: Contemporary Politics and Society*. Boulder, Colo.: Westview.

Martin, Allison. 2002. "The Legacy of Operation Baby Lift." Available at: <http://www.comeunity/com/babylift>.

McGuire, William. 1991. *Recent American Immigrants: Southeast Asians*. Princeton, N.J.: Visual Education Corporation.

Minority Health Resource Center. 2002. "Osteoporosis and Related Health Disease." Washington, D.C., May 13. Available at: <http://www.omhre.com.pub.osteo.dll>.

National Association of Women's Health Organizations. 2001. Asian Women's Reproductive and Sexual Health Empowerment Project. Available at: <http://www.nawh.org>.

National Center for Health Statistics. 2002. "Fertility Rates." *Population Bulletin: America's Racial and Ethnic Minorities*. Available at: <http://www.edc.gov/nchswww>.

National Institute of Health. 2001a. Report on Osteoporosis. U.S. Department of Health and Human Services. Available at: <http://www.nih.gov/osteoporsis>.

National Institutes of Health. 2001b. "Non-Cancerous Uterine Conditions." Available at: <http://www.grantsl.nih.gov/grants/guide>. Last visited November 19, 2002.

Sinnott, Susan. 1993. *Extraordinary Asian Pacific Americans*. Chicago: Children's Press.

Sotomyor, Martha. 2002. Summit on Elder Abuse and Victimization. Albuquerque, New Mexico Hispanic Council on Aging.

South Asian Women for Action. 2002. Telephone interview with Nancy Masuta. Available at: <http://www.sawa.net>.

Tessier, Marie. 2002. "Profiting from Abuse." Wenews. Available at: <http://www.unicef.org/sexual-exploitation>. Last visited March 2002.

Trask, Haunani Kay. 1993. *From a Native Daughter: Colonialism and Sovereignty in Hawaii*. Monroe, Me.: Common Courage Press.

UNICEF. 2002. "Seven Asian Nations Sign Pact to Limit Sex Trade." Press release, January 17.

U.S. Bureau of the Census. 2001. "Nation's Asian and Pacific Islander Population." *Current Population Survey*, March. Washington, D.C.: U.S. Government Printing Office.

———. 2000a. "Asian and Pacific Islander Population in the United States." *Current Population Survey*. Washington, D.C.: U.S. Government Printing Office.

———. 2000b. *Current Population Survey*, March. Washington, D.C.: U.S. Government Printing Office.

———. 2000c. National Center for Educational Statistics. Telephone interview with Janet Davis.

———. 2000d. *Ethnic and Hispanic Statistics*. Population Division. Washington, D.C.: U.S. Government Printing Office.

———. 1999a. *Current Population Survey*. Washington, D.C.: U.S. Government Printing Office.

———. 1999b. "We Measure America, Asian and Pacific Islanders." Washington, D.C.: U.S. Government Printing Office.

———. 1998. *Current Population Survey*. Washington, D.C.: U.S. Government Printing Office.

U.S. Federal Bureau of Investigation (FBI). 2001. "U.S. Crime Statistics on Women." Washington, D.C.: U.S. Government Printing Office.

Webster, Nancy. 2001. Interview, Albuquerque, New Mexico.
Women's Enews Inc. 2002. "V-Day Campaign to End Violence against Women." Available at: <http://www.equalitynow.org>.
Zinn, Howard. 2001. *A People's History of the United States*. New York: HarperCollins.

# CHAPTER 6

# Healing from Intolerance and Redefining Direction

By no means should the reader assume or try to twist my message to mean that there is hate on behalf of women and people of color toward Americans. It is surprising that there is not. This population has proven its patriotism by fighting in wars, defending their constitutional right to assemble and engage in free speech. Yes, they are critical, but they are constructive in their criticism. They prioritize respect above profit, unity over competition, and family, community, and nation over individualism. They believe in American freedom and participate in it to address their concerns. They simply want to define themselves, name themselves, and have input into what happens to them without ridicule. This is the American way. They want independence to speak English and their mother tongue. They want their lack of good health and political power, religious discrimination, poverty, racism, and sexism to be seen as America's problem, not just the problem of the victims. They want to participate in American problem solving and celebrate its successes. They want to live in a safe and beautiful environment and to believe in the promise of freedom and justice for all. First there must be healing. This requires that we recognize the enemy, capture him, bring him to justice, and take a different direction lest we repeat what has already been done and what has not worked to the benefit of the United States.

## RECOGNIZING THE ENEMY

In this book I have spent a considerable amount of time identifying and analyzing American values and it appears we are our own worst enemy. The truth is that violence and greed developed and sustained by patriarch is the enemy. I have discussed my contention that colonialism is rooted in violence and the desire for profit. More specifically, colonialism is about imperialist expansion needing and wanting more. American's capitalist history has ingrained into the American psyche that they need more money, more land, more cheap labor power, more status power, and more prestige. Colonialism has long deep roots. It is most often about greed and the attainment of privilege, facilitated by discrimination. Civilization has surpassed these modes of operation, and persecution is now, as it has always been, a crime, a violation of human rights, and even a sin as defined by Christianity.

It is assumed that the reader knows that many people in many countries, especial our own, love America. But in order to deal with why so many people hate Americans it is essential for us to deal with our internal contradictions. A major contradiction to American freedom as it is overtly and covertly marketed is that some are freer than others. Sexism allows the commitment of freedom to political, economic, educational, and spiritual security to be violated. These offenses are especially heinous because they target women, well over 51 percent of the population; the majority, and in America the majority rules. Critics of America cite that, indeed, the majority, women and people of color, do not rule. In fact, they are assaulted by poverty, a trespass to the human right to have adequate shelter, eat nutritiously, and dress adequately. Not only are women deceived, the lies batter their children.

War is especially violent on women. The pain runs a continuum of tears of sadness to physical destruction. Until recently only men went to war, and those wars involved men that women loved. Sometimes women have an undeclared war of their own that manifests in a contradiction, for the men they love may be their oppressors and their caretakers at the same time. Wynonia Cawyer (2002), a World War II wife who is now eighty-one years old, told me a story about how she loved her husband but he returned from the war "almost ruined." She missed him "like crazy" but when he returned he was addicted to alcohol and "downright mean." He beat her and "bossed" her. Eventually, she left him but had to return because she had his child and no money. Fortunately, he changed; but the heartbreak, pain, and love she had for him manifested in a life with her living with him for sixty years feeling "different" about the man she once loved. In *Bessemer: A Sociological Perspective of a Chicano Barrio* (Blea 1991) I focused on the U.S. war in Vietnam. Chicano women helplessly stood by while their husbands, brothers, and sons had to resolve their country's racism toward them by "serving their country" or go to jail. When they returned, women witnessed their loved ones maimed by the war. Many men were drug and/or alcohol addicted and some even committed suicide or went to prison because they could not make sound decisions and adjust to what they had experienced.

Unfortunately the women of Afghanistan have not been able to give voice to their war pain, which was devastating. They, unlike American women who lived through World War II and the Vietnam War, were physically, mentally, and spiritually wounded. They became political footballs in a male-dominated game. Some women have launched a war on war. Some of these women are women of color. I am one of them. Analyzing the impact of war on women and children will progress the civilization of the human race toward a more peaceful existence. The United States has the power to lead this movement, but male-dominated international politics prevents its participation in decision making. Engaging in such a dialogue to plot a New World direction would assist how the United States is perceived internationally. In the eyes of those who hate us, we would progress from being arrogant power mongers to leaders in a world of peace. President George W. Bush appeared to be striving for this goal, but his tactics were male and the persons he had to negotiate with male. Thus, he was stuck in a male mode that did not allow thinking "outside the box." Until the contradictions in female–male relationships and the plight of people of color are resolved in the United States and other countries, the world will continue in contradiction and violence. Those who hate us will hold the contradictions to the American Dream, to equality, to freedom and justice for all up to international scrutiny that will lead to Americans lacking legitimacy.

Violence can manifest in incarceration, and being trapped in a socially prescribed female role for some women is something like being in prison. Over a million and a half people are forced to live in jails in America. Approximately 120,000 of those people are women. The U.S. Department of Justice (2002) maintains there has been growth in the rate of incarceration of females. The common profile of the imprisoned female is that of a young, single mother with few marketable skills, a high school dropout who lives below the poverty level. The majority of the women are between the ages of twenty-five and thirty-four, and an estimated 90 percent have an alcohol- or drug-related history.

## THE NATURE OF VIOLENCE

There is something fundamentally wrong when things are violent. The hate and anger necessary to escalate and to be outraged to the point of rioting, social organizing, and even war robs humans of humanity, and crimes against humanity are the worst kind because they threaten not only human life, but also the life of the planet. They desecrate, another form of violence, that which allows life: the Earth that renders a place to walk, eat, and sleep. They destroy animals necessary to the ecological cycle of which we humans are a part, and pollute the very air and water vital to all existence.

Yet defining crimes against humanity has been limited by male approaches to crimes. Until very recently, defining crimes against women has not been a

priority for national leaders, but it has been one of the top concerns for feminists around the world. For over thirty years now, U.S. feminists of color have
struggled to make racism a feminist issue, and for that length of time the white-
dominated feminist movement has failed to serve our own country by taking
action to eliminate racism. This unwillingness to take national action has
disempowered the United States and adds to why persons in other countries
do not like America.

The plight of Afghan women has opened my eyes to the dehumanization of
a person as a strategy in creating an enemy. Unfortunately people of color in
the United States have been treated as if they were the enemy. Dehumanizing
them has made it easier to kill, maim, or humiliate other human beings. Many
women have been killed, maimed, or humiliated because they are women and
men needed to claim or sustain power. This has led some women to see men
as the "enemy." In my opinion the real enemy is the mode of gender and race
relations ingrained into the social fabric of American society.

In this context the dehumanization of feminists is a strategy by which men
and some male-identified women demonize women seeking to claim their
human rights. Male-identified women find it easier to remain within their oppression because they created a comfort zone, a life that they do not want
changed because they fear the consequence of seeking change and/or they
fear tending for themselves. In fact, I extend they are probably unable to tend
to themselves.

The treatment of Afghan women has opened the eyes of Americans to patriarchy, but most see patriarchy as something that happens in other "undeveloped" countries. To define a country as undeveloped or underdeveloped justifies
the belief that the suppression of women due to patriarchy does not exist in the
United States. In doing this, sexism is a problem rooted in the specifics of the
Taliban, not a social phenomena that characterizes women in our own households and is then exported in its unique American form throughout the world.

I have demonstrated how when white patriarchy was imposed upon women
of color it disempowered them. I have compared it to the AIDS virus. Patriarchy spread and was internalized by men of color. It attaches itself to immigrants and to conquered people by penetrating their culture, infusing it, and
setting up conditions to produce as a host that destroys itself. This is cultural
genocide perpetrated by the combined effects of sexism and racism. Fortunately, most people of color have developed coping mechanisms, sometimes
in the form of open resistance, and have managed to survive. The white-dominated U.S. women's movement can learn much from this experience.

The cultures I have discussed teach communal values, strategies that can be
used for coalescing American diversity that can be transmitted into global
citizenship. Globalization is a process, it does not happen overnight. Like it or
not, there is now a global scrimmage for power, and I believe most U.S. citizens are caught up in patriotic efforts to kill Osama Bin Laden and not paying
attention to the larger picture. I also believe that its people can manage the
direction the United States takes; and it can be done without violence. The

average women of color of the cultures I have discussed have demonstrated this. The global crisis demands that we cease insulting cultures created by people of color over thousands of years, and utilize what has sustained them for centuries to see what we can apply to our current global situation.

For dominant America the preoccupation with profit is translated into doing what will acquire more: more money, more clothes, more private property, more time, more of everything. Progress is akin to wanting and acquiring more and requires changing things: making them better, quicker, faster. In order to keep up the turbulent pace, Americans must be competitive. This perpetuates the idea of being better than everyone else and surpassing every-one who wants the same thing. Most of the cultures I have discussed teach communal values. People are members of the same human community and are not to compete against one another. In fact, competition is insulting. In-stead, the cultures teach that community members assist one another.

Some discrimination is institutional, part of the social fabric. Some of it is more direct. In either case, discrimination limits competition and gives social advantage to nonminorities. Through discrimination people are kept unen-lightened and in a state of false consciousness to the point where they fre-quently blame themselves for not succeeding.

The issue of imperialism, however, never surfaces because it is not called imperialism, and some people of color are a result of cultural imperialism, transporting U.S. culture onto other cultures. This approach has made critics of the United States unpopular and on the surface this can be interpreted as unpatriotic; to the contrary, self-criticism is highly patriotic because its objec-tive is improvement, empowerment, and unity with the goal of world peace.

In a world of advanced technology, global economics, and international politics, it appears antiquated to engage in dialog about colonialism and impe-rialism, throwbacks to an industrial era. But there is a cultural lag between what people know and do and the technology that makes it possible to have a global economy and international politics. In other words, the common citi-zen is still acting as if society was functioning under capitalist principles that worked for the good of only a select few. Thus, colonization continues and the masses are kept out of global power struggles until it comes to going to war to see who will control.

Social scientists since the late 1960s have extended the internal colonial model to explain race relationships in America. Rather than power and control being imposed by an external power, it is imposed internally by a violent force upon less powerful people and their descendents. The model was not intended to analyze immigrants in a capitalist country, but the class analysis upon which it is based makes it easier to accept its interpretation of the master–servant nature of race relations. An extension of the internal colonial model incorpo-rates these immigrants into its perspective when they inherit traditional domi-nant–subordinate relations.

Sexism is also an extension of a patriarchal class perspective. Women are relegated to the status of the underclass, which can be called into action during social crisis. This happened to women during World War II, when they were called to work during the war effort and dismissed after the men returned. A lack of commitment to extinguish sexist infractions demonstrates a lack of commitment to abandoning hierarchical elements of capitalism in an era of globalization.

A lack of commitment to the abandonment of sexism and racism combined, as in the lives of women of color, leaves women excluded from the multifaceted structured world. Put more simply, America is moving toward openly becoming a global powermonger. This not only leaves women, especially women of color, out of economic, political, and technological control, it leaves them open to physical and emotional abuse plus the crimes of murder and rape in a world of people who are quickly becoming useless in the age of cyberspace.

Are these the ravings of a mad social scientist? It could be, but there are patterns of oppression and there are patterns of liberation. America is venturing into a realm where only a few men have been. Increasingly, men are entering the frontier of outer space and are exploring it in order to plot its colonization. This, however, has become an earth mission, a mission of other countries that struggle to dominate the earth and perhaps outer space. Men plot war against each other and women are getting caught up in it.

Women have been excluded from planning and implementing the futuristic direction of the United States and its technology, especially its war technology. This leaves them in a vulnerable social, political, and economic condition. During war they are subject to war crimes and short-time labor participation. I contend that U.S. history, with its internal cultures and conquest, is now extended to gain a position in the Middle East, a place it does not control. If women do not want history to repeat itself, they must take a position on the nature of war.

## CULTURAL IMPERIALISM

The unwritten rules of a society, based on the violence of war, define the standards of conduct for the winner and the loser of war. From this arise two very different standards. In ethnic studies we speak of them as a dual economy, or class, race, and gender segmentation. The end result is that the conquered is expected to live at a lower standard, and social institutions serve as guidelines by which the society operates and sustains itself. This entire mode of operation is extended to other parts of the world as a way of life via ideology and the use of technology and consumer products.

For the purpose for furthering the discussion and action on the feminization of racism in order to promote tolerance within America and peace in the world, I shall limit myself to discussing controlling and liberating elements found in American society that affect women, especially women of color. In outlining the history of "minority" women I have laid out the social elements that control the conduct of their behavior. The steering elements of liberating U.S.

women from socially prescribed roles have had a strategy that can be recognized in retrospect. Women of color have now had over forty years of emancipating activism geared at disengaging the control of patriarchy. This procedure has maneuvered them into a position of power in a direction that is consistent with global feminism and global communication. In fact, they are prime candidates for the Office of Global Communication established by President George W. Bush in 2002. But some fear this office and the focus on protecting the "homeland" will lead to further human rights violations by invading citizen's privacy, something men have enacted upon women for centuries.

Terms frequently associated with the analysis of women of color are "colonialism" and "internal colonialism." This discussion is based upon the work of Robert Blauner (1969), who drew upon the work of Frantz Fanon (1963) and Albert Memmi (1965), both of whom wrote extensively about colonization. According to Fanon (1963), colonization is a process based upon violence. Unfortunately, violence against women has been at the hands, feet, and other weapons of men. This immediately sets men up to be the enemy, but theoretically the real enemy is patriarchy. Men and what men control are but the mode of delivery. They are in charge of the enforcement of a system of privilege based upon, until recently, them being lucky enough to be born male. Because of the abundance of privilege and the institutionalized threat that there is scarcity, men are hesitant to disrupt the patterns of female oppression.

Violence is used by the colonizers against the colonized to gain cheap labor, services, and land, and to retain the colonized in subservient positions. Such is the case with women of color in the United States and other parts of the world. Women of color in the United States have seen how violence is historical and takes different forms as times change and women gain more freedom in their gender role.

Discrimination is an intricate part of the remnants of colonialism; in the process the colonizers force the colonized to live separately in conditions inferior to those of the colonizers. Women have been forced to live isolated in their homes. Women of color are segregated on reservations and in barrios, ghettos, and set-aside sections of cities. In isolation, the oppressed are placed where they do not possess real privileges based on economic power, status, and prestige. Even the poorest of the poor colonizers have privileges over the colonized and believe they are superior.

To maintain control, the colonizers advance stereotypes about the colonized and their inferior status, thereby reinforcing discrimination and prejudice against the colonized. They become the losers in all competitions, are advertised as such, and the colonized are generally unable to get out of their situation. Their language and culture are devalued and any contributions they may have made to society are erased or appropriated by the colonizers.

Robert Blauner (1972, 1969) concentrated on the colonial model primarily in how it related to African Americans, but mentioned that it also served to explain the American Indian and Chicano experience. The generation of scholars of color whom followed Blauner expanded upon his internal colonial model and it is now one of the leading models explaining race relations in the United States. Women of color made grand contributions to that model.

First and foremost in the oppression of women is control of their bodies and movements; even within the reservations, the barrios, and the ghettos. This is witnessed in how women are taught to move, eat, sleep, walk, talk, and dress. Although women of color in the United States have not had to live covered by the *burqa* as Afghan women did in the twenty-first century, as recently as the 1950s and 1960s Hispanic women did cover their heads routinely with *tapalos*, scarves, and hats. Catholic brides and widowed women often covered their faces. These women did nothing wrong, and the men around them as well as other women did not see anything significant about this.

Some men have witnessed men interrelate with women in ways that are personally abhorrent to them. But they have felt like the Taliban leader who confessed to Goodwin (2000) that he had no choice when he had to tell his female employees they had to wear the *burqa* and then to stay home. He was forcing them to wear the veil, and admitted that when one sees women in *burqas*, it is easier to realize the power of covering a woman: "You don't treat them like people anymore, just bits of cloth carefully regulating how they move down the street." There is very little between this and walking in chains, having one foot bound, or walking three steps behind a man.

Some men rationalize female injustice. They feel that on a pragmatic level sexism is what has to happen to keep the society stable. Others just hate women, and like some Taliban men they assemble to watch and cheer a woman's degradation. Internalized contradictions force women to humiliate themselves in order to make a living. They do this by popping out of cakes at bachelor parties, stripping at conventions, and even getting "gang banged." There is not much difference between that and kneeling and being flogged and having men celebrate female pain in Afghanistan.

Several things motivate and manipulate male behavior beyond their self-interest. One of those things is the preferred and prescribed male role that they inherit when they are born. Even if men (like white people who do not like racial oppression) find some of their privilege based upon the oppression of women and even if they don't like it, they will hesitate to change it or they will intervene only to a certain degree. The degree, the line a man draws and does not go beyond, is based not only on his self-interest but on what other men will allow. We see this over and over again when members of the oppressed class and caste know that the massacre of Indians, slavery, and stealing land are wrong but would limit their efforts to stop it.

In summary, men are controlled and defined by social factors that guide their behavior, and one of them is their right to have more options and more social comfort than women. To end patriarchy is to educate women and to make better the relationships between women and men. To make better our relationship is to enhance our society and the world. Therefore, it is in the best interest of white women to promote putting a female face on racial discrimination, because in doing this they liberate themselves from limited roles, career options, and have defended their spirituality. They also liberate themselves from the contradictions they face, sometimes without knowing it, based upon the oppression of people of color. This is where women in one of the most powerful countries can contribute to the world. Unfortunately, September 11, the plight of Afghan women, and the war in the Middle East combined is the vehicle by which women can make this contribution.

To make the patterns of female oppression and liberation more clear, let us concentrate on what we know about Afghan women under Taliban control and about what we know about the oppression of women of color in the United States. To do this I shall rely upon my thirty-year experience as a Chicana sociologist, and heavily upon what has been reported on the Internet, television, and radio and printed in newspapers, articles, and books. The first thing Americans heard was that women Afghan women were being maimed and killed. For example, in an Internet article by Jan Goodwin (2000), "Buried Alive: Afghan Women under the Taliban," Goodwin describes that on February 27, 1998, 30,000 men and boys filled the dilapidated Olympic sports stadium in Kabul, the capital of Afghanistan. Street hawkers selling nuts, biscuits, and tea to the crowd engulfed entrances into the stadium. The male crowd was there to see a young woman receive 100 lashes, and to watch two thieves have their right hands amputated. The woman scheduled to be whipped was single and had been arrested walking with a man who was not a relative. This was a sufficient enough crime for her to be found guilty of adultery. Adultery was punishable by flogging. Had she been married, she would have been publicly stoned to death.

I have reviewed how women of color have been maimed and murdered. It may not happen as overtly today, but Chicanas, Indians, and African American women live with the flashbacks and anxiety of inheriting a social position as a result of rape, slavery, mutilation, and assassination. Their mothers, grandmothers, and great-grandmothers left the stories. American forefathers wrote it down. Our choice is to believe them or not, to accept the truth and do something about it.

Chicanas, Indians, and African American women have been hunted down, incarcerated, branded, and made to toil for little or no money. This is their experience today as it appears in government statistics and in movies. Declared or undeclared war has armed contemporary Asian and Pacific Islander women with the knowledge of being attacked, dehumanized, and traded for dollars. Like Indian women and Chicanas, they have seen their land and environmental resources stolen and disfigured. In their case the disfigurement came for many in the twentieth century in the form of nuclear bombs. Vietnamese women are more familiar with chemical warfare. What has made the dehumanization even more painful is that members of their own families, and sometimes even they, have had to give into the debasing elements of war, the ruination of their own environment, and even the national and international sex trade in order to survive.

The parallels between Native Americans and Chicanos in the United States and the colonization of people in underdeveloped countries in other parts of the world are too similar to dismiss. The conquest of the southwest created a colonial situation in the traditional sense, with Mexican land and population being controlled by an imperialistic United States. The situation exists today in the form of internal colonies.

Internal colonization has to do with how indigenous people had their land invaded by people from another country, Americans. The Americans used military force to gain and maintain control, and the original inhabitants involuntarily became subjects of the conquerors. The conquered then had an alien culture and government imposed upon them and became victims of racism and cultural genocide relegated to a submerged status. Like the Taliban, the conquerors of Indians and later Chicanos felt they had a mission from god to occupy the role they assumed. With regard to the southwest this was called "manifest destiny."

## DENIAL AS A COPING MECHANISM

Women of color in the United States and Afghan women have seen their religion bastardized. Members of the Taliban maintain they implement laws controlling women for the glory of God. Let us not forget that the savagery against women of color was for the glory of God, and in God's name women of color have had ancient spirituality desecrated, discredited, and relegated to the level of superstition and the work of the devil.

Religion and spirituality link the present to a larger sense of being. It helps explain the unexplainable and allows a human perception of reality. Among women of color religion is diverse, but in all of them spirituality permeates the soul, the core of what constitutes identity and how people relate to animals, the Earth, the heavens, and one another. This is more than political ideology; it is the belief in something larger than what is experienced on Earth, something grander than is explained by science. It is a belief in a supreme being or beings that permeate the social consciousness to influence creativity, hope, charity, and life pursuits.

When primarily Protestant Americans gained control of Indians and Mexicans, they bastardized the indigenous and Catholic traditions. For Indian women who had converted to Catholicism this was the second time they had their foundation disrupted. The first time was by the Spanish. When African and Asian immigrants entered the country, they inherited this desecration of spiritual belief, but they generally did not give up their religions. Among Latinos, the combined Spanish and Indian components are evident in *la Virgin de Guadalupe*, Jesus Christ, the saints, and the holy family, which is the model for the Latino family. Unlike African Americans, the Latino religious culture of origin is evident in the name of towns and cities, streets, and rivers. Even if Chicanos are not Catholic, they feel the impact of the indigenous, the church, and Christianity. It is part of Chicano reality and is often linked with the founding of communities. Catholicism plays a role during major rites of passage, in birth, baptism, *quincenieras* (community introductions of young women at the age of fifteen), marriage, and death; but it also is present in the art of the muralist, the studio painter, poets, novelists, and low riders, and on tattoos and t-shirts. The Native American and black struggle to regain their spirituality of origin is also evident in the form of dream catchers and libation practices, on the walls of buildings, in fashions worn by both men and women, in food, and in festivals.

Under the patriarchal rule of the Taliban, the religious restrictions for women impacted other areas of their lives. Female education, from kindergarten through graduate school, was banned. Employment for women was banned. It was illegal to wear makeup, nail polish, or jewelry; pluck eyebrows; cut hair short; wear colorful or stylish clothes, sheer stockings, white socks and shoes, or high-heel shoes; walk loudly; talk loudly; or laugh in public. In fact, the government did not believe women should go out at all; they could not step outside their residences. Although the rules are nowhere as repressive as Taliban rules, women in the United States very often fear venturing out of their homes. On the streets of America they are subject to sexual harassment, purse snatching, mugging, and rape.

Unlike the Taliban, where boys were authorized to use weapons and whips on women if they decided they were breaking the Taliban's laws, in the United States women are controlled by fear of male attack and by media and government reports on crimes against women. Women endure all this only because they are perceived as the "weaker sex" and easy targets for predators. Women of color are more frequently victimized. However, women are fighting back. One complaint often heard among feminist circles is the inability to fight back effectively. Thus far women have used self-education, self-defense courses, and the courts, but the violence against women continues, both inside and outside their homes. If a woman is going to be murdered, she will most likely be murdered by a male she knows, a husband, a male lover, or a relative (U.S. Department of Justice 2000).

The oppression of women depends on controlling their time and by also controlling what they think and do during their time. The Taliban banned virtually all forms of entertainment for the people of Afghanistan. The contention was that time should be spent serving the country and praying to God. Everything else was a waste of time and people were not allowed to waste time. American society evolved so that women's time was spent in learning how to keep house and have and raise children. Until the middle to latter part of the last century how women spent their time was not valued. U.S. women have fought for control of their own time and to increase the value of what they do with it.

I feel perhaps African American women have been most successful in bringing their talents before the public. Latinas are now emerging, but other women of color have made national contributions, and more create art and ideas. In the first five-year existence of the Taliban, they expunged all leisure activities. Their list of what was illegal grew to include music, movies and television, picnics, wedding parties, New Year celebrations, and any kind of mixed-sex gathering (Goodwin 2000). They also banned children's toys, including dolls and kites, card and board games, cameras, photographs, and paintings of people and animals, pet parakeets, cigarettes and alcohol, magazines and newspapers, and most books.

Once outlets of expression and unwanted influences are restrained, the next step is to get the victim to internalize that their worth is very little or nothing. These messages are both latent and overt. They are latent in that no mention is made of women of color and negative messages are fed to the larger society. The dangerous thing is that sometimes the stereotypes have a thread of truth to them; it is a very short and thin truth that is stretched to the outrageous. Because women are strong, resilient, competent, generous, and communal, it is said they are weak, not too smart, greedy, jealous, and cannot be alone. As a result of the low attainment imposed upon them, they develop low self-esteem and appear to be living up (down) to the stereotype. Continued low public achievements strengthens the stereotype and furthers discrimination and prejudice against the colonized.

To counteract some of the limitations placed by racial and gender inequity upon the cultures of women of color in the United States, women have taken a nonviolent means of addressing their oppression. They developed their own talents in music, movies, and television productions. They hold women-only gatherings like wedding showers and sweat lodges, and, of course, engage in mixed-sex gathering. But they have also created gender-neutral children's toys and games. They are now masters with cameras, innovative in taking photographs and painting and in producing magazines, newspapers, and books.

One of the major stereotypes against oppressed people is that they are unable to organize. A review of the 1960s and the history of women of color since that time reveals that they have an unrecognized history of organization. This was seen in the first chapter of this book in our discussion of the 1960s, and in subsequent chapters on the different ethnic and racial groups. Yet there is injustice. White women still have more privileges than women of color. Women of color are still dealing with the low value attached to their status in America. They have demonstrated that they are more diverse than anyone ever considered. Not only are they racially and ethnically diverse within their own groups, they are diverse by age, income, marital status, number of children, politics, spirituality, education, participation in the criminal justice system, immigration status, and language.

There is a distinct difference that impedes universal acceptance of Anglo colonialism in the United States. The land taken from the Indians and Mexico bordered the United States rather than being an area geographically distant from the "mother country." I maintain that Americans have accepted the myth that the area was meant to be U.S. territory; that the southwest was won in fair and just warfare as opposed to conscious and unjust imperialism. In the case of the U.S. war with Mexico, I think they want to believe that Mexico attacked peace-loving Anglos. They want to believe that imperialism is an affliction of other countries and not of their own.

## GLOBAL EXPANSION

Imperialism has to do with economic, political, and cultural expansion. Expansion is what some fear the United States is trying to attempt with its presence in the Middle East and fervor for patriotism. After the U.S. War with Mexico the original American colonies expanded in size and new American settlements sprang up on not only what was once Mexico, but also what was known as Indian Territory. These settlements added vast amounts of land and created nations within a nation. Psychologically, socially, and culturally the conquered remained Mexican and Indian, speaking their own language but with little other overt control over their political and economic lives.

In an imperialist war and in colonization it is important to gain control of the colonized's language. More recently we have seen state and federal government efforts to pass English-only laws. Blacks, Asians, Indians, and Hispanics have fought aggressively against these laws, because once the native tongue (the voice) is removed, much of how one structures one's reality is removed. One strategy is to silence the population, and if that fails to isolate the language to private use in households only. Thus, it is important to control not only what is thought and said, but also where it is thought and said. In the 1960s people of color in the United States held fast to their constitutional right to meet, organize, and speak about their living conditions. Culture-of-origin languages survived and those in danger of extinction continue to be regenerated.

Under a colonial and internal colonial structure the oppressed must interact with their oppressor. Interaction is dictated by both written and unwritten rules, and the best examples can be found in master–slave relationships. The colonizers will use members of the colonized who most resemble them by placing them on the periphery of both social groups. Encouraging colonized individuals to work for the colonizers is done by having them act as "go-betweens." This technique robs the colonized group of leadership and ensures that they will be kept in a subservient social position. In the case of slavery, one sees this in the form of house slaves and field slaves. Black Americans, unlike Chicanos, have a history of living closer to white people on white property and in their homes.

Often the colonized will reject their origin and identify themselves, as much as possible, with the colonizers. According to Memmi (1965), the colonizers will never fully accept the "go-betweens" because they believe colonized persons are of an inferior race with an inferior culture. Thus emerges the marginal person, the coconut, the apple, and the Oreo. Coconuts are upwardly mobile Mexican Americans that are considered by other Mexican Americans as brown (Mexican) on the outside but white in their world view on the inside. Indians are called apples and blacks are called Oreos. Until recently, not many women of color have occupied this position. Men of color have received more upward mobility, more education, and higher salaries because they were seen as less threatening. Women of color gently invaded the educational system, learned the white man's language and behavior, and quietly invaded his labor market. While they were doing this, women found men of similar social consciousness, married them, and teamed up with them to continue to advocate on behalf of their community. This explains how some members of the oppressed group gain upward mobility and why. Some, maybe most, will maintain they worked for what they got and that anyone can do the same. Maybe, maybe not; maybe it is a combination of the two strategies that produces marginal people who have to balance color, gender, and income in such a way that it does not cause them undue stress.

The women under the Taliban were not marginal to the Middle Eastern conflict with the United States. They were thrust, as all women are thrust, into the middle of the war. Although there is little comparison between U.S. women and women under the Taliban, injustice is injustice when one is the victim. In the United States men do not crowd into stadiums to watch women being dismembered, but they sometimes fall silent when luckless women are paraded in front of the media and made examples of. I noticed that such is the case of Heidi Fleiss, the white upper-class Hollywood madam, charged with various crimes surrounding the prostitution service she provided to wealthy men from all over the world. It was Fleiss who was prosecuted, not her male customers. They were not used as an example of how affluent people are to behave.

Much attention was given to the fact that Taliban men held up the severed hands of the women and announced, "These are the chopped-off hands of thieves, the punishment for any of you caught stealing." Then, to restore the party atmosphere, the thieves were driven in a jeep once around the stadium. This brought the crowd to their feet, sequestered the women, and warned the men (Goodwin 2000). I believe that women in the United States are sequestered in their roles, not only in their homes but in the educational system, in their lack of political power, and in their churches. Some are detained because they got pregnant, others because they are poor, old, or sick, but many because they do not speak English fluently and cannot read or write. Yet female illiteracy, health, and religious roles are not viewed as the same disability or with the same priority if the illiterate, elderly, or unhealthy person is male. American women's social circumstances are not like women's circumstances living under the Taliban. They are different forms of violence and control, different in degrees.

In spite of the fact that American women experienced dramatic changes over the 1990s and these changes have influenced women in other countries, they nevertheless still earn less money than men, even when they have the same jobs. They still are the primary health care givers, teachers, and home-makers. Now they also have to go to work. I believe this is causing women to delay marriage and childbirth and causing them to further distinguish men as the enemy. Out of economic necessity many more women are required to work. Children more frequently grow up in daycare or in front of the television because when women work outside the home they have to come home and engage in unpaid labor that is gender cast. Although there has been some effort to end this dual standard, it still goes on. The changes stimulated by women means that the life of men has changed, but it has only changed relative to what it once was. Men are resisting marriage until they can find a more comforting woman because feminists now expect men to fulfill responsibilities at work and at home.

I maintain that this expectation, however, applies only to the younger generation, those under thirty. For most married men over thirty little has changed except that the divorce rate is higher because women will no longer respect privileges based on gender alone. Men have little choice in the matter: They either change, live alone, or go through a series of relationships that fall apart or become downright oppressive to women in public view. In totality, the male secret is out. Yet some women follow traditional patterns despite the profound change that other women have tried to inspire in their lives. Much remains to be done to give every woman the opportunity to make a better life from birth. This includes launching a campaign to increase the worth of girl babies, demand childcare and maintenance until women can redefine their lives, and the ability to work in nontraditional jobs, engage in higher education, and enjoy a broader array of lifestyle choices.

However, my work with senior females in AARP and as president of the New Mexico Hispanic Council on Aging reveals that many women still do not look forward to a secure old age rooted in family values. Older women of color do not have the time left in life, as well as monetary resources, to take advantage of alternative lifestyles. They end their lives in family lifestyles they did not choose but had to accept. Women of color are significantly behind other women on almost every dimension of advancement. But, like other women, they continue to live longer than men do and their population keeps getting larger.

I have asked myself what keeps these women keeping on? During this century feminists should be paying more attention to the interaction of age, race, and gender relations. Combined, women of color are the majority of women in the United States and in the world. Asian and Latin American immigration and the higher fertility rate among women of color is leading to the gradual transformation of the United States into an increasingly multiracial female society of lower-level service providers. Put more simply, it is people of color who will be providing services for whites as they age. Given the hostility that older people are receiving now, with bad race relations one can only guess what kind of service white seniors will receive at the hands of younger workers of color, especially in the areas of nursing and home care.

Increased immigration in recent years accounts for much of this new population diversity and alternative ways of living. The 1980s saw the largest number of immigrants in the country's history. The 1990 census found 10.1 million girls and women who were born outside the United States, comprising 8 percent of the total female population (U.S. Bureau of the Census 1993). During the 1970s and 1980s the vast majority of immigrants to the United States came from Latin America and Asia and introduced new food into American kitchens and new entertainment.

Another consequence of the increase in the number of foreign-born women is an increase in the number of women without a fundamental knowledge of English. One in seven women over age four speak a language other than English at home, and Spanish is the first language for the majority of these women (U.S. Bureau of the Census 1993). Almost 4 million (3% of all U.S. women) live in linguistic disconnection in households where no one over age thirteen speaks English fluently. This separates them from English-speaking women, who are the majority in the country. This degree of silence and lack of connection, plus English-only laws adopted by several states, differs from the Taliban language restrictions on women, again, only in degrees

Women of color are severely limited and sequestered in their homes and in certain jobs—having to choose between maintaining family values and sustaining their lives. More women of color are urban. Many have had to leave their rural homes to live in metropolitan areas. Nearly 80% of U.S. women now live in metropolitan areas (U.S. Bureau of the Census 2001). Most rural women or women of color are ill-equipped to handle the city. For example, it is hard for Indian women to move from the reservation to the city and experiment with how to live. While they are trying to figure certain things out, they are robbed, raped, and become alcoholics while their mothers die of diabetes. Yet suburbs, not cities, have received most of the women of color population gain. Women who move to the suburbs tend to have extensive urban experiences. Most Chicanas, for example, have had over a century of living in cities like Los Angeles, San Antonio, and Santa Fe. Most of these women work. Women of working age (eighteen to sixty-four) are slightly more likely than average to live in metropolitan areas, and three out of four elderly women live in such areas, but most of the immigrants have rural pasts and many women of color, especially Native American and Latinas, are still rural (U.S. Bureau of the Census 2000e).

## SOCIAL CONTRADICTIONS

In psychology, if a person internalizes something it means they have taken it into their body of knowledge and made it true. A contradiction is knowledge that is in dispute. There is a disagreement between two things that are true. To deal with this conflict, some people manifest anger or denial, a refusal to reject one or the other. When such contradictions are not addressed there can be self-destructive behavior. This is what has happened to some members of the racial and ethnic groups in America. Not only are they prone to contradiction, the society that produces them is made sick and unharmonious. Racism and sexism, especially when combined, are a form of illness. They are America's symptoms of dysfunction due to inherent contradictions.

Blauner (1969) wrote that colonized populations have historically been rural and a result of imperialism. We are no longer a predominately rural society. The cultures of women of color, for the most part, began as rural, but the pressures of internal colonialism have forced them into cities. Even in the city the internal colonial model holds up, but it is in need of updating. There has been outside pressure to get people of color to move to cities where they are now most concentrated and can be observed. This removes them from the land and gives those with resources opportunities for land acquisition so they can extend their practices for profit.

As we move toward a global economy, the internal colonial model has to be revised in order to explain what will happen to people of color. For now, they have internalized contradictions that they struggle to resolve as they compete among social groups. They have internalized the white man's ways and grasp for bits of power while striving for upward mobility. At the same time, they are angry and tired. To participate in the process, they sacrifice aspects of language, culture, and spirituality and often find themselves in need of the white man's therapy, because the process of upward mobility is often too much for women and men, regardless of color.

There are patterns of resistance and liberation from contradictions. When the disturbance and outrage at discrimination is turned inward by the colonized, frustration emerges. Frustration can manifest as suppressed aggression, demonstrations, riots, revolutions, and wars. But these natural outcomes are buffered by minimal comfort, so the oppressed either comes to hate the oppressor or aspires to be like him. Because they have been taught not to hate by their native cultures and by Christianity, and because they have no weapons, they generally do not want to risk war. Until there is a gain in political consciousness this anger is at best internalized, it is rarely acted upon. When internalized oppression results in violence it is directed inward and manifests in depression and even self-destructive acts, not only against the self but against their own kind. Some examples of this include the high alcohol and drug addiction rates among women of color, the high suicide rate on Indian reservations, and gang activity.

Victimization of women is thus internalized anger at what one has to do to gain upward mobility. Victimization of humans reminds the oppressed of himself, but he is frequently unaware that he is angry, much less what he is angry at. He is angry at a situation that appears to have no perpetrator. What confines people to gender roles has no face. It is never just one person; it is a system of oppression with interrelated factors and players that does just as much harm to the victimizer.

When consciousness and anger manifest toward the colonizers, there is violence that frequently manifests in revolution. In the Middle East the Taliban acted upon their Soviet Union aggressors and what they saw as social–political intervention by the United States (Goodwin 2000). When the colonized acknowledges a real enemy, they seek to terminate or prevent colonization. Memmi (1965), Fanon (1963), and Blauner (1969) feel real social change can ultimately come about only through violence in the form of revolution by the colonized. The civil rights movement attempted to be a social revolution that was predicated upon the teachings of class divisions by Karl Marx and nonviolence by Mahatma Ghandi, who resisted British colonialism in India.

While there have been some advances in the lives of women of color in the United States, it is white women who have profited most from the civil rights movement that has for so long sought equality for people of color. The women's movement, combined with the fight for racial equality, has placed pressure on the society to change. The society has more readily accepted white women. This can been seen in U.S. census (1993, 2001) statistics that demonstrate an increase of white females in higher paying jobs and with higher educations. This once again proves to people of color the existence of white privilege, that whites take care of whites. White women have profits via upward mobility at the expense of combining their women's movement efforts with the gain of people of color and have remained silent about it.

While men and women who support them (some would say women acting under false consciousness) do not address the fact that the American economy now requires both men and women to work outside the home in order to live up to the American Dream, a white middle-class lifestyle. The middle class is often seen as the buffer between the lower and upper class in the United States, as the social position aspired to by people of color who also live under false consciousness and do not recognize their own oppression, and sometimes the oppression of others.

In response to this social situation, women are not only working more, but also having children later in life (U.S. Bureau of the Census 2001). One scenario is that they are often absent from the daily routine of raising children and are too exhausted to pay them adequate attention when they get home, especially when they are single parents. Another scenario is that women burn themselves out trying to do a good job of all that is required of them at work and at home and they end up with a variety of physical and mental illnesses.

It has been my experience that because of the need to control their own bodies and the need to support themselves and others, some women of color support population control and abortion. Even though, on the whole, women of color are more conservative on the issues of abortion than are white women, most have practiced some form of birth control, but fewer practice it consistently. Thus, most women of color do become mothers. I feel this is due to a high rate of religious affiliation among people of color, the spiritual value for human life and extended families, plus the fact that so many fear genocide, the killing of their people. This, plus the need to gain acceptance via the status and prestige attributed to motherhood, also explains why the proportion of families maintained by women of color is higher, and why the racial group with the smallest proportion of families maintained by women are whites.

I extend that whites fear parity and the freedom of racial and ethnic groups because they fear a lack of power. They know the process of oppression is violent, and have been taught that liberation is violent. Americans had to die for our freedoms. I have noticed some whites are so fearful they worry the white race will become extinct. This is what drives white supremacists. This also worries men who resist feminism. To prevent them from seeking to control their own bodies and their own lives, Christianity imposes upon women the idea of sin. Thus, women seeking alternative lifestyles walk around in guilt and fear of condemnation. This was my experience also. I grew up in the Catholic Church. Christianity, especially Catholicism, teaches that marriage is a sacrament, a way of getting holier and closer to God. Women are not taught that in the process they also become disempowered on earth. Sex is engaged in only to bear children. While fewer than one in ten never-married white or Asian women have had a child, one in four such Hispanic women, one in three such American Indian women, and nearly half of African American women have done so. The desire to be validated is so strong that America has young women and girls raising children when they are still children. After having taught students for almost thirty years, I can validate that a great number of these babies are the result of very young women with older men, but these men are rarely prosecuted.

So important is marriage and children to women that they experience "empty-nest" syndrome when they are no longer needed by their children. Women living outside what has been considered the typical American household are considered deviant. This is especially true for lesbians. There are symptoms of women attempting to resolve the contradictions of marriage and children. They involve women getting married later and having fewer children, and the divorce rate is high. Vast numbers of women are completing school or participate in continuing or adult education and are entering the workforce.

Except for African Americans, married women are still a majority of all women. The number of African American women who have never been married nearly equals the number of currently married African American women (U.S. Bureau of the Census 2001). Maybe they know something. Maybe they are like other women of color who are experiencing change. Among all racial and ethnic groups, the number of single women is growing faster than the number of married women. The most dramatic increase in the proportion of never-married women occurred among women in their late twenties and early thirties. This generation is sometimes call Generation X, because they appear not to care much about anything, and are therefore deviant.

There is a need in the United States for a new discourse on democracy, its ethics, and its values. I am not the first to call for such action. We need to embrace self-criticism as do some of our Asian citizens, and stop some of our denial about the nature of social–historical, physical, psychological, and spiritual trauma caused to women and people of color by discrimination. We must heal from this transgression. First we must be clear what it is we are healing from. For many this is difficult to see; for others it is so clear they suffer depression and suicidal tendencies.

The consequences of war and discrimination are depressing. Conditions were so deplorable for women under the Taliban that many were severely depressed and suicidal (Goodwin 2000). Without the resources to leave the country, some chose suicide as a means of escape. Suicide is rare in the Middle East. Afghan women were being treated for esophageal burns after swallowing battery acid or poisonous household cleansers. Household cleaners are easy to find and inexpensive, but it is a very painful way to die. Hundreds of Native American youth have suffered this kind of death (Kills Pretty Enemy 2001).

## A NEW DISCOURSE

Very few people are ready to engage in a discourse that suggests that the United States, like so many other countries, was founded and sustained upon violence. This is a factor of white, Euro-centered colonialism. Colonialism suppresses differences. From that violence is created a class, race, and gender structure that has caused suffering to millions and compromised the ideals of freedom and justice for all. It is a form of ethnic cleansing that no one wants to admit. The result is a culture that has limited access to elements of freedom for those who do not fit the white, male, Euro-centered norm, and granted privilege to others. Most Americans do not see or understand this, and they have not developed solutions to its social problems caused by their own a lack of democracy, which is masked under a message that all members of society can be rich and powerful if they work hard enough.

America has had numerous opportunities to engage in discourse and to heal from social discord. The most recent has been September 11, but there have been terrorist acts before, including the first bombing of the World Trade Center and that which took place in Oklahoma City. Prior to that we had the quincentennial of Columbus's experience in the Western Hemisphere. As mentioned in Chapter 1, it was a great opportunity for retribution and reconciliation, and to a limited degree some healing has taken place. It promoted healing of the fragmentation of the Americas by drawing to our attention that there was no discovery to be made by Europeans because indigenous people knew the Americas and had traveled them very well.

The quincentennial also promoted the recognition of the violation of human rights in our hemisphere, the destruction of the environment, and our dependence upon nature. Civil rights activists have been trying to enlighten us about the inhumanity of racism and sexism, and it is no longer the secret it was in the early 1960s. The lessons that could have and should have been learned were not incorporated into our general understanding of the development of the Americas to include a time when there were no man-made boundaries on maps. Today we live with those boundaries and with unlearned lessons in female courage, generosity, fortitude, and wisdom. Some of my students voice this as disrespectful to women, but to say this is disrespectful is to trivialize the neglect and victimization of women. For women of color there is also the threat of the appropriation of their culture and marketing it in watered-down, New Age products like aromatherapy, spa massage, and harmonic conversion.

Authors like those represented in *Native American Testimony* (Nabokov 1991) lament the loss of the continent's original life forms and the waste "modern" industry has rendered. This waste is supported by world views that include technology, profit motives, upward mobility, and individualism, attributes that have brought some indigenous people to the brink of extinction.

Indeed, some cultures have disappeared, and health practitioners, environmentalists, and the media stress that Americans are dying from stress-related illnesses. Those remaining struggle daily to survive the social toxicity that characterizes America. What is ironic is that so many people take political action to save endangered species of animals and even plants. These same people will not put the same energy into saving endangered cultures and people. The United States has no cultural policy. Most efforts to protect cultures from destruction have been those made by endangered cultures on their own behalf. There appears to be little value placed on human worth, their unique niche in the lifecycle, and their contributions to defining civilization. This neglect appears to be "ethnic cleansing." It manifests the same results as shooting, torturing, or beheading people in Bosnia and Afghanistan. This does not begin to compare or address the desecration of spiritual belief and role of women in creation convictions. The difference between desecration and death is a matter of degrees, based on how far the powerful take their violent action.

These beliefs are just as strong as the Adam and Eve story of Christianity, but only indigenous people seem to know them, and only they seem to care about or respect them. If nonindigenous people care, most Americans do not want to hear their voices and call them "radical." To most, this means abnormal.

In my studies of native cultures I have noticed that one tactic taken by indigenous people to protect their cultures is the use of treaties with the United States in the U.S. court system. This points out the contradictions and some white people deeply resent this. They feel the "Indian" is trying to cheat them, and that they do not have responsibility for something done in the past by their ancestors and the fact that they profit from colonization. In order to heal the nation, we must make retribution and correct history. To women of color this means not segmenting history from the teaching of morals, ethics, responsibility, and the truth about the nature of the reality in which we live. This is especially important for children, who grow up believing in certain "truths," thinking they know right from wrong, then finding out that they have learned a thought system that is misleading and full of lies. If not corrected, their discovery leads them to distrust adults and authority. It fosters a lack of a sense of civic duty and doubts about education and the political and economic structures. Thus, the most secure route to achieving social continuity is truth. Truth is essential for building the future and for teaching American youth pride and reliability for the care of the next generation. It teaches youth that they have a role in protecting freedom.

Correcting history and making retribution does not always involve a great deal of money. An example of this is the renaming of Custer Battlefield or the Little Big Horn Battlefield National Monument. The effort was led in Washington, D.C., by Senator Ben Nighthorse Campbell of Colorado and numerous grassroots activists. On November 1 the Washita Battlefield National Historic Site in Cheyenne, Oklahoma, was officially dedicated. The 326-acre site was established in 1996 to mark the site of the surprise attack and massacre of Cheyenne Chief Black Kettle's village by Colonel George Armstrong Custer and the U.S. 7th Calvary. The village consisted of mostly elderly, women, and children. Washita was a key event in the government campaign to force the Cheyenne onto a reservation and was named after the man who lost the battle, Custer. Advocates of the name change wanted equality. They noted that Civil War veterans, regardless of service on the sides of the North or the South, were honored at several battlefields for fighting for what they believe was right. They maintained American Indians were doing no less.

## RETRIBUTION AND ATONEMENT

The Washita effort was an effort to be inclusive. Indigenous populations noted the contradiction at the Washita site and maintained it was right for their ancestors to fight for their land and their way of life; yet they were not being honored. The Washita Battlefield National Historic Site name change was holistic, a change in "Indian" policy to include women and children as victims of war. It demonstrated how justice could be achieved and how other injustices could be corrected. It also demonstrated how it took both a liberal and a conservative approach.

Some lessons can be learned from focusing upon the Vietnam War Memorial in Washington, D.C. It took several years to note the participation of U.S. women in the war, and now a memorial to women who participated on the U.S. side stands not too far from the famous wall commemorating the 59,000 men who died in the war. It nevertheless pays no tribute to the Vietnamese soldiers and the thousands of women, many of who were raped, who endured that war, some of whom were forced to immigrate with children to the United States or lose their lives.

When women of color concern themselves with the past and the future, they must focus upon survival. According to Corrine S. Kills Pretty Enemy (1997), president of Tokata International in Alexandria, Virginia, survival has meant a career with the federal government, the entity that tried to destroy her people. It has meant working with the enemy. This is especially true if one works for the Bureau of Indian Affairs within the U.S. Department of the Interior and the Indian Health Service or the Public Health Service. Private practice or business is rarely an economic option, but many Indian women have been nurses to people of various races, and no nursing associations have paid tribute to these generous caregivers.

Such entities as the Women's Educational Equity Act Leadership Training Program, directed primarily at native women, attempts to sustain women in nontraditional fields. However, ingrained native patterns of behavior, fear, and lack of self-confidence and self-esteem when functioning in the "white man's world" prevent indigenous women from becoming entrepreneurs when women-owned businesses are increasing. Indigenous women often have difficulty balancing the goal of being in business, profit, with their spirituality, generosity, and communal nature. Most Indian beliefs at one time or another are in contradiction with the goals of business. Indigenous cultures hold people who share their material resources with the less fortunate in high esteem. Often those who work for government entities are considered "apples"; white on the inside, red on the outside; traitors.

Reconciling these differences or inventing another way for indigenous to become self-sustaining is imperative. One thing is clear: We must get away from a description of the United States as monocultural. As our Indian ancestors knew and still know very well, we are all related. The notion of a single society with one cultural norm must be abandoned, not only because it is not true in the United States; it is not true worldwide.

There are microcosms of societies that make the United States, and there are several cultural models and modes of human relations. All of these offer healing solutions from intolerance. All of them can provide insight into social and cultural stability. The majority of them are nonviolent, predicated upon the teachings of people like Ghandi to not hate your enemy but to pray for him. In times of duress I have often had to rely on the teaching of our Apache ancestors that I am as powerful as my enemies are. African cultural wisdom was used by Hillary Clinton (1996) to express her understanding of how humans are intereliant in *It Takes a Village*.

The philosophy that it takes a village to raise a child is nonviolent, but in America it took violence to end the slavery of those who gave the former First Lady her famous quotation. Citizens, including children, were bruised, kicked, and thrashed before rulings by the U.S. Supreme Court during the 1940s and 1950s brought major victories for African Americans. In several decisions between 1948 and 1958, courts ruled that separate educational facilities for blacks and Chicanos must be equal to those for whites. Other Americans have inherited these rights. Largely because of federal court rulings, laws permitting racial discrimination in housing and recreation were also struck down. As an increasing number of people of color began to move into all-white areas of cities, many whites moved out into the suburbs, but human rights activists persisted in making America the land of justice for all.

Organizations like the National Association for the Advancement of Colored People (NAACP) and the Mexican American Legal Defense and Educational Fund (MALDEF) won historic victories when the U.S. Supreme Court ruled in the case of *Brown v. Board of Education of Topeka, Kansas*. It ruled that segregation in public schools was in itself not only unequal, but was unconstitutional. The *Brown* decision was the result of an effort brought about by the school board, which had voted not to allow a black female student, Linda Brown, to attend an all-white school near her home. The Lemon Grove incident, an educational decision prohibiting segregated education for Mexican Americans in California, and the *Brown* decision held up a public mirror to white America and most did not like what they saw. I witnessed that they were angrier when in their own court system it was ruled that they were wrong in discriminating in public education.

Nonviolence and using the judicial system seems to work, but it takes a long time. It took riots and the killing of young people before President Kennedy and his brother Robert outlined the Civil Rights Act, later presented by President Lyndon B. Johnson, who persuaded Congress to pass it in 1964. This act prohibited intolerance and injustice based on race in public places and called for equal opportunity in employment and education. In 1965 President Johnson declared that it was not enough simply to end segregation and separation of the races by law. It was now also necessary to eliminate de facto segregation, racial separation in fact and based largely on custom. Johnson called for programs of affirmative action that would afford people of color equal opportunity with whites in areas where discrimination still existed. Many businesses and schools, oftentimes begrudgingly, began to adopt affirmative action programs. These programs, some of which were ordered by the federal government, gave hundreds of thousands of people of color new economic and educational opportunities.

The opportunities enabled many to increase their incomes, permitted the development of a Mexican American (Chicano and Mexican immigrant) working-class income group, and greatly expanded the black and Asian lower-middle-class income group. American Indians sequestered on reservations did not reap the same benefits, but AIM organized a large move to better the quality of life and promote equality for Native Americans.

During the early 1960s many of the old traditions and laws were still being practiced. The best known female civil rights activist was African American, Angela Davis (1998). Davis was also a scholar and author who was fired from her teaching position in 1969 for her "radical" politics. In 1970 she was on the FBI's most-wanted list for escaping from a California county courthouse, and being implicated in a violent incident led to her arrest on murder, kidnapping,

and conspiracy charges. Davis was incarcerated sixteen months and then ac-
quitted (Davis and James 1998). Davis's ordeal has inspired three decades of
writing from a revolutionary female perspective. The analyses of these women
on gender, capital, and race expanded the scope and range of social and political theory. They challenged the foundations of mainstream beliefs and schol-
arly discourse on theory and praxis (the difference between stated beliefs and
actual social practice), and forced a paradigm shift. No one gives them credit
for it.

Only a few students in universities know about these scholars, who have
not only engaged in social change, but published articles and books on women
of color, helped develop Ethnic Studies departments, and then taught in them.
I have been among them. Activist scholars have forced Americans to take
alternative perspectives and forced the social sciences and university administrators to accept female scholarship and Chicano, Latino, Black, Asian, and
Native American Studies departments and programs. Yet I know young people
in high school do not know about them.

Women of color have struggled against white women, involved themselves
in revolutionary struggle, and then taught Americans about prison reform, political restraint, civil disobedience, and resistance to the internalization of colonialism. These brave women have examined revolutionary politics and
intellectualism to illustrates how progressive political movements and social
philosophy can and will change with involvement of the masses. Their stances
are political, philosophical, and critical, and for this the majority have endured
isolation, ridicule, and abandonment.

We have seen how people of color share most issues: discrimination based
on race, highly limited access to education, little or no political and economic
power, injustice in the criminal justice system, and persecution targeting
women. Women of color are also linked to the issues of social policy about
language, especially code switching (switching between two languages in one
sentence, paragraph, or entire discourse) because of the children they have in
schools, but the effects of language use are different for women and men. The
genders make certain use of language. Both females and males are reared to
know there are unwritten rules, not only with regard to the words they use, but
also how and when they are used, with whom, and what body expression
accompanies the use of words.

Furthermore, there is cultural diversity in how language is used, and this is
linked to how Americans would like to simplify the world. They would like to
presume that women are generic and do not differ among themselves. They
are not generic and they do differ. We have discussed how they differentiate
by race, class, gender orientation, sexual preference, age, income, education,
political activity, immigration status, amd region or country of origin. This is
one thing that the U.S. white-controlled feminist movement has been negli-
gent in recognizing, celebrating, and extending. Diversity is too confusing for

the culturally deprived, and the U.S. white feminist movement has heard about it in various forms. Some women of color have international experience in addressing the issues. In 1995 women from other countries were more widely informed at the U.N. Fourth World Women's Conference.

This American Dream, or myth, motivates members of the society to not question the assumptions of the society. After all, we live in the richest, most powerful country in the world. Until recently few have paid attention to the fact that we are not as highly esteemed by other countries on the globe. When this became apparent, the American government quickly moved to reestablish its position by going to war and launching a massive public-relations campaign. For the first time the male-controlled government presented itself as the victim. It did not inform its citizenry that there was a perspective that war is a male activity and that in America it is in the white male's interest to sustain their global power position.

My extensive work in both the civil rights and women's movements confirm that women do not want absolute power. They know that the ability to control everything can lead to phenomena like the Taliban. As mentioned before, some women think that equality with men means being like men. It does not. It means having women's lives and work valued the way we value the lives and work of men. On television I saw that many American women went to Afghanistan to fight against terrorism. Why do some women want to go to war, to be equal to men in killing? I extend they have internalized that competition and being successful in a male domain is equality. Males dictate their standard of conduct. Perhaps they are in desperate need of power, money, and prestige, but participating in a male-dominated world that involves taking human life is counterproductive to the feminization of racism because when they are involved women are supporting the very structure that oppresses and defines them.

They have internalized that what men do gets them what men have—justice, freedom, and control—and that this is good. Men of color have fallen into the same mindset; so have poor people. If one is poor, of color, and a female with few options, the military, education, the legal system, and the corporate structure offer opportunities to escape a powerless position. They submit to its teachings, do what it asks of them, and expect to gain some of its rewards. Even though a few succeed, entire racial and gender groups do not. The structure that has produced them produces many of them. They do not want to reward too many "minorities" because the white-dominated structure's assumptions cannot and will not tolerate too many with too much power. To appease the oppressed groups, it allows some of its members to be marginal, a buffer, between the oppressor and the oppressed. The presence of the member exhibits to those who dare to criticize America that America is truly the land of opportunity, freedom, and justice for all. The strategy is not working internally and it is not working internationally.

## STOP THE VIOLENCE

Before we can heal our nation, we have to stop the violence. We must face our contradictions, the fact that we have not been doing what we have been taught to do, and that some people want it this way and will kill to keep it this way. In addition, we must accept the fact that we have not really constructed a model for other countries to follow. In spite of all it accomplishments, the United States has failed to advance itself toward its ideals, and other countries are exposing it, but intolerance, racism, and sexism are evasive and ever changing. They shift shape and color in the form of policy, use its victims, and is evil, like the Taliban is evil.

People of color will no longer tolerate discrimination. They sue, fight back, and heave such treatment upon their oppressor that the profit margin is beginning to narrow. This happened when President Bush's $300 million plan to encourage marriage among single female-headed households on welfare was announced in late February 2002. Feminists quickly got on national television and radio programs, on the Internet, and in print to criticize the plan to subject those who already have problems with their men to marry them. They noted discrimination against children who were being raised in married household and who would receive certain services versus those raised in unmarried households who would not receive the same services. This policy would not help grandmothers raising children on behalf of their daughters, and it neglected the fact that over 50 percent of the women who leave men do so because of domestic violence (Kills Pretty Enemy 2001).

President Bush's plan to promote marriage was quickly exposed as sexist for targeting women, classist for targeting the poor, and racist because more women of color are poor. It was a psychologically violent proposal because every time women get blasted in the press by the president of the nation they get scared. Yet this is not seen as abuse. It is psychological abuse. The trauma leaves wounds that may heal, but the scares serve as monuments to the wrong that has been done. Further, the Bush plan was at worst evil, at best sneaky and mean. He attempted to sneak it into public policy while his popularity rating and patriotism were high.

The barbaric practice of discrimination is duplicated in social institutions such as the media, public schools, education, and the family. Children learn it very young. Feminists are not antimarriage or antifamily, they simply note that in these institutions values are taught that reinforce the hierarchical structures that work against women. There is a class element to when the system responds to certain issues. When social concerns and violence affect men, they get addressed. This is followed by when it affects white women, then white middle-class youth. People of color see this. They know this and they talk about this, but they do not get invited on national television to comment on the situation unless they are black. Many white people fear blacks. Once in a while we see a conservative Hispanic comment on social policy, but for the most part all others are invisible. Foremost among the invisible are women of color. This is not dialogue. This is not discourse. This does not promote better race relations in America and it does not promote world peace.

Healing involves mourning and Americans cannot skip any phase of this process, especially this one. Healing requires inclusiveness. It requires that the majority of white Americans join with people of color to mourn their misdeeds. This involves a holistic approach that includes recognition of the trauma, structure, and function of our social divisions. It must recognize that this trauma is historical. We must teach it and embrace the anger, the rage, the fear, and the guilt, and engage in atonement with a discussion of what is enough. Where do we go from here? People of color have been telling this country that it has a problem for years, but no one really wanted to hear, much less do anything about it. Last, we must engage in forgiveness. If we do not forgive and make atonement we hurt the human rights efforts that now need to be implemented globally; we hurt ourselves.

I have seen the pain we have caused ourselves among the youth. I counted the young women among the students killed in the Littleton, Colorado, shooting at Columbine High School. Some of the boys killed were of color. The issues of sexism and racism were raised in discussioms om cp,,unitites of color but were hushed by the media during this national trauma. Women do not exist in social or historical isolation. They exist in and are all too frequently defined by state and federal governmental policies, their history, what people did to their people, how they feel about what happened, and how they relate to what was happening to the next generation. Women inherit communities when they are born or move into them. Thus, they inherit what has gone on before them. Some women grow up and live the life that is outlined for them, wishing it would be different. Others strive to change it, but change for women has not come without consequence: being threatened, resisted, hurt, and murdered.

All too often there is violence. I have witenessed this violence. I have seen that from violence has been created a gender caste in which women of color hold the lowest status and are frequently murdered by husbands and lovers. At its worst, violence limits the life chances of women by compromising their self-identity. How people choose to identify themselves is important because labeling imposes a definition. When a label is used, one either lives up or down to a standard that denotes value. Some things are known about how labels emerge and how they work to define groups, but not much is known about how groups come to define them. Nevertheless, labeling is a process that defines "in groups" and "out groups," the normal and the abnormal, the legitimate and the deviant, and labeling that does not come from within is subjective to whomever is doing the defining. It not only reflects group values; it also renders a framework for understanding as well as misunderstanding. The danger attached to labeling is stereotyping, making generalizations about a group based upon cruelty and insufficient knowledge.

Labeling not only leads to stereotyping; it can lead to associating groups of people with physical space. For African Americans the space is the ghetto, and for Chicanos the space is generally the barrio. Closely aligned with the physical space is the deteriorated appearance of the segregated community. As has been discussed, it is not always true that only poor people of color live in predominantly "colored" communities. Whites and members of other groups live there also. However, these communities are easily identified by being characteristically isolated or distanced from Anglo communities by freeways, railroad tracks, industrial corridors, airports, or dump sights. These communities have names and possess other symbols and physical boundaries: bridges, streets, ditches, rivers, and factories mark the beginning and ending of the physical space.

The community is not only a physical and social space; it is a psychological space where people have been conditioned and where they learn to love and learn the meaning of family and neighbors. The community is not in one geographical location. It is a creative place, with emotional boundaries that exist in the mind and throughout the nation. The segregation messages are strong. They can create a mentality not allowing individuals to go beyond the community's borders. The sad reality is that too many do not recognize that segregated communities are a form of discrimination. Some communities are self-sufficient. People do not have to leave them to interact with Anglos. They do not even need to know how to speak English. Other communities are more interdependent. People leave them every day to go to work, the doctor, the community college, or the university. Some of them are middle income and others are working-class neighborhoods.

## A COMMITMENT TO PEACE

There are many forms of work for peace, but it takes a commitment to peace at a fundamental level of personal existence and transference into action. Is it part of our humanness to go to war? No, many man-made forces work to produce it. What is naturally human is to protect oneself against violence, and some women have lost the ability to do this. As long as there have been humans there has been a need to engage in conflict resolution that is nonviolent. Americans have even taught it in their universities. Yet we have refused to see one another as resources for one other, and because of our ingrained self-interest we refuse to monitor what we think, what we say, and what we do to others in order to sustain that self-interest, that greed. We have refused to think communal thoughts about the nature of community and nation and world, and we have refused to stop getting upset at differences and do not care that some see the world as God living in all of us and that others are a reflection of ourselves. This is why some countries hate Americans. This is why some Americans hate other Americans. This is why we have terrorism.

Yet patriotism in time of war is dangerous because injustices, even atrocities, can be committed in the name of patriotism. It is possible that we hide our racism and sexism behind this mask. Underneath the mask of patriotism may be fear, resentment of religious differences, and a lack of value for human life. Many have discussed the war in Afghanistan as a religious war, an armed conflict pitting the secular "modern" world view against the traditional or indigenous religious world view. As Afghanistan found itself strangled within the grip of religious fundamentalism, human rights across the nation were being grossly violated. The conditions were even worse than they were during the Soviet occupation period (Goodwin 2000). The nature and range of crimes perpetrated against Afghan women by fundamentalists has no precedence in modern history. Afghan fundamentalists, particularly the Taliban, treat women as degraded souls whose only function is to satiate men's lust and reproduce. These men could not have conceived of women's rights through reasoning. But as fundamentalists continued to create turmoil in Afghanistan, the Revolutionary Association of the Women of Afghanistan (RAWA), a resisting force of Afghan women, held that women could not achieve their rights or attain meaningful freedom. They felt women had to continue their struggle against fanaticism and carry it through to the end.

RAWA believed that the United Nations had not been able to address women's concerns properly. Prior to U.S. intervention, they often wondered why the United Nations did not send a large number of peacekeeping forces to Afghanistan. It was unfortunate that world powers were limited to negotiating with fundamentalists, and it was apparent that the United Nations was not willing to take any steps that would annoy them. Meanwhile, women were dying. RAWA advocated that the United Nations view Afghanistan as the homeland of the Afghan people, and not as the property of a few armed militias.

In order to resolve the Afghan crisis, RAWA interpreted the presence and activities of armed fundamentalist bands as the root cause of the current disaster in Afghanistan. Therefore, they were the targets of Taliban surveillance. RAWA believed that the only way to restore stability to Afghan was by disarming all the armed groups and their accomplices. This was possible only by a peacekeeping force not including troops from countries that had involved themselves in the Afghan infighting and that might support any bandit groups. The same peacekeeping force could supervise the convening of the *Loya Jirga* (grand assembly) and the formation of a government based on democratic values and comprised of neutral personalities. Some of their ideas were instituted, but RAWA was not given credit for them.

The government they wanted was very simple: It should be based on democratic values and it should ensure freedom of thought, religion, and political expression while safeguarding women's rights. Does this mean that RAWA wanted Afghanistan to be Americanized? RAWA still demands a separation of religious and political processes in Afghanistan. This is not solely American, it is democracy. Though the fanatical groups label secularism as a communist idea and call it the "faith of the infidels," RAWA (2001) firmly believes that only a government with a secular orientation can thwart the design reactionaries from the Dark Ages would like to impose. It is only a secular government that can prevent the religion of Islam from being used as a retrogressive tool in the hands of fanatics to govern. The Taliban did not represent the people of Afghanistan, who have been Muslims for centuries.

In the future, RAWA will not allow fundamentalists to decree what women should or should not wear. They feel they have no right to impose the veil upon women. As far as RAWA was concerned, its members would not wear the veil as far as security and social discretion would allow. They regard rejection of the veil as a symbolic form of resistance and defiance of the fundamentalists. To wear or not to wear the Islamic veil is a completely personal issue, not one that is imposed on women. Wearing the veil is also a cultural issue, not a religious one. Fundamentalists try to present this issue in religious terms. RAWA maintains that by forcing women to wear the veil the Taliban unleashed their misogynist tendencies through terror and oppression. In summary, their ultimate objective is to keep women under control, in the status of chattel.

Resistance becomes a strong social force when the power and ideology of the dominant group is threatened by the minority group. Struggles for power are evident in the legal cases that women and men of color have had to file in order to gain equal access to hiring at college and university campuses. Once on campus, many have to sue for promotion and tenure. In spite of this, the work of women of color is gaining national and even some international importance. Chicanas, for example, have been part of political and academic dialogues in Mexico, Central and Latin America, Europe, and even the Soviet Union and Israel. In cultural and academic exchanges, Chicanas and other women of color engage in discussion on the impact of patriarchy upon their lives. There are also dialogues with international and Anglo women for profit ventures and national and international philanthropic organizations. Many women of color are no longer allowing Anglo women to dominate these exchanges. They have created their own elevated space. The space they occupy is important and changing as more of them develop a feminist experience connecting theory to practice.

## LINKING THEORY TO PRACTICE

An area in strict need of linking theory to practice is the two-party political system in the United States. While there are other parties, like the Green and Socialist parties, the Republicans and Democrats have struggled and succeeded in maintaining control for most of America's existence. To many, this is not democracy. It is highly suspicious when power is centered in the hands of a few white men decade after decade. Women of color demand that both parties change to address their issues, but both parties have been slow to act, and have acted only when it was in their self-interest. People of color have been disillusioned and sought to start their own parties, such as the Chicano Raza Unida Party and the latest multicultural attempt with the U.S. Rainbow Coalition.

The reason America is having problems within and outside of its boundaries is that what is left is a culture that has not updated itself as fast as it has updated its technology. What we have is leftover sentiment, social structures, and ways of behaving that prevent the advancement of the culture to create a great civilization, a global civilization. It did not take civil rights activists long to find out that to control knowledge and resources is to control people and information and the propensity to use violence.

They are highly aware of the historical trauma they have endured in the land of the free, and they live the huge discrepancy between the ideal and real social conditions in a country that promises justice for all. Thus, people of color and women and those who are knowledgeable about their disenfranchised history have come to lack trust in those that symbolize the offenders of these promises. Some have said to me that freedom and justice for all are simply promises, not guarantees. The difference is semantics. They have come to fear justice and seek to rationalize it by splitting fine fibers in the mantle of human rights, and women of color fear this last-minute effort of white men to hold on to a disintegrating way of life.

Perhaps the biggest fear for women of color is the injustice of having to give up the fragile hold they have on their own children. Put simply, they no longer want to be exploited by dominant Americans and they do not want to be absorbed by their values, but their children have to live in the culture they have inherited. Women of color want the inconsistent standards for social participation based on ethnicity, race or color, and gender to be eradicated. They do not want to have individualistic, profit-oriented, competitive dominant American values imposed on their communal way of life. They also do not want talented women with resources to be lost to the community of color because they have to choose between upward mobility and their families. Perhaps what Anglos fear most is that if people of color come into power they will treat Anglos the way Anglos have treated people of color. Perhaps if racism ends Anglos fear they will lose their privileged position in the society that values their skin color. Perhaps Anglos fear that the basis upon which their society rests will be revealed as a lie, as cruel, and that it will crumble.

Dominant Americans must understand that America pledged freedom and justice for all and that people of color believe it and expect it. They have tried to Americanize, to work within the system, and it has not delivered what it promised. From their perspective the system is rigged against them. Basically, they feel they have kept their share of the bargain and dominant American culture, Anglo controlled, has not delivered on its share. Because both sides have retreated into a world that is hostile, people of color have been left angry, empty, lost, fearful, or confused. Anger is the most threatening. It costs lives. As I write this book, people of the Middle East lash out at those who have been defined as their oppressors. The violence is causing individuals and entire groups to kill innocent women and children. Women and children have become disoriented, depressed, self-destructive, and without cultural reference and therefore human reference, and without harmony, beauty, or peace.

Although the general population of the United States has not noticed it, it is a nation at war since riots broke out in the 1960s. The race war combined with the war between the sexes all over the nation, but the entire nation chose to focus upon what they believed was self-destruction by the people who lived in ghettos and barrios, reservations, and ethnic enclaves. Contemporary technology is such that the bombings and beating and killing of women in wars caused by men can no longer be disguised, concealed, or kept secret.

It is cliché to note that the United States is a violent culture. International statistics on violent attacks, executions, and incarcerations uphold this contention (Amnesty International 2002). Competition is a well-defined dominant American cultural attribute and is recognized around the world. People of color are experiencing frustration at not succeeding. It has and will breed violence when the cloak of patriotism is removed. Violence and competition are most apparent in riots, but are also apparent in how people of color are forced to think and act in a culturally inconsistent manner that is hierarchical in structure. But they must live in it in order to survive. This is not natural. This is not in balance. This is wrong for them. Yet they have consciously or unconsciously tolerated the situation. In doing so, they have given the system permission to continue treating them this way, but they have given it a chance to change.

The violence, competition, and individualism of the dominant culture are central to most things women and people of color have to contend with. It is apparent in the dichotomies and in the racist language they have learned to use: "Uptown, downtown," "in groups, out groups," "in the black, in the red," "a Mexican standoff," "Indian-giver," "yellow peril," and "lowest man [not women] on the totem pole." White values are apparent in how academic progress is graded from A to F; first grade, second grade; K through 12 versus higher education; and girls bathroom, boys bathroom. Most white Americans have not learned to speak another language, and most are perceived as not having learned about respect for people of different cultures, for the elderly, and for anything beyond their own lives. If they had, there would be no sexism and no racism. There would be home health care for the elderly and decent prescription drug cost regulation.

If society valued women, antidiscrimination laws and domestic violence laws would be enforced and these ills would finally disappear. If the society valued the environment, there would be strict enforcement of environmental protection laws and an internalization of a connection to the land, the air, the water, and plants. In other words, if Americans were equal, there would not be status cars and status neighborhoods, "old heaps," "clunkers," reservations, ghettos and barrios, and Miss America contests. There would be no such thing as historical trauma.

Historical trauma is the physical, spiritual, and emotional damage women of color have endured due to prolonged periods of social, physical, and psychological abuse. The abuses are well documented. The fact that they exist is evident in that there is legislation to prevent the abuses and that women are using legislation to protect themselves from abuse. There are data to prove it.

Even in death the law is involved. The cost and funeral business rules governs how the body is displayed, when it may be viewed, where it may be viewed, how mourners are received, and how the body is disposed of. Policies and laws plus the cost of moving the body do not allow for three-day overnight vigils in the home. Historical trauma is simply the contention that anything not Christian is the work of the devil. People have been treated in exclusionary and demeaning ways for a very long time. In its most severe manifestation historical trauma renders the wounded with a lack of ability to thrive in their society. To a lesser degree it impacts the victim's self-esteem, and manifests as bad health, low education, a lack of political power, higher rates of incarceration, and poverty. These manifestations validate Anglo culture as favorable, the true culture, and the correct culture, and allow privilege and status to those who conform to skin color and gender in behavior and body type. This elevates discriminatory practices into the ongoing institutional and cultural mechanism. When viewed from an outsider's perspective, women of color may appear to suffer from a loss of self-concept and self-esteem, but when viewed from the inside they are highly motivated to protect their culture. This motivation involves high self-esteem and a concept of self that connotes value, and dominant Americans need to learn to respect this.

## DECENTRALIZING PATRIARCHY

As more racial and ethnic "minorities" and women learn to value themselves and their cultural productions, the distrust for established norms erodes. Not only the victim, but also the perpetrator lives in a state of distrust. They fear the outcome, and the fear is compounded by the knowledge that traumatization is bad for both; it is stressful. The oppressor knows what he is doing. In the case of discrimination, the racist, the sexist, and the homophobic can be stressed to his limits. This person causes harm to other members of white society by robbing it of talent that could have made generous contributions to civilization.

Communities need to openly discuss the fact that discrimination comes with some very high costs. It not only affects the bottom line of corporations by taking workers' time away from production. It costs them in other ways. Fewer people volunteer when they are made to feel uncomfortable. It costs the community in police relations and keeping the peace. It makes the community less safe for children to play in. Persons with abilities to contribute music, song, poetry, dance, lectures, urban planning, local government leadership, and security to elders cannot contribute fully or cannot contribute at all. Some of this human resource is missing from that which is already at the forefront of discussions and actions on drugs, the homeless, gangs, and graffiti. Those who are not now participating can assist a community in creating beauty and harmony and healing from discrimination.

Discrimination creates ambivalence and antagonism, and this has its costs. Ambivalence and even antagonism by some people of color toward life outside the barrios, ghettos, and reservations often denies them good health. There is incongruity and strife toward those who love members of the opposite group, or toward those who have friendships with those of the opposite group. Antagonism toward Anglos can be encountered for no other reason than that they are Anglos, and there can be hostilities toward anything that is considered middle class and therefore white. Sometimes "in group" members who have adopted lifestyles that are middle class are called *agrindado* or *gringos* by Latinos or apples and Oreos by Native Americans and blacks. This intolerance toward the Anglo and Anglo ways is in contrast to a tolerance demanded from people who have long been oppressed, and it does not end oppression.

It is time to link theory to practice; time to get ride of prejudices in order to get rid of our contradictions and hostilities and attempt to get closer to our ideals of true democracy. Here the role of women can be more helpful. Most women have assumed the caretaker responsibility for themselves and for their men. Thus, women can play a big role in helping society heal from its male dominance, sexism, and racism. Caretaking for contemporary women is no longer limited to childbearing. They now bring home a major part of the family paycheck. On the job it means guarding against racism, sexism, and class discrimination, and taking responsibility for sexuality and childbearing. It means the teaching of morals, values, and ethics, not only at home, but also in the workplace. It means tending a personal emotional, physical, and spiritual life for themselves and for those around them. The truth is that because of changes in society, men have inherited, or at least have to share in, some of the work that women once did.

Some women of color have demonstrated how to forgive past social illness, but they will not stop short of decentralizing patriarchy. Recognizing the enemy does not mean they will forget what he did. It means making sure he does not do it again. In fact, forgetting might not be a good idea. Remembering and learning from the past builds a solid foundation that will prevent mistakes from being repeated. When Americans join in healing from their losses; psychological, spiritual, physical, and environmental attacks; and the death of major parts of a past civilization, they can serve as role models to the rest of the world. In healing our atrocities we can find liberation. This process can begin in kindergarten and preschool. We need to go beyond offering students skills in reading, writing, and math. We need to make them culturally literate.

In making American citizens more culturally literate we prepare them for a global existence and for resistance to responses to colonialism like those witnessed in Afghanistan by the Taliban. The Taliban lacked the mental resources and foresight to educate themselves on how women of color and many others throughout the world have nonviolently dealt with not trusting values that became part of an education system that excluded them. From these women we learn about resolving contradictions, how some circumvent the impact of exclusion by learning to speak at least two languages, and how to deal with hypocrisy and remain true to oneself.

To decentralize patriarchy means to decentralize material goods that reflect patriarchal values for profit over humanity. Some things intentionally and unintentionally hurt women; things like high-heeled shoes that ruin women's feet, pantyhose that cause poor blood circulation and yeast infections, and cigarette smoking. Cigarette smoking for women was severely punished by the Taliban, but it was condemned more out of disdain for the American tobacco industry than for the health of women. Thus, women must be vigilant about products marketed to them before they purchase them. They must ask who is producing the product and why. At the center of the answers she will generally find it is being produced first and foremost to make money. By doing this women can decide what will and what will not be produced.

It would probably be easier to list what the Taliban did not ban during their regime. The regime even outlawed paper bags. This would be amusing if the penalties for disobeying the laws were not so severe, especially on women. The women of Afghanistan, like women of color in the United States, can have a leading role in healing from discrimination because they have been the victims, and because so many of them have developed coping mechanisms that can strengthen the social fabric of society. Healing, of course, requires that the dominant culture recognize that wrongs have been committed and that people of color who have survived have the knowledge to heal them. For most of these groups this knowledge is built upon ancient civilizations.

Atonement, forgiveness, and linking our knowledge to practice reinforces a society and honor and respect to humanity. This is a journey that changes not only attitudes and behavior, but also the very future of the nation. It is a long journey, pitted by obstacles, but not impossible. The oppressors must be confronted with twisting injustice for their own good. Despite its disastrous and very public record on the violation of human rights, the Taliban was petitioning the United Nations for a seat in the General Assembly in May 2000. Its New York representative, Abdul Hakeem Mujahid, claimed his government was protecting human rights and liberties in Afghanistan (Goodwin 2000). He also stated that, having put a stop to the miserable living conditions under which women were living, they had restored women's safety, dignity, and freedom. This twisted message was no worse than decreeing that there is freedom and justice for all in America and then supplying statistics that support arguments that this is not true for women, especially women of color.

Also central to decentralizing patriarchy is the redefinition of the girl child. The assumption of the majority of the roughly 30,000 women who met in China for the U.N. Fourth World Women's Conference was that women allow men to have too much influence on their lives. While attending the conference I witnessed women from various countries testify that this is a process that begins with parental expectations before a girl child is born. She inherits it before she exits the womb and it affects her through death. Males have defined what women wear, where they can go, what they can do, how they do it, and whom they marry. They define how women adorn their bodies, how they walk and sit, who they pray to, and who they have sex with. Male dominance and the internalization of patriarchy have made women dislike their own lives, their bodies, and other women. Because of internalized patriarchy women have gone on diets, had emotional collapses, acted as unpaid servants, been trafficked as sex objects, and even committed suicide. Male attitude and influence in women's lives have subverted the feminist movement by demeaning female opinion and stifling the development of female consciousness. In many cases men have made women afraid to become involved. The male need for control is so intense that it frequently drives him to violence against women, thus making him highly emotionally impaired.

The U.N. Women's Conference agreed to make racism a feminist issue (Blea 1997). The United States must catch up with this international effort. Light-colored skin has been centralized around the world and efforts are in force to end it. International marketing, especially by the United States, made it extremely valuable and frequently subjected women to the dual impact of gender and race. Add to sexism and racism class discrimination and then ageism, immigrant status, and physical or emotional impairment, and the victim is bombarded by several intersecting social blows. Intersecting variables cross over into one another, thereby compounding their impact. If the woman being affected is a lesbian woman of color, the affront to patriarchy is so intense that her very life is at risk.

Women of color have lived and struggled in a world cemented by patriarchy. This has taught them what they do not want. Now they are ready to take action. Attempts to decentralize patriarchy, to remove the impact of men in women's lives, has not required guns. What has been required, and is still required, is insight into internalized racist and sexist messages and a woman of color strategy for decolonization from the remnants of internal colonialism for women. To get rid of the antiquated vestiges of colonialism is to get rid of patriarchy. Feminists have prevented many women from getting involved or continuing relationships with men that are not good for them. American women are realizing that they are paying too a high price for male activity. They pay it in not only their personal relationships with them, but also in the costs of policing, representing, and jailing men who abuse them or engage in activities that do not enhance the quality of women's lives (Stephenson 1991).

Women of color can and do advocate on behalf of a certain kind of men, but when men do not take women seriously in this or in most other arenas women of color have moved forward to better their own lives. More women are moving past being codependent and are allowing men to "stew in their own mess" or "get it together." In the end, only men can stop their own violent oppression as males who have to fight wars. They cannot stop it by simply leaving violent scenes. They must remain in the dialogue with women and they must boycott violent messages. They especially need to be vocal when violence targets women of color and their children. They are among the most valuable assets in American society; they are our cultural treasures, equal to other endangered animals and the environment in which they live.

Finally, men must teach other men how to relate to women and to other men, especially young men. Men have to work with other men to teach them to value community, and that to empower their community means empowering women. There are a few men who truly feel and act this way. They need to be more vocal about it, and about the nature of the impact of sexism upon the lives of males. They need to educate themselves about the concerns of women of color and they need to educate themselves about the global feminist and peace movements. They need to be brave to be more international, like so many women of color who are moving forward, with or without male permission, in their efforts to resist sexism. Women of color now must organize to feminize racism around the world. They have no choice. Racism and sexism and the patriarchy inherent in them are too high a price for the United States not to be liked in many places on the planet.

## REFERENCES

American Association of Retired Persons Population Reference Bureau. 1990. "What the 1990 Census Tells Us about Women: A State Factbook." Washington, D.C.: American Association of Retired Persons.

Amnesty International. 2002. "USA." In "Amnesty International Report 2002." Available at: <http://www.amnesty.org.web/ar2002.nst/amr/usa>.

Blauner, Robert. 1972. *Racial Oppression in America*. New York: Harper and Row.

———. 1969. "Internal Colonialism and Ghetto Revolt." *Social Problems* 16 (Spring): 393–408.

Blea, Irene. 1997. *U.S. Chicanas and Latinas in a Global Context*. Westport, Conn.: Praeger.

———. 1992. *Bessemer: A Sociological Perspective of a Chicano Barrio*. New York: AMS Press.

Cawyer, Wynonia. 2002. Interview by author, Albuquerque, New Mexico, May 12.

Clinton, Hillary Rodham. 1996. *It Takes a Village and Other Lessons Children Teach Us*. New York: Simon and Schuster.

Fanon, Frantz. 1963. *The Wretched of the Earth*. New York: Grove Press.

Goodwin, Jan. 2000. "Buried Alive: Afghan Women under the Taliban." *AOL Internet*, January. Available at: <http://www.infoshop.org/gulag/women.html> (updated February 22).

Gunn Allen, Paula. 1992. "Sky Woman and Her Sisters." *Ms.*, September–October.

Hill Collins, Patricia. 1990. *Black Feminist Thought*. Boston Unwin Hyman.

James, Joy, and Angela Davis. 1998. *The Angela Y. Davis Reader*.Oxford: Blackwell.

Kills Pretty Enemy, Corrine S. 2001. "Native Women Move Beyond." Lecture at the North Valley Community Center, Alexandria, Virginia, September 16.

———. 1997. *Business Tips for Women*. Alexandria, Va.: Tokata International.

Memmi, Albert. 1965. *The Colonizer and the Colonized*. Boston: Beacon Press.

Nabokov, Peter. 1991. *Native American Testimony: A Chronicle of Indian–White Relations from Prophecy to the Present, 1492–1992*. New York: Penguin Books.

Revolutionary Association of Women of Afghanistan (RAWA). 1997–2001. "Under the Tyranny of the Fundamentalists." Available at: <http://www.rawa.fancy marketing.net/women>.

Stephenson, June. 1991. *Men Are Not Cost-Effective*. New York: Harper Perennial.

The American Gulag. 2000. "Women in Prison." Available at: <http://www.infoshop.org/ gulag/women>. Last visited May 21.

U.S. Bureau of the Census. 2001. "Women's Research and Education Institute 2001." Washington, D.C.: U.S. Government Printing Office.

———. 1993. *We the American Hispanics*. Washington, D.C.: U.S. Government Printing Office.

U.S. Department of Justice. 2000. "Corrections Statistics." Available at: <http://www. ojp.usdoj.gov/bjs/correct>.

# Selected Bibliography

African American Women's Archives. 1999. "American Perspectives on African Ameri-
    can Women." Manuscript sources at the Special Collections Library, Duke
    University. Also available at: <http://www.scriptorium.lib.duke.edu.collections>.
————. William T. Bain Papers, 1850–1865 (89 items). Raleigh, North Carolina.
————. Archibald Boyd Letters, 1841–1897 (46 items). Lenox Castle, North Carolina.
————. William George Matton Papers, 1859–1887 (4 items). High Point, North Carolina.
————. John Moore McCalla Papers, 1785–1917 (1,813 items and 40 volumes). Lex-
    ington, Kentucky, and Washington, D.C.
————. John Parker.
————. John Rankin–John Parker Collection ca. 1880. (3 items). Ripley, Ohio.
————. John Richardson Kilby Papers, 1755–1919 (39,489 items and 19 volumes).
    Suffolk, Virginia. Personal papers of John Richardson Kilby (1819–1878) and
    Wilbur John Kilby (1850–1878).
AFRO-America. 1999. Afro-American Newspaper Company of Baltimore. "UPS
    Donates Nearly One Million Dollars to Support Groups for African Americans
    in Atlanta, Georgia." Available at: <http://www.afroam.org> (revised March 8, 2001).
American Association of Retired Persons Population Reference Bureau. 1990. "What
    the 1990 Census Tells Us about Women: A State Factbook." Long Beach, Ca-
    lif.: AARP.
American Hypertext Workshop. 1996. Corcoran Department of History, University of
    Virginiam Charlottesville. Available at: <http://www.virginia.edu.history,.htm>.
American Online News. 1999. "Jefferson's Slave Kin Shunned." *Associated Press*,
    May 16. Available at: <http://www.womenhistory.about.com//library>.

Amnesty International. 2002. "USA." In "Amnesty International Report 2002." Available at: <http://www.amnesty.org.web/ar2002.nsf/amr/usa>.

Anzaldua, Gloria. 1999. *Making Face, Making Soul/Haciendo Caras, Creative and Critical Perspectives by Women of Color*. San Francisco: Aunt Lute Books.

Arango, Raul. 2000. "Candidates Seek Cuban Vote." *USA Today*. Available at: <http://www.usatoday.com>.

Blauner, Robert. 1972. *Racial Oppression in America*. New York: Harper and Row.

———. 1969. "Internal Colonialism and Ghetto Revolt." *Social Problems* 16 (Spring): 393–408.

Blea, Irene I. 2002. *Maria Josefa Jaramillo: Spanish Frontier Wife of Kit Carson*. Unpublished manuscript. Albuquerque, New Mexico.

———. 1997. *U.S. Chicanas and Latinas in a Global Context*. Westport, Conn.: Praeger.

———. 1995. *Researching Chicano Communities*. Westport, Conn.: Praeger.

———. 1992. *Bessemer: A Sociological Perspective of a Chicano Barrio*. New York: AMS Press.

———. 1992. *La Chicana and the Intersection of Race, Class and Gender*. New York: Praeger.

———. 1988. *Toward a Chicano Social Science*. New York: Praeger.

Brave Bird, Mary, with Richard Erdoes. 1993. *Ohitika Woman*. New York: Grove Press.

British Broadcasting Corporation (BBC). 1987. "Hawaii: Islands of the Fire Goddess." Bristol: British Broadcasting Company Nature Series, vol. 1, no. 3.

Bush, George W. 2001. "State of the Union." Public address by the President of the United States televised nationwide, January 30.

Chambers, Veronica, and John Leland. 1999. "Lovin' la Vida Loca." *Newsweek*, May 31. Available at: <http://www.thundersearch.com/JenniferLopez/jlnewsweek.htm>.

Clinton, Hillary Rodham. 1996. *It Takes a Village and Other Lessons Children Teach Us*. New York: Simon and Schuster.

C-SPAN. 2002. Wilson Center for National Affairs. New York: The New School. Book TV, June 27.

Cuban Information Archives. 2001. "Cuban Immigration." Available at: <http://www.cuban exile.com>.

Deloria, Vine. 1977. *Indians of the Pacific Northwest: From the Coming of the White Man to the Present Day*. New York: Doubleday.

Dudley, Michael Kioni, and Keoni Kealoha Agard. 1990. *A Call for Hawaiian Sovereignty*. Honolulu: Na Kane O Ka Malo Press.

Ethnic NewsWatch. 1999. SoftLine Information. Available at: <www.ethnicnews.org>.

Fanon, Frantz. 1963. *The Wretched of the Earth*. New York: Gove Press.

Fleet, Cameron, ed. 1997. *First Nations–First Hand*. Seacaucus, N.J.: Chartwell Books.

Freedman's Bureau. 2002. Available at: <http://www.freedmansbureau.com/search/kkk>. Visited November 16, 2002.

Frink Brown, Janice. 1999. "Girl 12, Pleads with Mayor, Police Chief to Reopen Case of Slain Brother." Baltimore: AFRO-America. Available at: <http://www.afro am.org>.

Fritz, Jean. 1983. *The Double Life of Pocahontas*. New York: G. P. Putnam's Sons.

Fuentes, A., A. Afflick, and B. Hessol. 1997. MEDTEP Research Center on Minority Populations, 145 (2): 148–155. (Unpublished grant report.)

Gonzales, Patrisia, and Roberto Rodriguez. 1999. "Getting into Political Trenches Brings Results." *Universal Press Syndicate*, August 19.

Goodwin, Jan. 2000. "Buried Alive: Afghan Women under the Taliban." *AOL Internet*, January. Available at: <http://www.infoshop.org/gulag/women> (updated February 22).

Gridley, Marion E. 1974. *American Indian Women*. New York: Hawthorn Books.

Grimes, Joel. 1992. *Navajo: Portrait of a Nation*. Englewood, Colo.: Westcliff.

Gunn Allen, Paula. 1992. "Sky Woman and Her Sisters." *Ms.*, September–October, pp. 23, 28.

Hale, Janet Campbell. 1993. *Bloodlines: Odyssey of a Native Daughter*. New York: Harper Perennial.

Hart, George. 1995. "U.S. Should Try Turning Juvenile Corrections into Private Enterprise System." *Ojibwe News*, September 26, p. 61.

Haubegger, Christy. 1999. "The Latino Century." *Newsweek*, July 12, p. 25.

Holmes, Steven A. 1998. "Black Couples Are Favoring Small Families." *New York Times*, April 5, p. B-1.

hooks, bell. 1996. *Killing Rage: Ending Racism*. New York: Owlet.

———. 1989. *Talking Back: Thinking Feminist, Thinking Black*. Boston: South End Press.

———. 1981. *Ain't I a Woman: Black Women and Feminism*. Boston: South End Press.

Jacobs, Harriet. 2001. "Incidents in the Life of a Slave Girl Written by Herself." Available at: <http://www.xroads.virginia.edu>.

James, Joy, and Angela Davis. 1998. *The Angela Y. Davis Reader*. Oxford: Blackwell.

Juneteenth.com. 2002. "History of Juneteenth." Available at: <http://www.juneteen.com/2000>.

Katz, William Loren. 1986. *Black Indians: A Hidden Heritage*. New York: Atheneum.

Kills Pretty Enemy, Corrine S. 1997. *Business Tips for Women*. Alexandria, Va.: Tokata International.

Larmer, Brook. 1999. "Latino America." *Newsweek*, July 12, pp. 48–51.

Leland, John, and Veronica Chambers. "Generation ~N." *Newsweek*, July 12, pp. 52–58.

Liliu'okalani. 1991. *Hawaii's Story by Hawaii's Queen*. Boston: Charles E. Tuttle.

MacDonald, Donald Stone, and Donald N. Clark, eds. 1996. *The Koreans: Contemporary Politics and Society*. Boulder, Colo.: Westview.

Mankiller, Wilma. 1993. *Mankiller: A Chief and Her People*. New York: St. Martin's Press.

MarketResearch.com. 2001. "Hollywood Looking to Expand Its Market." Available at: <http://www.MarketResearch.com>.

MarketResearch.com. 2001. "The U.S. Hispanic Market." Available at: <http://www.MarketResearch.com>/ProductID+234615>.

Martin, Allison. 2002. "The Legacy of Operation Baby Lift." Available at: <http://www.comeunity/com/babylift>.

Martinez, Maria. 2002. Several books available at: <http://www.amazon.com> and <http://www.maria pottery.com>. Articles featureing her potery available at: <http://www.pueblopottery.com/sans>.

McDonald Boyer, Ruth, and Narcisus Duffy Gayton. 1992. *Apache Mothers and Daughters*. Norman: University of Oklahoma Press.

McGuire, William. 1991. *Recent American Immigrants: Southeast Asians*. Princeton, N.J.: Visual Education Corporation.

Memmi, Albert. 1965. *The Colonizer and the Colonized*. Boston: Beacon Press.

Moraga, Cherrie. 1981. *This Bridge Called My Back: Writings by Radical Women of Color*. Delhi, N.Y.: Persephone Press.

Morenus, David. 2002. "The Real Pocahontas." Available at: <http://www.geocities. com/Broadway/1001/pocah>.

Nabokov, Peter. 1991. *Native American Testimony: A Chronicle of Indian–White Relations from Prophecy to the Present, 1492–1992*. New York: Penguin Books.

National Center for Education Statistics. 1993. *We Measure America: Women and Education*. Washington, D.C.: U.S. Bureau of the Census.

National Center for Health Statistics. 2002. "America's Racial and Ethnic Minorities." Population Bulletin. Hyattsville, Md.: Population Reference Bureau.

National Parks and Conservation Association. 1998. "Custer's Battlefield or Little Big Horn." *National Parks* 72, no. 1–2: 1.

National Women's Health Information Center. 2002. "Chronic Illness among Indian Women." Available at <http://www.rwomen.com>.

Native Women's Health Education Resource Center. 2002. Lake Andes, South Dakota. Available at: <http://www.rwomen.com/index/cfm>.

Naverette, Ruben. 1997. "Private Schools Latino Education." *Los Angeles Times*, July 6.

New Mexico Spanish Genealogy Society. 2001. Available at: <www.nmgenealogy.org>.

Ochoa, Gilda Laura. 1999. "Everyday Ways of Resistance and Cooperation: Mexican American Women Building Puentes with Immigrants." *Frontiers: A Journal of Women Studies* 20, no. 1: 1–20.

O'Connor, Anne-Marie. 1998. "Many Latinos Fare Better in Catholic Schools." *Los Angeles Times*, August 3, p. B-1.

Oregon Public Broadcasting. 1998. "1968: The Year That Stopped a Generation."

Parker, Sara C. 1999. "Urban Natives and Urban Issues." *The Circle* 17, no. 4: 22.

Piccione, Peter A. 2001. "The Status of Women in Ancient Egyptian Society." Available at: <http://www.cofc.edu/~piccione/main.html>.

Quaife, Milo Milton. 1935. *Kit Carson's Autobiography*. Lincoln: University of Nebraska Press.

Revolutionary Association of the Women of Afghanistan (RAWA). 2001. "Under the Tyrrany of the Fundamentalist." Available at: <http://www.rawa.org>.

Robinson, Joynty Maya Angelou, and Tritobia H. Benjamin. 1996. *Bearing Witness: Contemporary Works by African American Women Artists*. London: Rizzoli International.

Schafe, Anne Wilson. 1995. *Native Wisdom for White Minds*. New York: Ballantine Books.

Schlissel, Arthur, Lillian Schlissel, and Vicki Ruiz. 1988. *Western Women: Their Land and Their Lives*. Albuquerque: University of New Mexico Press.

Sheldon, Kathryn. 1996. "Brief History of Black Women in the Military." Women in Military Service for America Memorial Foundation. Available at: <http://www. womensmemorial.org/BBH1998.html>.

Simon, Naomi A. 1996. "Suburban Natives Strive to Keep Culture Alive." *The Circle* 17, no. 4: 23–28.

Sinnott, Susan. 1993. *Extraordinary Asian Pacific Americans*. Chicago: Children's Press.

Smith, Amanda. 1893. *The Story of the Lord's Dealings with Mrs. Amanda Smith, the Colored Evangelist*. Chicago: Meyer and Brother. Special Collections Library, Duke University.

Smitherman, Geneva, ed. 1995. *African American Women Speak Out on Anita Hill–Clarence Thomas*. African American Life Series. Detroit: Wayne State University Press.

Snider, Sharon. 1990. "The Pill: 30 Years of Safety Concerns." Available at: <http://www.fda.gov/bbs/topics/CONSUM/CO00009.html>.

Sonneborn, Liz. 1998. *Encyclopedia of Women: A to Z of Native American Women.* Available at: <www.Goodminds.com>.

Stephenson, June. 1991. *Men Are Not Cost-Effective.* New York: Harper Perennial.

Suaro, Roberto. 1998. *Strangers among Us: How Latino Immigration Is Transforming America.* New York: Alfred Knopf. Also available at: <http://www.pbs.org/newshour/bb/race_relations>.

Tessier, Marie. 2001. *Profiting from Abuse.* Wenews. Available at: <http://www.unicef.org/pusgen/profiting> and <http://www.unicef.org/sexual-exploitation/index>.

The American Gulag. 2000. "Women in Prison." Available at: <http://www.infoshop.org/gulag/women> (last accessed May 2002).

Therborg-Penn, Rosalyn. 1998. *African American Women in the Struggle for the Vote, 1850–1920.* Blacks in the Diaspora Series. Bloomington: Indiana University Press.

Time-Life Books. 1994. *The Indians of California.* Alexandria, Va.: Time Warner.

Trask, Haunani Kay. 1993. *From a Native Daughter: Colonialism and Sovereignty in Hawaii.* Monroe, Me.: Common Courage Press.

Trujillo, Charlie. 1990. *Soldados: Chicanos in Vietnam.* San Jose, Calif.: Chusma House.

UNICEF. 2002. "Seven Asian Nations Sign Pact to Limit Sex Trade" Press release, January 17.

U.S. Bureau of the Census. 2001. "Americans with Disabilities." Washington, D.C.: U.S. Government Printing Office.

———. 2001. "Characteristics of American Indians." Public Information Office memo March 17, 2001.

———. 2001. "Latino Population in the U.S. Mainland." Current Population Survey. Washington, D.C.: U.S. Government Printing Office.

———. 2001. "Minority-Owned Firms Grow Four Times Faster." Public Information Office. Report by Eddie Salyers and Valerie Strong, July 12.

———. 2001. "Revenues for Women-Owned Businesses Show Continued Growth." Washington, D.C.: U.S. Government Printing Office.

———. 2001. Slide presentation, Ethnic and Hispanic Statistics Branch, Population Division. Slide 3 of 22. Last revised January 4, 2001. Washington, D.C.: U.S. Government Printing Office.

———. 2001. "The 'Nuclear Family' Rebounds." Census Bureau Reports, Public Information Office. Report by Jason Fields, April 13.

———. 2001. "Update on Country's African American Population." Public Information Office. Washington, D.C.: U.S. Government Printing Office.

———. 2000. "Black Population in the U.S.: March 2000." PPL-142. Current Population Survey. Washington, D.C.: U.S. Government Printing Office.

———. 2000. "Census Facts for Women's History Month," and "Women-Owned Firms Compared to All U.S. Firms by State." (CB97-FS.02). See also memo from Laverne Vines Collins, Chief of the Census. Public Information Office, February 2, 2000. Washington, D.C.: U.S. Government Printing Office. Also available at: <http://www.census.gov/Press-Release/cb96-07.html>.

———. 2000. "Half of All Mothers with Infants Return to Labor Force after Giving Birth." Washington, D.C.: U.S. Government Printing Office.

———. 2000. "Population Projections of the United States by Age, Sex, Race and Hispanic Origin: 1995–2050." P25-1130. Washington, D.C.: U.S. Government Printing Office.

———. 2000. "Profile of the Nation's Women." Public Information Office. Washington, D.C.: U.S. Government Printing Office.

———. 2000. "Projections of the Total Resident Population by 5 Year Age Groups." Washington, D.C.: U.S. Government Printing Office.

———. 2000. "Race and Hispanic Origin with Special Age Categories: Middle Series, 1999 to 2000." Washington, D.C.: U.S. Government Printing Office.

———. 2000. "Women in the United States: March, 2000." PPL-121. Current Population Survey. Washington, D.C.: U.S. Government Printing Office.

———. 2000. "Women-Owned Firms Compared to All U.S. Firms by State: 1992–2000. "Washington, D.C.: U.S. Government Printing Office.

———. 1999. "Educational Attainment in the United States." Washington, D.C.: U.S. Government Printing Office.

———. 1999. "We Measure America, Asian and Pacific Islanders." CB01-111. Washington, D.C.: U.S. Government Printing Office.

———. 1998. "Younger Women Surpass Young Men in Educational Attainment." Washington, D.C.: U.S. Government Printing Office.

———. 1997. "Three in Ten Households Were Maintained by Women in 1996." Washington, D.C.: U.S. Government Printing Office.

———. 1997. "We Measure: Women and Their Racial and Ethnic Backgrounds." Washington, D.C.: U.S. Government Printing Office.

———. 1996. "Age at First Marriage at Record High." Public Information Office. Washington, D.C.: U.S. Government Printing Office.

———. 1996. "One-Third of Nation's Businesses Owned by Women." Washington, D.C.: U.S. Government Printing Office.

———. 1995. "About 40% of Food Stamp Mothers Never Married." Washington, D.C.: U.S. Government Printing Office.

———. 1995. "Child Support for Custodial Mothers and Fathers: 1995." Washington, D.C.: U.S. Government Printing Office.

———. 1995. "Five Never-Married Women Have Children." Washington, D.C.: U.S. Government Printing Office.

———. 1995. "Single-Parent Growth Rate Stabilized." Washington, D.C.: U.S. Government Printing Office.

———. 1994. "We Measure America: Women and their Housing." Washington, D.C.: U.S. Government Printing Office.

———. 1993. "We Measure America: Women as Crime Victims." Public Information Office. Washington, D.C.: U.S. Government Printing Office.

———. 1993. "We the American . . . Hispanics." Washington, D.C.: U.S. Government Printing Office.

———. 1992. "Women-Owned Firms Compared to All U.S. Firms by State: 1992." Washington, D.C.: U.S. Government Printing Office.

U.S. Commission on Immigration Reform. 1999. "Binational Study: Immigration between Mexico and the United States." Available at: <http://www.utexas.edu/bj/uscir/binational>. Visited November 16, 2002.

U.S. Department of Health and Human Services. 2000. "A Profile of Older Americans." Administration on Aging. Washington, D.C.: U.S. Government Printing Office.

U.S. Department of Justice. 2000. "Correction Statistics." Available at: <http://www.ojp.usdoj. gov/bjs/correct>.

———. 2000. "Victim Characteristics." National Crime Victimization Survey. Available at: <htt[://www.inforshs.org/galus/women>.

U.S. Department of Labor. 1993. "We Measure America: Women and Work." Washington, D.C.: U.S. Government Printing Office.

———. 1965. "The Negro Family: The Case for National Action." Washington, D.C.: U.S. Government Printing Office.

U.S. Federal Bureau of Investigation Crime Index. 2002. "United States Crime Statistics: United States Crime Index: Rates per 100,000 Inhabitants." Public Information Office. Washington, D.C.: U.S. Government Printing Office.

———. 2001. "United States Crime Index: Rates per 100,000 Inhabitants." Public Information Office. Washington, D.C.: U.S. Government Printing Office.

———. 2001. "U.S. Crime Statistics Total and by State: United States Crime Index: Rates per 100,000 Inhabitants." Public Information Office. Washington, D.C.: U.S. Government Printing Office.

———. 1996. "Women's Statistics News Release." "United States Crime Index: Rates per 100,000 Inhabitants." Public Information Office. Washington, D.C.: U.S. Government Printing Office.

Walker, Alice. 1983. *In Search of Our Mother's Garden*. New York: Harcourt Brace Jovanovich.

Williams, Maxine, and Pamela Newman. 1970. *Black Women's Liberation*. New York: Pathfinder Press.

# Index

## ABOUT THE AUTHOR

**Irene I. Blea** is the former Chairperson of the Chicano Studies Department, California State University, Los Angeles. A leading scholar in the field, Professor Blea published four earlier volumes with Praeger, *Toward a Chicano Social Science* (1988), *La Chicana and the Intersection of Race, Class, and Gender* (1991), *Researching Chicano Communities* (1995), and *U.S. Chicanas and Latinas Within a Global Context* (1997).